THE
WITCH's

EIGHT PATHS OF POWER

THE

WITCH's

EIGHT PATHS OF POWER

a complete course in magick and witchcraft

LADY SABLE ARADIA

WEISERBOOKS
San Francisco, CA / Newburyport, MA

First published in 2014 by Weiser Books

Red Wheel/Weiser, LLC
With offices at:
665 Third Street, Suite 400
San Francisco, CA 94107
www.redwheelweiser.com

ISBN: 978-1-57863-551-1

Library of Congress Cataloging-in-Publication Data available on request.

Cover design by Jim Warner
Cover image © Vibrant Image Studio / Shutterstock
Interior by Deborah Dutton
Typeset in Adobe Garamond, ITC Franklin Gothic, Nuptial Script and Trajan

Printed in the United States of America.
EBM

10 9 8 7 6 5 4 3 2 1

For my teachers in the craft: Lady Vichary, Lord Grunnar, Lord Maphis, Lady Dolphanie, and Lord Redleaf. I cannot offer you any greater gesture of my gratitude than this, to teach what you have taught, informed by what I have learned. May these pages be a part of your legacy.

And the Wicca should be properly prepared and purified, to enter into the presence of the Gods.
—GERALD GARDNER, *THE GARDNERIAN BOOK OF SHADOWS*

CONTENTS

INTRODUCTION

As a Witch, I believe the most misunderstood element of what we do is the practice of real magick (first spelled with a "k" by Aleister Crowley to differentiate the art, or craft, of magick from magic as illusion). We are taught in our culture that magick is somehow wrong, or that it is dangerous and mysterious, and only the truly gifted can do it.

But magick is really about self-empowerment. The practice of magick uses a language of symbolism and metaphor to circumvent that little voice in the back of our mind that tells us something will not work. It speaks to our subconscious in primal symbols which set forces in motion to bring about our True Will.

Gerald Gardner, the founder of modern Wicca, wrote in his *Book of Shadows*,[1] about "The Eightfold Way," or the eight different methods of performing magick:

1. Meditation or Concentration.
2. Trance, projection of the Astral.
3. Rites, Chants, Spells, Runes, Charms, etc.
4. Incense, Drugs, Wine, etc., whatever is used to release the Spirit.
5. The Dance and kindred practices.
6. Blood control (the Cords), Breath Control, and kindred practices.
7. The Scourge.
8. The Great Rite.

---

1. Gardner's Book of Shadows is believed to have been written from 1949–61. The materials were later compiled by Aidan A. Kelly and posted online in the mid-nineties. The full text can be found online at www.sacred-texts.com/pag/gbos/index.htm.

Since I teach the Eightfold Way as workshop intensives, the creation of which led to the writing of this book, people ask me if these methods need to be practiced in any particular order. Gardner tried to answer this in his theory of the Five Essentials:

1. The most important is "Intention": You must know that you can and will succeed; it is essential in every operation.
2. Preparation: You must be properly prepared according to the rules of the Art; otherwise you will never succeed.
3. The Circle must be properly formed and purified.
4. You all must be properly purified, several times if necessary, and this purification process should be repeated several times during the rite.
5. You must have properly consecrated tools.

Each chapter in this book covers one point of the Eightfold Way. I would suggest that chapters 1–3 are the most essential. Chapters 4 and 5 lead to deeper practice, but they are optional. Chapters 6–8 represent advanced skills and practice. The vast majority of my students drop out before they begin the work of the last three paths. The ones who persist usually also take their Second and Third Degree initiations and go on to found covens. They are among the most effective Witches I know.

Gardner says these five essentials and Eight Paths, or Ways, cannot be combined into one rite:

> Meditation and dancing do not combine well, but forming the mental image and the dance may be well combined with Chants. Spells, etc., combined with scourging and No. 6, followed by No. 8, form a splendid combination. Meditation, following scourging, combined with Nos. 3 and 4 and 5, are also very Good. For short cuts concentration, Nos. 5, 6, 7, and 8 are excellent.

I don't entirely agree with him, but it's often not necessary or desirable to combine paths. Still, there's no hard and fast rule about this in my experience. As a matter of fact, one of the exercises I've included here combines dancing and meditation to great effect.

My tradition, Star Sapphire, was founded twenty-five years ago in Canada by Gardnerian and Alexandrian initiates connected to the Hereditary Celtic tradition through Sybil Leek. In addition, most in this motley crew were avid martial artists, or they practiced with Dianic and Reclaiming groups. Before I was a Star Sapphire Witch, I was an eclectic Witch, solitary and then coven-ing, for many years. I have practiced yoga quite seriously, am a Reiki master and teacher, and have dabbled in Tantra and Ritual Magick. As a result, my background borrows from a variety of sources: British Traditional Witchcraft, Reclaiming methodology, Ritual Magick symbolism, Eastern mysticism, and energy work. This book will draw upon these sources to show you how to develop each of these eight techniques to hone and refine your magickal skills. I'll break them down into component elements and then assign exercises, reading, and practice to improve those skills. As I tell my students, magick is just like any other skill or talent; some people are born with more natural ability than others, but if you want it badly enough, with practice you can be brilliant—regardless of where you started!

So, if you are serious about mastering magick, and you're willing to do the work and study, then let's explore the Witch's Eight Paths of Power!

part one

THE BASICS OF THE
EIGHTFOLD PATH

chapter one

INTENT

1) Meditation or Concentration. This in practice means forming a mental image of what is desired, and forcing yourself to see that it is fulfilled, with the fierce belief and knowledge that it can and will be fulfilled, and that you will go on willing till you force it to be fulfilled. Called for short, "Intent."
     —GERALD GARDNER, *THE GARDNERIAN BOOK OF SHADOWS*

Magick is the Art and Science of causing change in conformity with Will.
     —ALEISTER CROWLEY, *MAGICK IN THEORY AND PRACTICE*

Intent is the wellspring of all magick. I find that many people believe they know what this means and how to do it, but in practice, forming clear and precise Intent, and willing it to happen, is not nearly as simple as it sounds. It takes training and effort! Quite a few things must come together at once. You must:

- Be able to visualize, clearly and concisely, what you want as if it has already happened.
- Have sufficient focus to keep this goal clearly in your mind while performing the ritual that announces your Intent to the Universe (what we traditionally call "casting a spell").
- Be able to induce a sufficient altered state of consciousness so that your magickal act is happening on both the astral plane and the physical one.
- Invest your Intent with passion and direction.

- Have a clear enough idea of what you want that you will not get something else instead (this is harder than it sounds!).
- Know yourself well enough to be able to trust your own motivations, so that you don't end up accumulating "karmic debt" with the Threefold Law ("What you do shall be returned to you threefold").
- Trust that the Universe will fulfill your desire.
- Circumvent, or rewrite, any negative programming in your behavior or beliefs that might cause you to undermine your own work.
- Do the real-world work to help give your Intent an opportunity to manifest itself.

Not as basic as it initially seemed, is it? Most Witches practice and study for years to eventually achieve a state by which their Wills are effectively manifested. But I am here to tell you that if you persist, eventually you will be capable of simply wanting something with the power of Intent and it will come to you—without spells, rituals, or charms! Just be careful what you wish for, because you just might get it!

VISUALIZATION

When it comes to utilizing magick, the most basic skill I can think of is the ability to clearly visualize what you want. It's also probably the most difficult to learn. With constant distractions and noises clamoring for our attention, is it any wonder we have no attention span anymore? Each day we process a great deal of information, hold it in our minds for a few seconds, and spit it out once we're done with it. It's a twenty-first century survival skill. But in doing this, we lose the ability to completely focus on one thing, let it fill our thoughts, understand every aspect of it, savor its essence, and hold it forever.

So for our first task, I want you to practice *really seeing* something with your whole being. Try to understand every part of it, and then clearly visualize it in your mind's eye. I want you to be able to recall that item with perfect clarity at least a week later. This isn't going to happen right away, but we'll keep practicing.

Exercise 1: Five Things

"Visualize" is really not the best word for what I'm trying to communicate, but it's the name given to the skill in most magickal books, so we'll use it here as well. If you want to "see" something clearly in your mind's eye, you need to use as many senses as possible. It's like a piece of poetry; the more senses you bring to bear, the better you will be able to visualize.

Let's start by making full use of our senses!

First, look all around you and notice five different objects. Don't focus on the details in this case, just their existence and what they are.

Next, close your eyes. Pay attention to five separate sounds. They must be entirely separate sounds, but they could be related to the things you saw, as long as you are clear that you are indeed hearing them and not thinking that you should be hearing them because you saw them in the first round!

Do you remember everything that you saw and heard? Good!

Now, keeping your eyes closed, pay attention to five entirely different things that you feel. Is there a breeze? How warm are you? Are you itchy? Do your clothes have a texture? What about your jewelry?

Last round: Focus on five entirely different things that you smell and taste! Yes, you really can do this; the air has all kinds of scents and flavors in it. Maybe your perfume has an odor, for example, or maybe the neighbor is barbecuing. Maybe you can still taste a hint of the coffee you drank in the morning. Can you smell dust or moisture in the air?

Now, cycle through all the senses again, this time noticing four things instead of five. They must be different from the first five things.

Repeat this cycle of the senses three more times, noticing three things, two things, and then just one thing for each sense.

Open your eyes. Do you remember everything that you noticed?

Practice this once a day for at least three months. After a while, it will become a habit, and you will always notice the world in this complete and all-encompassing way.

There is no test. Other than you, no one will know whether or not you've done the homework. But if you have the persistence to go the distance, the end result will pay off. And the world really is much prettier than we give it credit for, if you just take the time to pay attention! Consider that a study bonus!

Exercise 2: Onesight

To help us appreciate the real details of things, this exercise will have you practice visualizing one object with complete recall, using as many different sensory aspects as you can.

You will need:

- An object, such as a large piece of fruit or a small statue or painting; something three dimensional that has texture and scent
- Paper and pencil
- A small piece of fabric or a towel large enough to cover the item
- A timer

1. First, place your item on the table in front of you with no other distractions. Set the timer for one full minute, and then examine the item as thoroughly as you can. Look at it, touch it, smell it, taste it. Appreciate each detail with all five senses.
2. After one minute, cover the item and write every detail you can remember about it. No peeking!
3. When you have exhausted every element you can possibly think of, uncover the item and study it again. Was there anything you missed?

I find that when people start doing this exercise, either they notice only the obvious things (e.g. the orange is orange,) or they notice the things that stand out (e.g. the orange has a blemish near the top of it), and miss the obvious things (e.g. the orange is orange!). Take note of which one seems to be true for you, because it tells you how you look at the world. Are you missing the fine details of things? Or are you "missing the forest for the trees"? In order to completely visualize something, you have to be able to consider both the minute details as well as overall context.

Try to do this exercise at least once a week, and work on the aspect in which you are weakest.

Magickal Visualization

The exercises you have just completed will hone your skills of observation and prepare you for the next step: magickal visualization. This is when you attract something into your life by investing it with emotional energy and the power of your Will. The more clearly you can visualize something, the more effective you will be at bringing it into your life.

How does this work? Well, the answer might actually be found in the field of science. At the quantum level, when you measure subatomic elements as particles, particles are what you get (protons, electrons, neutrons, etc.). But when you measure subatomic elements as waves of energy, waves are what you get! In other words, our expectations determine the nature of our physical reality. The wider implications of this for the Witch are awe-inspiring.

Understanding this essential principle, why don't we now consider how to visualize energy directly?

CREATIVE VISUALIZATION AND DAYDREAMING

In your work so far, have you noticed favoring one sense over the others? When you visualize, do you feel things before you see them? There's nothing wrong with that. Just keep it in mind when you begin to sense for things like the movement of energy, or auras, or how a person is injured when you are about to do energy healing work for them. I felt auras as vibrations long before I ever saw them because I'm very tactile.

You were probably taught that daydreaming was bad for you, but this is how new ideas are born! Do you create any form of art? Do you make things with your hands? How do you come up with the idea that you later create? You daydream about it!

The same skills that used to make you a good daydreamer as a child are the ones that make you good at visualization. Shakti Gawain's classic book *Creative Visualization* explains this very well. If you consciously visualize something, you are actively creating it in the astral plane. You are forming a concept and giving it life. If you do enough work to make it real in the astral plane, it becomes real in the physical world as well, though it does help to do some real-world work to back it up and reinforce it.

Let's make some things in the astral plane!

Exercise 3: Visualizing Symbols

Using the index finger of your dominant hand, draw a pentagram in the air starting from the bottom left-hand corner. From the bottom left, go up to the top, then down to the bottom right, up to the upper left hand corner, across to the right, and back down to the bottom left where you started. Something like this:

Figure 1: Earth Banishing Pentagram

Do you see it? Now see the pentagram emitting a brilliant blue gas flame! Does it sparkle and crackle? Does it make a vibration, like being too close to an electrical wire? My pentagrams make a whooshing fire sound when I draw them, like a fireplace being lit.

Now turn to your right and draw another pentagram in the air, identical to the first.

Turn to your right again. Draw another.

Turn to the right once more, and draw a fourth pentagram.

Turn right to come back to your original position. Do you see and feel the four pentagrams on each side of you? Nicely done!

Now, let's create a circle. Starting in the east or the north, according to your desire and/or tradition, extend your index finger of your power hand and visualize a glowing white light radiating from its tip. Draw that line all the way around you and the area you're working in, making a complete circle. Face the original direction you started in. Visualize that circle expanding to form a big, glowing white soap bubble of protection surrounding you top and bottom; first one dome, then the other.

This basic white bubble will serve you well in your magickal practice. You can expand it to cover your entire house (convenient when the coven is over—you can all use the bathroom without breaking circle) or you can contract it to just cover yourself (a good shielding exercise that never hurt anyone to practice).

Practice this visualization every day, at least once a day. And yes, I really mean it!

MEDITATION

Most of you are probably already familiar with the concept of meditation. So why is an Eastern mystical practice important to Wiccan magick? Meditation is the simplest way I am aware of to still your mind, remove distractions, and induce a slightly altered state of consciousness that accesses the astral plane.

It is traditionally recommended that you practice meditation in the morning when you are fully rested, but any time of day when distractions are unlikely, regardless of when or where that is, will work. It is better to meditate for even a short period of time, and frequently, than to not do it at all. Find five to fifteen minutes every day to meditate. Relax all the muscles in your body as well as your mind and emotions. It may help to lay on your back with your arms at your sides and your legs straight out, feet relaxing outward. In yoga this is called *shavasana,* or "corpse pose."

Exercise 4: Candle Meditation

People new to meditation are often under the impression that they need to completely blank their minds in order to succeed. This is only one form of meditation, and it is really more for seeking enlightenment and visions. Most forms of meditation involve contemplation of one particular thing without active consciousness. Let me share the method that my first mentor taught me.

Light a white or a beeswax candle and place it on a table or on the floor in front of you. Dim the lights and make yourself comfortable. Look steadily into the flame with a softened, unfocused gaze. Consider the way it flickers, the intensity of the light, the color. Fill your mind with this, and nothing else. Allow yourself to blink when you need to, and close your eyes if they get tired, but continue to visualize the flame in your mind's eye. If you get distracted, bring yourself gently back to the moment. Allow any intruding thoughts to float away like a soap bubble on the breeze without judgment or emotional attachment.

When you are ready, bring yourself back to conscious awareness.

Practice this exercise whenever you feel the need and desire, and try for that "unfocused focus" for longer periods. And you know what? Congratulations, that's meditation!

CENTERING AND GROUNDING

After doing the candle mediation, you should be centered. Centering is feeling focused in your energy and your sense of self. There is a place in your body which likely feels like the center of your being; some say it is in the navel, just below the navel, or in the solar plexus, but it's wherever feels right to you.

Centering also involves aligning your physical, mental, emotional, and spiritual selves. When you are centered, you feel connected within yourself, and you can access the spiritual and astral plans with relative ease. Highly empathic people often have trouble centering, because they can't discern which of the many emotions they feel are theirs and which are other people's. If this describes you, put up that white bubble of protection around yourself first, and if necessary, add the pentagrams.

Running a lot of magickal energy is a great deal like running an electric current. Sometimes it even has effects in the physical world that people can see or react to: your watch might stop or start in bizarre ways; you might give people electric shocks or feel extremely warm when you touch them; or your computer could malfunction. This is due to the changes of energy in your body, and that's where proper grounding comes in. Once you're centered within yourself, you must establish that connection to the earth so that you can allow excess energy to dissipate into the earth instead of remaining stored in your body.

The next exercise is one example of grounding. You might also simply touch the earth with the palms of your hands or the soles of your bare feet. There are many ways to ground; the key is to establish a physical or energetic connection to the earth.

Exercise 5: Tree Meditation

Picture yourself as a tree. You can be any kind of tree you want—a birch, a yew, a pine, a poplar. Close your eyes, and reach your roots from the soles of your feet through the floor if you are indoors, through the foundation of the building you are in, through the rich topsoil beneath it, deep into the sand and rocks, past the bones of your ancestors. Feel your roots take in the deep, nourishing, rich elements of the soil. Draw them up into your roots, and your trunk, nourishing you.

Now extend your roots farther, through the soil, into the bedrock, then past the rock into the groundwater beneath. Draw that water in through your roots, past the bones of your ancestors, wet and thirst quenching, deep into your trunk and through your leaves or needles. Feel that water wash through your whole being, slaking your deepest thirst. *Aaaahhhhhh!*

Now, take your awareness from your deep roots, and bring it back up, through those roots, into your trunk, back up through your branches, and into your twigs and leaves. Feel a lively, warm spring breeze running through your leaves or needles. Feel the air giving you breath, absorbing and seeping into you. Smell the scents in the warm spring air.

When you have sensed that, stretch those leaves, twigs, and branches up toward the soothing spring sun. Absorb that life-giving warmth into your leaves, spreading throughout your branches, trunk, and roots, into the very core of you.

You are balanced between heaven and earth, between all four elements, and ready to enter into sacred space.

You can adapt this exercise for a group by having someone read and direct the meditation, and everyone else follows along.

GROUP MEDITATION

I generally find that trying to get many people to meditate together, unless you are using a guided meditation, is more trouble than it is worth. Not surprisingly, trying to get multiple people to be silent and unmoving at once takes some work, and often seems to breed more frequent coughing, fidgeting, sneezing, and bathroom breaks. But go ahead if you wish to, especially if you have several more experienced Witches who can guide the inexperienced ones. You might want to experiment with Exercise 4: Candle Meditation and Exercise 5: Tree Meditation in a group setting.

Exercise 6: Visualizing Energy

Building on the work you've done, the next step is to visualize something that does not (yet) exist in your physical reality.

Put the palms of your hands together and rub them back and forth for about ten to fifteen seconds to create friction. Then, keeping your palms facing each other, draw your hands slowly apart. Can you feel the tingling between them? Still feeling that energy, form it into a ball and turn it around in your hands. Now see the ball glowing a beautiful golden color. Close your eyes if necessary. Once you have that, add sound effects. Perhaps the ball might make a low hum, or a vibrating noise like a finger on the edge of a wine glass, or maybe an electric buzz. Do you still feel the warmth of it? Has the sensation of it changed at all? Are your hands tingling or feeling prickly? Has the heat increased or decreased?

Now play with the ball a little! Reach your hands up above your head, set the ball on your crown, and circulate it around your body, starting with your front. Draw a deep breath in, and as you exhale, move the ball down your forehead, nose, chin, neck, collarbone, sternum, diaphragm, belly, lower belly, genitals, and perineum (you may find it easier if you tighten your perineum, like in a Kegel exercise—if you do this, be sure to take the ball back into your hands before releasing). Pause, and as you inhale move the energy up the back of your body—up your tailbone, kidney area, lower back, middle back, upper back, back of the neck, back of the head, and back to the crown. Repeat this process twice more, exhaling as you send the ball down your front, and inhaling as you draw the ball up your back. This is actually a Yoga practice called Circulation of the Body of Light which centers you and prepares you for magickal work.

You can also try fancy maneuvers like rolling the ball over your arms and over the back of your neck like a Harlem Globetrotter, if you like! Just don't dribble it; energy often dissipates when it comes in contact with the ground.

This is also a good way to learn how to work magick in consort with other people. If you have the opportunity to practice with a friend or covenmate, try passing the energy from one set of hands directly into the other; then try passing it one-handed; then try throwing it back and forth to see if you can maintain a consistent image between you. You can also use this as a coven exercise by passing it around or across the circle.

When you're ready to release the ball, take it back in both of your hands and bring them together, making the ball smaller and smaller, until you have squished it between them. Then break your hands apart and push your palms toward the ground, directing all excess energy down as you do so. Clap your hands together or shake them like you're trying to get water droplets off in order to safely dissipate the energy you've built up!

YOUR BOOK OF SHADOWS

After you have completed a meditation session, take time to journal about it. Many Witches have a book that they record their magickal experiences in, along with dreams, spells, and whatever information they have copied out of books that might be handy. They call this their Book of Shadows, and it's a good idea to start one if you haven't already. You will need it later.

Exercise 7: Magickal Journaling

Make a habit of recording your spellwork. Name the day, the date, the time, the phase of the moon when you performed the spell, any significant astrological events, who was involved, your emotional state, what you did, the symbols you used, what your divination result was regarding the spellwork, and the ultimate outcome. Use this information to fine-tune your spellwork to be more effective as you become aware of the different factors that can affect what you are doing.

BEATING THE "I CAN'T" FACTOR

When you set out to learn magick, what you wish for in your heart, and what you think about and focus on, is what you receive. So in order to effectively manifest what you want, you have to learn how *not* to manifest what you *don't* want. I don't think anyone is ever entirely successful at this process, but you can become more skilled over time at not getting in your own way.

SUBCONSCIOUS BELIEFS

Malcolm Gladwell's excellent book *Blink: The Power of Thinking Without Thinking* describes how we, as human beings, "thin-slice" a topic in order to make a quick decision. We sift through a great deal of information in a split second that we aren't even aware that we know, stored by our subconscious. Some of that information could have even been obtained through psychic abilities (we are talking about magick, and I do believe in such things). So, a split-second decision can be just as effective, or even more effective, as a decision made after careful analysis.

The disadvantage of this human trait is that sometimes we pick up subconscious beliefs we don't really want, such as prejudices. When I started promoting the classes I teach at my metaphysical shop, I realized I had promoted my herbalism class more effectively than the others because I had an outstanding turnout. I tried to figure out why.

What I realized was that I believed fully in myself and my knowledge of herbalism because I had taken a yearlong course on the subject from an accredited herbal college. I didn't have the same level of confidence in the other topics I taught. But, I have been a Witch for more than twenty years! So what a ridiculous thing to think! I realized then that I had the following subconscious belief: One year of formal instruction is better than twenty years of practical experience. Isn't that ridiculous?

Where did I get this idea? It may have come from my parents, who put great emphasis on going to school and getting a formal education. Because I chose not to continue with university after high school, they never seemed to regard my work as anything but an amusing hobby. I was urged to "get a career to the pay the bills," and ephemeral pursuits such as writing and music were dismissed as career options. The recognition of this subconscious belief, in this case, was enough. I knew that consciously I didn't believe such a thing, and so I was able to get over it and promote the work I had done more effectively.

Let me share with you some exercises that helped me to process and overcome these sorts of harmful blocks.

Exercise 8: Affirmations

The secret to your subconscious mind is that it believes anything you tell it, and it doesn't hear or understand tone. So the way to program your subconscious mind is to repeat something over and over again until it becomes ingrained. The way to your superconscious (also known as your superego or your Higher Self), which is how you can access your divine cocreation powers, is through your subconscious. Hence, the art of affirmation.

An affirmation is a positive statement you make to yourself in order to fix an idea in your mind. You repeat it until you believe it. When you believe it, you make it happen around you, almost by accident.

To begin, consider a belief you would like to counteract and create a statement that is the opposite. For example, let's take that original belief I had: "One year of formal instruction is better than twenty years of practical experience."

In order to counteract this, I would create the following statement instead: "My twenty years of experience in Wicca qualifies me as an expert in my field."

Notice that I did not say: "Twenty years of experience is equal to or superior to formal study." That would just negate the previous belief, and that doesn't work! This is an important lesson.

Trying to counteract a previous belief is not effective. Your subconscious does not understand negations. It does not compute the word "not." So, if a woman believes she is overweight and you say that she is "*not* fat," it will not sink in—especially if this body image is a core belief absorbed from childhood. But if you instead tell her, over and over again, that she is beautiful, that her dress emphasizes her figure and her lovely curves, that you noticed how good she looks this morning and did she change her hair or get a spa treatment, then she will start to absorb it and believe it. (Take note, gentlemen and ladies who love ladies; many women come to their adult life with body image issues.)

So, how can magick that focuses on a negation be entirely effective? It can't. You have to find a way to turn a negative into a positive.

Many of our limitations are self-imposed. The reason we can't do things most of the time is because we *believe* we can't. And that belief comes from subconscious programming that we absorbed as children.

THE THREE LEVELS OF CONSCIOUSNESS

Freud's model of consciousness discusses three levels of mind: the conscious mind, or *ego;* the subconscious mind, or *id;* and the higher consciousness, or *superego.* Feri Wicca refers to these respectively as the *talking self,* the *younger self,* and the *higher self.* The conscious "talking" mind cannot communicate directly with the higher consciousness; it needs the subconscious to be a conduit.

Unfortunately, the subconscious isn't always a reliable messenger. It is like a very small child. It does not understand things in rational terms, and speaks only in the languages of symbol and emotion. As any psychologist can tell you, the subconscious also picks up everything it is ever told. The problem is that it does not understand irony or context. This is why you should never tell your children they are stupid, even as a joke, and especially not over and over again. Even if you don't really mean it, your child's subconscious mind will not be able to tell the difference!

One of the things that imprints on our subconscious through repetition is *limitation.* If someone tells us repeatedly—or we tell ourselves—that we are stupid, we can't sing, we have no money, or we are fat, we believe it. And then, the subconscious takes the message to the superego, and the superego does what it thinks we want it to do—it makes it true! As Jerry and Esther Hicks tell us in *The Law of Attraction*, if we focus on our poverty, we remain poor. If we focus on our fatness, we can't be thin. If we dwell constantly on how badly things are going for us, they continue to go badly.

So how do you change these beliefs if they are ingrained? The first step is silencing the ego. Next, we have to make our subconscious an ally, and we do this by meditating and self-examination. Affirmations can change the way we think, and help us heal. Or, we can speak to our subconscious in a language of symbols, colors, and feelings, which is what the craft is all about.

It is said that the doors of Eleusis boasted the inscription, "Know Thyself." We have to quiet the mind long enough to know what the subconscious is really saying. What do we really believe about the world and ourselves at our core? There are many ways to work toward this goal, from psychoanalysis to soul retrieval. They are all effective, and the more healing you do for your subconscious (and the better you understand it), the better you will be at changing consciousness according to Will.

Exercise 9: Know Thyself

Do this exercise about once a month to reflect on how your perspective may affect your beliefs and your magick.

First, make a list of ten things you don't like about yourself. These might be things such as:

- Physical features
- Personality traits
- Mental concerns
- Spiritual aspects

You can list anything at all, but please make sure it is you that you are considering, and not someone else. Don't list things you dislike about others, and don't write something down just because someone else has criticized you. Be honest, direct, and courageous!

Once you are finished, make a list of ten things that you *do* like about yourself, in those same categories—physical features, personality traits, mental and spiritual aspects. Again, this can cover any of the four realms and be anything at all. Please be as honest and courageous as you were with your list of things you did not like. Remember, no one will ever see this list but you.

Now, examine your list. Which of the four realms—physical, emotional, mental, or spiritual—received the most attention from you, either positively or negatively? That tells you something about the way you think, and if it's primarily negative attention, where you lack self-confidence. Perhaps you might consider reexamining your self-image in this area, rather than changing all these "negative" aspects.

Next, did you find it easier to be critical of yourself or complimentary? That also tells you something. There is a pendulum between low self-esteem and arrogance. Somewhere in the middle you will find a healthy self-image, based in self-confidence, humility, and an honest assessment of your own strengths and weaknesses. Having a "right-sized" ego is essential in your magickal practice.

Compare your likes to your dislikes. How many are related? How many are potentially synonymous? For instance, I found that I was both "stubborn" and "determined." Well, don't the two sort of go hand in hand? Maybe being stubborn isn't such a bad thing after all!

Of the dislikes, which are changeable? Which are unchangeable? Which are changeable but feel like impossible issues to surmount? Ha! Trick question. Everything is essentially changeable. That is part of what you are learning how to do by reading this book! Even if something seems impossible, it likely isn't.

Nothing Is Impossible

My husband was in a near fatal car accident six years ago. I was aware that the situation was grave; the tight-lipped looks from the nurses, and the fact that I was allowed to bring anyone I wanted into the ICU at any time, day or night, were strong indicators. But no one ever told me his survival was impossible, so I never for a moment doubted that he would not only survive, but recover.

While my husband was on a respirator in a medically induced coma, I called every Witch and Pagan, every praying Christian and every healer I knew, and I asked them to go to work. Hundreds of people I didn't know that I knew—cab customers, long-lost relatives, friends we hadn't spoken to in ten years, friends of friends of friends, prayed and lit candles and performed spells and sent Reiki. Hours became days; days became weeks. I left everything and stayed at his side and did Reiki each and every day for as long as I could stand it. A diligent intern spent six hours off-shift poring over his X-rays to determine the problem and found a tiny spot in his lung that had been ignored previously, though they were treating him for an infection. It turned out to be a pulmonary embolism. He was given blood thinners, and at last he began to recover and came out of the coma.

Between the accident itself, the pulmonary embolism, the long coma, and the other combined factors, he had less than a one in ten thousand chance of survival and recovery. But he is still here! He suffered severe nerve damage from the long period in ICU, but no head injuries, and no spinal injuries. He had lost his leg in the accident, and he was given a prosthetic and started relearning how to stand and how to walk. Though they didn't tell us this until much later, my husband's prosthetist looked at his physiotherapist and questioned, "Are we wasting our time here?" To which the physiotherapist replied, "I don't know, but let's give him some hope."

Well, my husband has learned to walk again. Not for long periods, and he gets tired easily and is awkward on his feet; but he can do it.

Did you know that there have been two recorded cases of people growing their arms back after they were amputated? My husband's leg hasn't regrown yet, but he is working on it! Though, I admit, this does seem unlikely. Maybe it is far too difficult to surmount. That, then, becomes the work of grief and acceptance. We'll be covering that, too.

Nothing, nothing, *nothing* is impossible!

Understanding Your Motivations

I cannot stress enough how important it is that you understand your own motivations. You really can be your own worst enemy. Ask yourself why you want whatever it is you are doing magick to obtain.

Suppose you decide that you want to do magick to get a promotion at work. Why do you want that promotion? Is it because you hate the job you are in and you would rather have another one? Is it because you need more money? Is it because you want more responsibility in your life? Is it because you would like the prestige of having a higher position? Maybe you should be doing magick for more money or more prestige instead of the promotion.

Also, why do you want whatever it is that you think you want? Are you keeping in mind the greater good of all involved? Do you only think that you know what that greater good is? Let others determine what is in their own best interests, as you would want to do.

You've probably heard of the Wiccan Rede: "An it harm none, do what thou wilt." I believe that the Rede admonishes us to consider our actions. When you would "harm none," that gives you permission to do things freely and enjoy them without unnecessary guilt. (Sex can be a lot more fun under the Rede, for example!) But when you can't avoid harm, then you have to think about it. What is the best course of action for you? A true Witch acts according to her own moral beliefs and accepts the consequences of that decision. She takes personal responsibility for her actions.

When Magick Goes Wrong

Sometimes, you will find that your magick actually is effective, but it seems to go horribly wrong. Let's discuss what can go wrong and why.

I do believe that sometimes the gods, or our higher consciousness, know what is best for us better than we do, and our ego might be confused about what that actually is. But most people use this as an excuse for their own failures. Not every failure of magick is the Lady's will. More often than not, things don't go according to plan because you've screwed something up. Let me explain how.

Magick fails primarily when there is not a clear line of communication between the ego and the superego. There are four main communication issues that will cause spell failure:

Problem: The Magick Didn't Work the Way You Wanted It To

Perhaps you did a spell to give you more time on your hands. As a result, you lost your job and now you are on unemployment. Not helpful. But you did get exactly what you asked for, didn't you? Remember, magick takes the path of least resistance. The subconscious doesn't understand that you need to make money to pay your bills, and the superego doesn't either because it has no material needs, so the superego simply processed the request by removing the offending work that was costing you so much of your time.

Solution: You Have Been Unclear

Lay down your parameters. Consider what you would be willing to sacrifice in order to get what you want, because you may be forced to make a choice. Maybe what you need is time management, not "more time." This is part of why most good books on magick recommend that you do everything possible in the physical world first to get the result you want.

Perhaps it's your phrasing or your choice of symbols. Perhaps what you've asked for is too long or too complicated. Maybe you're asking for six things at the same time instead of one, and the Universe is confused as to which one is actually your priority. Maybe you are using a negation instead of an affirmation. In any case, it's not going to work.

Problem: The Magick Worked, but You Didn't Want to Pay the Price

It's important to include the following caveat in almost any magick you do: *an it harm none.* Because magick takes the path of least resistance, unfortunately sometimes it will run people over. My husband and I did a spell to bring our household more money. The path of least resistance was a life insurance policy that paid $100,000 for dismemberment. Now my husband is missing a leg. Not worth it.

Another example occurs when somebody does a spell they believe is in another's best interests but which interferes with their free will. When I was still new to magick, I had a couple friends in high school who started dating. They were constantly fighting, breaking up, and getting back together, and of course they would complain to me all the time because I was close with both of them. It was a regular nuisance. I came to the conclusion that they had some kind of negative tie that was pulling them together and it had to be cut. I made paper dolls of them with their names in Theban script, tied them together, and ceremonially cut the string. They broke up all right, but both of them descended into a depth of depression that resulted in one of them trying to commit suicide.

I really didn't intend to harm them, but I was self-righteous. I believed that I knew better than they did. I did not, and you never can, no matter if that other person is your spouse, your best friend, or even your child. The only spells you should ever do for anyone else without their permission is a spell of healing or protection (or a protective hex, if someone is causing harm and you believe that the greater good is served through this), and even then you should include a caveat that they must accept what you offer.

Solution: Your Will May Be in Conflict with Another's

The Goddess will give us anything we want; but just like any other mom, She doesn't love you more than your brother, and when you want something and he wants the opposite, She won't take sides. The strongest Will, or the one with the most support, will win. And in this case, the status quo is more likely to win out than change, because magick takes the path of least resistance.

Problem: The Magick Worked, but It Didn't Take the Form You Expected

Magick will often—often!—show up in a form that surprises you. Sometimes it accomplishes what you actually wanted, and sometimes it doesn't. The key is to be careful what you wish for.

I sent out the Intention that I wanted a dedicated temple room for my coven and me to work in. Shortly thereafter, some resource-draining roommates of one of my newer coveners moved out, and he turned the empty room into a temple. Well, I didn't say I wanted it to be at my place, did I? But this worked out just fine. My coveners had a really wonderful place with lots of room and we used it for all our Sabbat gatherings and Esbats. It wasn't what I was expecting, but it was what I really wanted.

Solution: Maybe You Don't Really Want What You're Asking For

Be specific about what you want, but be open-minded about how the Universe chooses to give you what you need. Decide if the form that the result chose to take suits your needs, and if it doesn't, perhaps refine your request or change your parameters. Maybe you really want something else, or you just don't care enough about the outcome to invest it with the necessary emotion.

Problem: The Magick Worked, but It Wasn't Powerful Enough

Perhaps you did a spell to bring more money, and you found a twenty-dollar bill lying on the sidewalk. What you really needed was enough money to pay your rent. But you didn't clarify that, did you? Go back to the drawing board and be more specific next time.

Solution: Maybe You Are Sabotaging Yourself

It's easy to overthink things, to put more effort into worrying about how your magick can go wrong than planning how it can go right.

ASKING FOR WHAT YOU REALLY WANT

Remember: Be specific, and be simple, or you will confuse the subconscious, which will not be able to translate things for the conscious mind effectively. The subconscious probably has the comprehension of a three-year-old. You can't write essays for her. She doesn't understand them, and it's not fair to expect her to.

Let's say you're doing a spell for a new house. You have some pretty specific ideas about what you would like in this house. Maybe you want four bedrooms, three and a half baths, a fireplace, a dining room, a study, an attic, a mud room, a workshop, a garage, a big yard, trees around it, a nice view of a lake, places for the dog to run, you want it to be on a golf course . . . You see the problem here, right? Too much to remember in written form!

Here are some things you could do instead:

- Draw a picture. Maybe a floor plan would be sufficient to fix the idea clearly in your subconscious mind.
- Write it into poem form. Perhaps your subconscious will find that kind of thing easier to remember (most of us do). I'll teach you how to do this in chapter 3.
- Make a collage with images like the things you really want. Cut photos out of a homebuyer's magazine, or print them from the Internet. You're speaking in pictures, then, not words.

You also need to speak to your subconscious with symbols that she actually comprehends. This is especially important for Witches who like to cast spells out of recipe books. I do think those can be fun; but if the spell calls for you to draw an image of a pig to represent financial well being, I hope you actually like pigs! If you don't, then this is not a good symbol to use. Perhaps you think of pigs as lazy and dirty. That certainly doesn't represent financial security in your mind.

If you ask for too much at the same time, you will frustrate your subconscious, which won't know what to deal with first. Break down what it is you're asking for to find the root of it; don't try to cover too much at once, or make things too vague. Also, you may have to accept that a very large goal might take time to realize. How do you eat an elephant? Well, you break it down into smaller chunks, and then you eat one piece at a time.

Facing a Conflict of Wills

Magick takes the path of least resistance. It is *lazy*. Like most energy, it will do what is easiest. We've all heard that an object at rest tends to stay at rest, while an object in motion tends to stay in motion. This is as true in metaphysics as it is in physics. Fighting the established flow of energy (or lack of it) is like swimming upstream. So why make it work harder than it has to?

There are a few different ways to handle this, and some are more effective than others. The first, and the most traditional for Witches, is to do it in secret. No one can argue with you if they don't know what you're up to. For individual acts of magick, this may be the most practical tactic. On the other hand, keeping some things, such as the core elements of one's being, a secret is harmful. For example, I believe most gay or bisexual people in the Western world feel the need to come out because hiding their sexual orientation denies too much of who they are and restricts their genuine feelings for others.

The second way is to put oneself in the position of eternal victim. This person goes around bemoaning how the whole world is against them. There is always an excuse as to why other people have caused their failure, or why they can't do whatever it is they say they want to do. This is not a practical tactic, nor is it helpful. If you spend enough time worrying about why things won't work, or finding reasons they won't work, you'll be right!

The third way is to become what I call "a rebel without a clue." Some people just like the idea of being the one who disturbs the fecal matter. These people generally got into Witchcraft because it was perceived as "devil worship" and countercultural. They are angry and they want an excuse to keep being angry. If the whole world is against them, then they can always blame someone else for their failures. Anger is only helpful when you are ready to turn it into practical action.

The best solution is to reach a point in your life when the good opinion of others is no longer important to you. Though I didn't consider it a choice at the time, my husband and I chose to swim upstream when our friends and we fought magickally for his life. I went from silently healing him with spells and Reiki when the nurses weren't looking to the "why is all this crap happening to us?" whining to my friends stage, to the "screw you, Universe, you can't have him!" stage in which we consciously challenged the forces of death. All these methods were successful on some level; they managed to stave off what seemed inevitable. But only when he and I reached a point where the healing process became the single priority; when I stopped answering the phone, when I stopped letting my frantic mother-in-law goad me into dealing with the endless bureaucracy, when my friends and I started doing ritual in the hospital room whether the hospital liked it or not, and when my goal became simply to love my husband however I could; only then did his truly miraculous recovery really begin.

All these stages may be necessary to pass through in our spiritual development, especially in a mystery tradition with initiations. I laugh now when I see it in myself (though like most people, I usually have to have this pointed out to me, preferably gently by a friend rather than receiving the Lady's "clue by four" upside the head, but I'm not immune to that either!), and I have more patience with it in others than I used to. We all must come to the place where we are free to exercise our own True Will in our own ways. If that way involves feeling the anger, then do it! Just don't get stuck there.

Exercise 10: The Witch's Pyramid (Four Powers of the Magician)

You may have heard of these. We're going to use the pyramid to create more effective spellwork. Let's start in the east.

Figure 2: The Witch's Pyramid

Noscere "To Know" (East, Air)

Air is the place of knowing. Start with a wish. "I wish that I were wealthy." "I wish that I could be a bestselling novelist." "I wish that I would never get a cold." It really can be anything.

Before you can begin effective spellwork, you must know things. Make a clear Statement of Intent. Ask for what you want specifically. Know what you need to get it. Know the magickal symbolism you will need to make it happen. Know how to express your desires clearly enough that the Universe will comprehend what it is you're asking for.

Velle "To Will" (South, Fire)

Fire is the place of Will. This is where desire is created. This is where things change from "I wish" to "I want."

Consider your wish. Do you desire it sufficiently to change it to an "I want"? Are you willing to ask the Universe to help you with your desire? How can anyone, including the Divine, know what you need unless you ask for it?

Audere "To Dare" (West, Water)

Water is the place of daring. Magick is an act of courage. We are told our whole lives that magick is impossible, or if it is possible, that we are not worthy. If you wish to succeed at magick, you must dare to ask, and dare to receive! You must also dare to proceed even if you feel that your knowledge is less than perfect. You must risk that things will change by your request, and that only you are responsible for the consequences.

Tacere "To Keep Silent" (North, Earth)

Earth is the place of silence; but silence isn't really what is meant. Others will tell you that your idea is a bad one, that it's impossible, that you're selfish for asking, etc. It was once believed that speaking about your magick reduced its power. Exposing your desires to others who may have desires that conflict with yours will create interference, and exposing magick to those who doubt it means that your Will must now contest with their doubt as well as your own! Now you have brought your desire into the world of ego, and people have a lot invested in their egos and belief systems. Successful magick may challenge that investment. Why set yourself up for this? Just do it and discuss it after it is achieved. Or, if you are going to discuss it, then do not associate with people who are going to rain on your parade. As Doreen Valiente said, "Keep pure your highest ideal; strive ever towards it; let none stop you or turn you aside."

A cautionary note: bragging, boasting, or threatening others is ill advised—especially about your magickal abilities. The rest of the world will say, "Oh yeah?" and set their Wills to making sure that your magick fails so they can laugh at your pretensions. Don't wish harm on others or spread gossip, and be careful what you wish for; you just might get it!

It's always a good idea to gauge how a spell will turn out before you actually set about casting it. Perhaps you are already familiar with some form of divination. Maybe you like runes or Tarot cards, pendulums, playing cards, or tea leaf reading. If you aren't familiar with any of these, get a six-sided die. Ask the following question: "What will the consequences be if I choose to cast this spell?"

Draw a card, watch the pendulum, etc. Or, if you are using the die method, use odd numbers to indicate a bad idea, and even numbers to indicate a good one; set your Intention so that the higher the number rolled, the better the idea. In this example, one, three, and five would be negative, with one being the worst possible outcome and five being only mildly inconvenient; and two, four, and six would be positive, with two representing a fairly decent outcome, and six being the most beneficial idea you could imagine. Record the result, and then choose whether or not you will heed the advice.

TRUE WILL

Ceremonial magicians often speak of something called "True Will." True Will is your innermost desire, as well as a sense of destiny. People in the New Age community call it "serendipity." Some people believe that the gods sent us here for a specific purpose, and when we have accomplished this purpose, we will pass into the next realm and perhaps return later for a different purpose. Magicians believe in a similar philosophy, except that they believe we have chosen this said purpose before we were matter. Sometimes that True Will is at cross-purposes with what we think we want at the time. We feel thwarted, and we think our magick hasn't worked, but this is where understanding what you really want is so important.

A personal example—I tried for two years to have a baby, and I finally got pregnant and I was so happy. I did everything the midwife said to do. I joined prenatal yoga, I ate right, I drank teas that were supposed to be helpful. At about three months I miscarried. My husband and I were heartbroken and angry. I had done everything right, but it all went wrong anyway.

Two and a half years after that, I was in Port Coquitlam staying with a dear friend and sister priestess while my husband lay in Vancouver General Hospital literally on the brink of death. He was in surgery when I realized with a start that if I had carried that baby to term, she would have been two years old. I was incredibly relieved and grateful that I did not have to go through all this horror and chaos with a two-year-old! My True Will knew this experience was coming down the pipe and I could not do both.

INVESTING YOUR INTENT

So here's the kicker about real magick; you have to care whether or not it works! And then you have to invest it with energy to make it happen. I call this process "Investing Your Intent."

Exercise 12: Prioritizing

Consider something you would like to bring about in your life. Everyone has something they want, and I hope if I have communicated nothing else thus far, I have succeeded in imparting that it is not selfish to want some things for you! However, before doing any act of magick, you should ask yourself the following questions:

- Is this something I really want, or is this something that somebody else wants for me?
- Is this something I really need?
- How badly do I want or need it?
- What are the possible consequences of making this happen in my life?
- What might I be willing to sacrifice in order to make this happen?
- Which of these possible consequences and sacrifices am I not willing to accept?
- Why do I want or need this?
- Can I trust my own motivations?
- Will anyone possibly be hurt by this action? If so, am I willing to accept the consequences of that? (Remember the Threefold Law.)
- Am I, intentionally or unintentionally, interfering with anyone else's free will?
- Is there a more effective way I can phrase my request so that it goes to the heart of what I actually want?

When you have answered these questions to your satisfaction, move on to the next exercise. We are going to cast a spell!

Exercise 13: The Spell

First, consider your responses in the previous exercise.

Begin by coming up with a phrase that expresses your desire as clearly and concisely as you possibly can. Be specific! For instance, if you are doing a spell to bring a male lover into your life, and you don't like hairy men, say that! You are allowed to set conditions. Write it down. Revise it. Revise it again until you are satisfied that it is exactly what you want.

For example, I want recognition for my accomplishments, and financial success. So I might write it like so: "I want financial success and professional acknowledgment and achievement as a writer and a Witch."

Next, write a statement that phrases your Intent as though you already have it. You might begin it with "I am" or "I have," or end it with "this is so" or "I will have this by X date." Consider any clarifications you might want to add or limitations you may wish to establish. What are you willing, and unwilling, to sacrifice in order to make this happen? If you are happy with your statement, move on to the next exercise.

Exercise 14: Manifestation

Now, we need to take this statement and translate it into something your subconscious understands. My statement is too long; I need to simplify it. Perhaps I could draw a picture of me signing books in a bookstore. Or I could use a language of symbols, such as drawing the sign for Jupiter for success and a dollar sign for making money, along with a quill to represent writing.

We'll discuss more about planetary symbols and associations later, but for now, just draw a simple picture or use symbols that mean something to you. Don't overthink it or you'll second-guess yourself!

Take this symbol or drawing and write your Statement of Intent on it as detailed in the previous exercise, so that the two are associated.

Now that you've done this, concentrate on visualizing the successful result with all the clarity and intensity you can! You should be fairly good at this by now, since we've been practicing these skills from the beginning. Add all your senses!

Now—and here's the real trick—invest this image with enough emotional intensity to communicate your passionate desire to see it happening in your life right now! And believe; believe with the whole of your being that it will happen! Call upon the Divine as you understand it to help you, to make this part of your life. Say out loud a phrase that fixes it in your mind as having been completed, such as "Amen," "It is done," or "So mote it be."

FROM THE ASTRAL TO THE MATERIAL

Magick doesn't end with the casting of the spell. Now it's time to bring your Intent into the physical realm. There are a couple things you need to do (and not do!) in order to make your Intent manifest.

Exercise 15: Seal the Deal

Now that you have your piece of paper with your spell on it, what do you do with it? You use it as a tool to perform an act of ritual that seals your Intent in your mind. There are a few different options. Please trust your intuition and do whichever one feels appropriate.

1. You can release the paper to the elements, visualizing this as the act that takes your Intent out into the Universe. You can toss the statement into a stream and watch the water carry it away. You can fold it into a paper airplane and toss it off a windy mountaintop. You can burn it and visualize the obstacles preventing it from manifesting in your life turning to ash. You can bury it under your house. (If you're trying to get rid of something, washing it away in running water, burning it, or burying it at a crossroads is also traditional.)

2. You can carry your Intent with you, and visualize it attracting that desire into your life; in which case, you keep it until the spell has manifested. You might carry it in a medicine bag around your neck or in your purse or vehicle, put it in your pillowcase or at the head of your bed, or tape it to your mirror or computer screen. Then you thank the Divine and release it through one of the elemental methods. Visualize the energy of the paper being released back into the Universe with gratitude now that the spell is fulfilled.

3. You can place it in a special box that you have set aside specifically to hold spells until they manifest. (A treasured jewelry box might work as well, especially if it has powerful emotional or sentimental associations.) When the spell has manifested, dispose of the paper using one of the methods described above: throwing it away, burning it, washing it away, burying it.

Make your choice, and send your act of magick into the world like a sail-boat on a river, or a message in a bottle.

Don't Give the Universe an "Opt-Out" Option!

Every day, people are straying away from the church and going back to God.

—Lenny Bruce, satirist

No matter which name we choose to call the Divine, I believe we are co-creators with divinity, and the Divine spark exists within us all. The Divine expects us to take personal responsibility for our own actions. So since we are partially divine ourselves, don't you think the Divine trusts us to know what we're doing (or at least think we know)?

We know that sometimes, your True Will might stop you from doing something that you believe you want to do. Or, perhaps you might have mixed feelings about something and so you end up fighting yourself. But this is your own interference! This is not the will of the gods (or demons) stopping you from getting what you want. Hexes do happen, but they are exceptionally rare and easily broken if you train your Will to not allow them to affect you. You always have a choice, even if it doesn't feel like it. It's just that the consequences of doing other than what you have done, or not done, may be something that you are unwilling to accept. That's not the same as not having a choice.

And sometimes, the Divine will have a mission for you, and you will feel Her hand upon you. That's a beautiful experience, but trust that the purpose asked of you is something that is also in accordance with your own True Will.

Believe your magick will happen and the Divine wants you to succeed; and then trust the Universe to take care of it (though it may take some time and you may need patience). And if you decide, after a time, that the magick you have instigated really has failed, troubleshoot it, figure out why, and if necessary, cast the spell again in a more beneficial way.

Doing the Real-World Work

The Gods help those who help themselves.
—"Hercules and the Waggoner," *Aesop's Fables*

Sometimes, a spell might take so long to manifest that it seems like it's a hopeless cause. You would be amazed how often I hear about this! A friend of mine did a spell to get a new job, and it took her months and months to find beneficial employment. Her spell seemed sound, her training was sufficient to the task, and she didn't have any immediate enemies who were likely hexing her. But then I asked her, "So where have you applied?" thinking that maybe she was looking for work in fields she hated and was radiating her true lack of interest when she went to interviews, and she said, "Oh, I haven't." I blinked at her. "Have you called anybody? Have you written any emails for positions advertised online?" I asked. She said she had not. Apparently, she was waiting for the job to find her! Well, I thought it should be common sense that your chances of finding a job increase significantly when you actually go out and look for one!

In order to increase your chances of success, you need to actually do what you can in the real, physical world to bring about your Intent through the "normal" channels. Magick influences probabilities in your favor, but so does footwork in the real world. You need both on your side if you want your magick to be quick and effective!

Even magick for other people works better this way. If you're trying to cure your friend's cancer, she will do better if she seeks medical treatment. If there's nothing else you can do—perhaps your friend's cancer is inoperable— then you might as well do magick too, because you've done everything else you can.

Remember this, though: First, interfering with someone else's free will is dangerous, and maybe your friend is tired of living with the pain and the disability and wishes to take another kick at the can in the next life. That's her choice. When doing healing work, it's fine to send healing without direct permission, but it is better received if your patient aligns his or her Will with yours to the purpose. If you can't ask direct permission, always include the caveat "if this is for their Highest Good" or "An it harm none."

Second, sometimes there are significant forces allied against your purpose. While I don't believe anything is impossible, sometimes it's really, really difficult and maybe you just can't do it right now. Just do your best. Go back to the discussion on a conflict of Wills and consider how best to beat that.

Exercise 16: Doing the Footwork

Make a list of the real-world steps you will need to take to implement your magick. Which ones can you do right now? Which ones have to wait because something else is required first? If there are first steps you can do right away, go out and do them. Check them off your list. Then work on the next steps. Work through this process one piece at a time to its conclusion.

LETTING IT GO

This is the part that is hardest for me, and it may be very difficult for you too. There is a fine line between being empowered and being a control freak. You can't control everything. There are millions of other Wills that you share the world with, and they need what they need too.

Trust the Universe to fulfill your desire; try not to worry. Know deep in your heart that this thing you want will happen, that the Universe, the Divine, loves you and knows you need it, and it will happen when it needs to and not a moment before. And it may take a form you do not expect. Do not fret about what could go wrong. This is the purpose for the act of ritual that "seals the deal." You've done all you can do now. Let it go, and don't look back.

Exercise 17: Releasing Your Spell to the Universe

Take a moment to commune with the Divine. Speak with an attitude of gratitude. Preferably just after your act of ritual to "seal the deal," but any time afterward, whether the spell has manifested yet or not, thank the Divine for helping you cocreate your Will in this Universe. Like leaving it in the hands of good and reliable friends, trust the Divine to fulfill your request. Don't micromanage. Let it go.

WORKING MAGICK WITH OTHERS

You may reach a point in your practice when you prefer to work in a group. You can gather some like-minded friends (I recommend Amber K's *Coven Craft* and Judy Harrow's *Wicca Covens* for advice on how to do this), or you can find a local coven to join. Witches are usually easier to find in large urban areas. Try searching Facebook, Google, or your most popular local event listing service. A couple good websites are *www.witchvox.com,* which lists groups and events by region, or *www.paganpride.org,* which lists Pagan Pride gatherings by location. Local coordinators tend to know a lot of people in the community and can probably recommend you to someone. You can also try asking at your local metaphysical store.

With group magick, everyone's Intent must be in as perfect alignment as possible. Otherwise, you will end up with a conflict of Wills working against the same spell! Using common symbols, and a common framework to visualize in, gives everyone involved something to focus on together, so that everyone is taking part in the same story. This is also why most religions, Wiccan traditions, and magickal lodges have a consistent pattern to their ceremonies every time; that's why we call it "ritual." We'll be breaking down the process of Wiccan ritual in chapter 3.

When meeting as a group, you'll have much more success with your Willworking if you clear away as many outside influences as you can. Always be sure that you are working in sacred space. Many groups choose to practice in a dedicated area—a temple, so to speak—specifically for the working of magick and the sharing of ceremony. Most Witches don't have this, so they make sacred space wherever they are by casting a circle.

Always be sure that you take some action to clear negativity from the area, thus symbolically clearing the space for your work. Here are some suggestions:

- Smudging—burn sage and other herbs to clear the area energetically, making sure to get every corner.
- Besoming—sweep a broom counterclockwise around the room (mostly in the air) while visualizing all negativity and distractions in the area being swept out with it.
- Using crystals—good choices include hematite and black tourmaline, quartz, or citrine.
- Taking a ritual bath—sit in the tub and relax until all negativity and distractions drain away, then open the drain and visualize all that stuff being carried away with the bathwater. Stay in the tub until it is done. Adding salt to the water enhances the effect.

Exercise 18: Solitary Energy Clearing

Practice one of the methods of energy clearing prior to ritual work, whether that is meditation or a spell.

Exercise 19: Group Energy Clearing

As a group, join hands and visualize positive energy radiating out from all of you at the epicenter, like a glowing, white-gold light. See it drive all the negative energy and distractions before it out of the area, or destroy them on contact. It may help to have one person direct the meditation through narration.

Alternatively, starting in the north of the room, take turns besoming with a broom as described above. Pass it around the circle and let everyone take turns sweeping negative influences away from the center of the room.

SELF-EVALUATION

We have come to the end of the first chapter! Good job for sticking with it! How do you feel you are doing so far? Take a moment now to review what you've learned, and consider what you might be able to do to improve upon that work. You can write in your Book of Shadows, or simply run through a mental evaluation for your own purposes. Remember, you're the only one who is ever going to know what you said, and if you don't answer honestly, it is only you who will be harmed!

chapter two

TRANCE

Magick is the art of changing consciousness in conformity with Will.
—DION FORTUNE

What exactly is a trance?

Technically, any state of consciousness—awake, asleep, comatose, hypnotized, and otherwise—is a "trance." But when Witches refer to a trance, we are generally speaking of an "altered state of consciousness," or a state that differs from what we think of as "normal" waking consciousness. Much of the training in magick and Wiccan mysticism involves altering your consciousness from one state to another. There are two ways to do this. We can "go deeper" by relaxing and descending into deeper levels of meditation, or we can reach for higher states through stimulation. Different brain waves (measured in cycles per second, or hertz (Hz), indicate different levels of consciousness, and the ability to change consciousness at will is the only real ability that is required for successful magick.

TRANCE THROUGHOUT TIME

Throughout human history, mystics and shamans have used trances to heal, seek knowledge, and gain insight beyond our conscious capabilities. Shamans use trances to conduct healing work that the more scientifically minded would recognize as psychotherapy from very ancient times, and to interact between the spirit and physical worlds. In Ancient Greece, pilgrims visited the Temple of Asclepius at Epidaurus for "dream incubation" and healing sleep, in which dreams were interpreted in much the same way that modern psychoanalysts do (though omens were also read). Mystics in most of the world's major religious traditions, including Yoga, Sufism, Buddhism, Islam, Shamanism, Native Spirituality, Aboriginal traditions of Australia, and medieval and American Christianity used trances to seek divine insight and religious communion and ecstasy, which you can find in the writings of Hildegard of Bingen, St. John of the Cross, Meister Eckhart, St. Theresa, St. Francis of Assisi, Crazy Horse, and modern writers Carlos Castaneda, Lynn Andrews, and Stuart Wilde.

Trances used for divination have an ancient history. Most of the cultures of the ancient classical world speak of *sibyls*; or prophetesses, whom leaders and generals would consult before waging war or making major political decisions. Oracles, serving a similar role, have also been significant in most ancient cultures, including Ancient Greece, China, India, Mesoamerica, Nigeria, Hawaii, and Celtic Europe, where Druids and Ovates served that function. The *völva* of Norse cultures were much like the sibyls or the frenzied oracle at Delphi, and the Nechung Oracle continues to serve a significant function in the religion and government of Tibet. All these seers would achieve either a meditative or ecstatic trance state to deliver their words of wisdom.

Military trances also have a long history. The Berserkers of the Norse (the Vikings) were famed for their rage-driven madness, their apparently superhuman strength, and their immunity to pain. Similar trance states are described in the writings of the Romans referring to the blue woad painted Pictish warriors, and in the description of the Celtic "warp-spasm" that Cuchulain was legendary for. Muslim "assassins" in the age of the Crusades were actually called *Hashishin,* named for the hash oil that they reputedly smoked to achieve their legendary determination and precision in combat. From as early as the sixteenth century, march music was used to entrain an army into a battle trance: marching and attacking as one and feeling little pain or fear.

Franz Mesmer and Milton Erickson's work in hypnotherapy is used by modern psychologists to treat neuroses, obsessions, addictions, and anxiety disorders. Modern shamans and mediums use trances much as they always have—to communicate between the spiritual and physical worlds. Mystics all over the world continue to use trances to achieve astounding feats such as levitation, piercing, scourging, hibernation, and walking on hot coals. Modern Witches, channels, and mediums use trances to call spirits and gods into their bodies to communicate with us.

METHODS OF TRANCE INDUCTION

There are hundreds of different methods of inducing a trance, which can be classified by the means used:

- Auditory and rhythmic driving (drumming, music, guided meditation)
- Kinesthetic driving (dancing, mudras, ritual, yoga, breathing, and sexual stimulation)
- Visual driving (visual meditation, mandala, pendulum, film, art, yantra, strobe lights, cloud watching)
- Olfactory driving (perfume, incense, oils, pheromones, flowers, and any scent that has emotional associations)
- Gustatory driving (herbs, starvation, hallucinogens, alcohol, stimulants, aphrodisiacs and other drugs)
- Disciplines (Yoga, Sufism, transcendental meditation, ritual)
- Trauma (traumatic accident, piercing, scourging, sleep deprivation, decompression sickness, fever, sensory deprivation)
- Naturally occurring (dreams, lucid dreams, euphoria, ecstasy, psychosis, out-of-body experiences, visions, ESP, and channeling)
  In the course of this book, we'll cover all of these.

ALPHA CONSCIOUSNESS

You reach alpha consciousness (8–14 Hz) when you are relaxed and daydreaming. Increased memory, light meditation, and psychic intuition take place here, so it's important for a Witch to be able to attain this state.

Exercise 20: Daydreaming

Make some time during your daily meditation to work on your daydreaming skills! Visualize yourself doing something in your life that you have always wanted to do. Maybe you always wanted to be a rock star, a doctor, a ballerina, or a bestselling writer (ahem). Don't censor yourself.

What might your new activity feel like? Listen to the sounds, smell the smells, see the sights. For example, if you want to be a rock star, imagine the cheering roar of the huge crowd in the sold-out stadium when you take the stage, the smell of sweat and metal, the songs you'd sing and the crowd's reaction to it. If you have a guitar, feel the pressure of the strings on your fingers, the weight of the strap on your shoulder, the pick in your fingers, your wrist vigorously strumming. If you are singing, feel the cold metal of the microphone in your hand and hear your voice ringing out through the speakers and the monitors. You get the idea. It may help to put on music that fits the scene, especially if you have headphones to plug in so that you can hear nothing else.

Spend at least ten minutes a day on this, visualizing it as clearly as you can. Do not firmly direct the daydream, but as long as it remains positive and encouraging, allow it to go where it will.

Beta Consciousness

Beta consciousness (12–20 Hz) is our normal, waking state, when we study, communicate, and use our logical left brain. You have been using beta waves merely by reading this book.

Exercise 21: Study Hall

To practice beta state, study something that interested you from the previous chapter, and have a friend quiz you on it.

Theta Consciousness

Theta consciousness occurs at 4–8 Hz, with "shamanic consciousness" occurring at 4.5–6 Hz. This state takes you to deeper meditation or what people typically think of as a "trance" state. We enter this level during sleep, and trance channeling or drawing down the moon (when a priestess aspects the Goddess through her body) takes place here. Sometimes we enter theta accidentally while performing rote tasks, and we don't remember driving the last ten miles or putting the dishes away.

Exercise 22: Self-Hypnosis

To practice reaching this state, you can use any deep guided meditation. This exercise demonstrates how to put the hypnotic state of shamanic consciousness to work for you.

Visualize a cave opening in your safe place, and a staircase heading down into the earth in a counterclockwise spiral. Descend gently and slowly, taking your time. At the bottom of the staircase is a pool of comfortably warm water. Descend slowly into the water until you feel like you are gently floating and you are a little numb. Your heart may begin to race as you enter the water; this is perfectly normal and it will pass.

When you feel yourself floating, consider a problem you are attempting to deal with. Then visualize three boxes floating in the water that contain positive elements to heal the problem. As you open them, narrate what is happening in the present tense in a positive way that avoids using negatives. (For example: "I open the box and a radiant light engulfs me. I feel warm and supported. I am loved and respected. This is a part of me now and can never be taken away.") Adapt this to your individual needs. Repeat your statements as many times as you wish, though two or three times should be enough.

When you are satisfied with what you have accomplished, and you feel you are ready, swim back to the stairs and begin to ascend in a clockwise direction. When you emerge from the water, you may suddenly feel heaviness on your shoulders or body. If this is distressing, wait until this passes and continue. When you have reached the top of the stairs, step back out from the cave.

When you are ready, bring yourself back to beta consciousness. You can visualize a door to the outside world opening, or you can repeat "wake up, wake up, wake up," or perhaps something that your mom used to say to wake you up in the morning. This will return you to a conscious, wakeful state.

DELTA CONSCIOUSNESS

The lowest level of brain functioning is delta consciousness (4 Hz or less). This is the state of deep sleep, deep trance, and coma. Most of us don't remember delta consciousness. People who do not get sufficient levels of delta wave sleep suffer from all the symptoms of sleep deprivation, whether they have slept or not.

If you are having difficulty remembering your dreams, or you believe you do not dream at all, this next exercise may help.

Exercise 23: Dream Recollection

Before you go to sleep at night, place a notebook and pen (or a computer, or a dictation machine, etc.) beside your bed. Make a conscious decision as you fall asleep to remember your dreams. Repeat this as a mantra and use it as a form of meditation. If your thoughts start racing over the day, bring them back to this mantra. When you wake up in the middle of the night from a dream (which happens much more frequently than we think), record as many details of it as you can remember. Do this right away, because dreams begin to fade immediately after waking, and if you have not made an effort to preserve that information, most of it will be lost within ten minutes.

If you struggle with this, you can try setting an alarm in the middle of your sleep cycle. This is the time that you are most likely to be actively dreaming, and waking then will increase your chances of remembering.

You will be amazed at what starts coming to you through your dreams! Most of us have significant flashes of personal insight and even psychic experiences when we shut down beta consciousness for a little while.

This exercise will prepare you for astral travel, psychic work, and lucid dreaming, and it is also helpful training in interpreting visions. Keep at it until it is reflexive. It takes twenty-one days of repeating a behavior until it becomes a habit, so be persistent!

GAMMA CONSCIOUSNESS

Gamma waves range from 20–40 (considered the ideal) up to 250 Hz. The greatest mysteries of the human mind might be found here, from "battlefield consciousness," to eureka moments, divine inspiration, satori, kundalini risings, and out-of-body experiences. I call this "being in my muse" when I am driven by something beyond myself in creative projects, and the writing or the music is pouring from me like water without any conscious effort on my part. There is a reason Druids linked bardic creative inspiration and divine inspiration. They called it *awen,* or "fire in the head."

Exercise 24: Awen

The next time you find yourself inspired to create a great work of art, write something amazing, play music like a genius, or run like your feet have wings (especially if it is something you are exceptionally good at), take note of the heightened state of awareness that you find yourself in. Absorb it for a while. How do you feel? What is happening physiologically? How can you increase your chances of repeating this experience? Write about it in your Book of Shadows.

Inducing Trance

Some people find trancing really easy—almost too easy, maybe. Others find it extremely difficult. There are two major factors that seem to affect this ability: imagination and brain chemistry. People who read novels voraciously, engage in artistic and creative pursuits, or simply daydream frequently have a much easier time of learning how to trance than those who spend most of their waking hours engaged in left-brain beta consciousness, such as people who work in office jobs like data entry and taxi dispatching. Also, because meditation is a form of trance, if you have trouble meditating, you are likely to have trouble with other forms of trance as well.

People who suffer from seizures, sleep disorders, mood disorders, or mental illnesses, especially those requiring medication, may also have difficulties.

> **Warning: Consult with your doctor if you are doing this work and have seizures, because a change in consciousness may trigger one. Mood balancing or antipsychotic medication may also make this work more challenging, but *do not stop taking your medication without consulting your doctor first.* It takes more work, but your mind will adapt.**

If you find trancing easy, you may end up daydreaming or accessing altered states of consciousness without intending to in your daily life at first. You may feel the desire to stop practicing if it becomes extremely inconvenient. If you intend to persist, constant grounding exercises can be helpful, as can eating or drinking tea to diffuse an inconvenient trance. You might also try carrying a grounding stone such as hematite or lodestone in your pocket. Hold the stone in your hand when you find yourself beginning to drift.

Trancing might bring up the sludge of your subconscious. You may encounter "negative entities," since you are accessing the otherworld in your altered state. Most of the time, these negative entities either come from your own subconscious mind, or they are drawn by the sludge you bring to the surface. You may even begin to see them in your waking consciousness out of the corner of your eye when you are not looking directly at them. They have no power over you, and they cannot harm you without your permission. Create your bubble of protection before you begin any trancework and you should have very little difficulty with them.

How It Works

Stimulating a trance is usually accomplished through a process called "brain wave entrainment": Your brain waves will try to match noticeable rhythms from the outside world. Most of the methods of inducing trance involve using rhythmic or shifting sounds, body movements, or visual triggers. We're going to examine some of the more common or easily accessible methods and put them to work.

Visual Driving

Visually driven trances work according to a principle called photic driving. Certain visual stimuli, such as types of art, flickering candlelight, shifting clouds, pendulums, and strobe lights induce an echoing production of brain wave frequencies through oscillation, or pulses, of light and shadow or movement. Hypnotists put this principle to work in the classic pendulum-swinging procedure. There are all kinds of videos using light and oscillating patterns on YouTube (most of them are marked "Visual Acid Trip" and so forth). This principle and practice is also utilized in color healing and at rock concerts and raves.

Exercise 25: Visual Driving with the Elements

You have already practiced the use of visual driving with Exercise 4: Candle Meditation Now we are going to use visual driving in other ways. Many things will induce a trance simply by watching them or the way they move.

Find something in the natural world to focus your visual attention on for a minimum of fifteen minutes. Allow your thoughts to drift over shifting of light and shadow, speed of movement, shapes and images, etc. Allow memories to occur, but do not dwell on them. When you are finished, pick up a pen (or computer) and write whatever comes to you. Sometimes you will find this amazingly inspirational, and sometimes you will receive Divine insight or psychic messages.

Practice this at least once a week for a full month. In the first month, choose any of the Earth methods. In the second, choose any of the Air methods. In the third, use Fire methods, and in the last, use Water methods.

TABLE 1: Visual Driving with the Elements

Week One: Earth	Stare up into the leaves of a tree (the Druids practiced this in oak groves); stare into the depths of a crystal; study a rock face; draw patterns in sand; watch insects crawling along the ground.
Week Two: Air	Watch the clouds; stare at the grass or flowers blowing in the wind; study wind chimes twisting and turning; watch mist swirl; observe a storm; watch a bird circling; study a moth or butterfly fanning; contemplate the moon and the stars.
Week Three: Fire	Practice your candle meditation; stare into the depths of a campfire; watch dust motes in a sunbeam; stare into a fireplace; watch a meteor shower; contemplate the stars.
Week Four: Water	Watch waves drift back and forth on a beach; stare into the rain; look into the depths of a deep lake; watch a creek or stream run; stare into a reflective pool; scry with water; contemplate a waterfall.

AUDITORY AND RHYTHMIC DRIVING

One of the most effective methods to induce trance is through sound. People have been using this method for thousands of years, right back to drums and rattles in dancing, meditation, and shamanism, but recently we have begun to understand the science behind it.

Exercise 26: Your Safe Place

For this exercise we are going to use a guided meditation, which is a form of auditory driving. This is a technique in which you are directed to visualize a particular scenario and your participation in it. You'll need those visualization skills you were practicing in chapter 1!

For best results, record the following guided meditation on a tape recorder or your computer, or get someone to help you out by reading it to you. Within a coven structure, a facilitator can read the meditation while everyone else participates. Try to use a soothing, relaxing tone, like when you are telling a small child that everything is going to be okay. Read slowly, and allow time for visualization when a scene is described or an action is suggested. Lulling your listeners to sleep actually is your goal! Play instrumental music, if that helps. Perhaps lie in shavasana. Do whatever feels comfortable for you.

Once you are completely relaxed, realize that you are standing in the most beautiful place you have ever seen. This is a natural place, and it is just perfect for you. Perhaps you are on the shores of a lake, or in a green glade, or perhaps an ocean lagoon. Wherever you are, the temperature is perfectly comfortable. If you like things warm, they are warm, and if you like them cooler, there is a lovely cool breeze. Maybe you share this space with other creatures, be they natural or mystical. But no other human beings are here; this place is yours alone. No harm can come to you here.

Just take a moment now, and enjoy the beauty and peace of this lovely, natural place. Spend some time, look around, and enjoy your sacred solitude.

Allow ten minutes to meditate on this safe place and visualize. At ten minutes, you are likely actually relaxed and in deep healing meditation.

Now that you have spent some time in this safe place, it is time to say goodbye. Gently say farewell to any creatures, beings, or special features. Know that you can return here at any time.

When you are ready, start moving your fingers and toes, stretching and reacquainting yourself with your physical body. Become aware of your itches and the clothes in contact with your body. When you feel ready, open your eyes.

Practice this exercise whenever you want to.

Exercise 27: Drumming Circle (Rhythmic Driving)

For this exercise you'll need a drum, a rattle, or some other percussion instrument.

Get together with some other drummers and practice drumming. You could get a group of friends together, do this as an exercise for your magickal circle or coven, or join a drumming group (which you can often find in public parks or at metaphysical stores, raves, festivals, or yoga studios.) Note the effect on your brain through auditory and kinesthetic driving. There's a reason why we've used this technique since before the dawn of human history!

Isochronic Tones

Isochronic tones are regular beats of a single tone, often repeated in very quick cycles, which entrain your brain waves to cycle at the same tonal frequencies. There are many software companies and New Age musicians taking advantage of this technology, but we've been using it for millennia. Isochronic tones are sometimes produced in nature by campfires, wind, rivers, and rain, but they can also be found in machinery such as engines, the thrumming of train tracks or electric fans, the click of playing cards in bike tires, the whir of a pinwheel, and even in music—especially music designed to induce a trance, such as shamanic drumming, rattles, droning, chanting, or modern forms like trance music and dubstep.

Binaural Beats

Two tones close to each other will induce a response in the brain equivalent to the difference between them. These rhythms are known as binaural, or "two sound" beats. The ears do not actually hear the sound, but the brain creates the tonal effect. You would use a binaural beat to relax, visualize, and daydream, so it's probably perfect for casting a spell. One ear must hear something entirely different from the other ear, so headphones (or a really brilliant surround sound system with speakers at opposite ears) are necessary to make use of these frequencies.

Monaural Beats

Monaural beats are created by presenting two different tones at slightly different pitches, creating a rhythmic increase and decrease in amplitude. However, these beats are carried in the open air and result from the brain trying to "locate" the source of the sound with its differing tones based on phase. This is rare in nature but very common in manmade objects, such as fans, the thrumming of two jet engines running at differing speeds, vibrating crystal bowls, didgeridoos, sitars and other droning instruments, and drumming circles. The throat singing of northern cultures such as the Norse and the Inuit and toning used as a vocal exercise in numerous Pagan and New Age circles have the same effect.

Exercise 28: Auditory Brain Wave Entrainment

If you have an Internet connection, log on to YouTube and search for "isochronic tones," "binaural beats" and "monaural beats" in turn. Select something that sounds appealing to achieve an effect you want and have a listen.

Many of these require headphones, so be sure to get a good pair! You can find audio tracks to increase your effective intelligence, help you focus, relieve pain, attract money, and much, much more. Most of them include visuals that are also designed to induce trance—kaleidoscopic patterns, fractals, spinning spirals, shifting colors, tunnel effects, and so forth. If you want to watch the visuals, go ahead, but keep in mind that it is the auditory effects you are after.

Some of them are just the tones, and some of them imbed the tones in music. I found the music videos much more effective and appealing than the tones alone, but they worked okay if I kept them on a very low volume that I could barely hear.

I even created my own album that utilizes isochronic tones and binaural beats for brain wave entrainment called *Elemental*. I wrote a song for each of five major types of brain waves that you can entrain, inspired by the four cardinal elements plus spirit, and I used a carrier frequency for each that is suited to those elements and the magickal working you might wish to do with the music. You can find the songs on my YouTube channel at www.youtube.com/user/SableAradia or you can order the CDs or digital downloads at sablearadia.bandcamp.com. Please feel free to distribute them to your friends as long as credit is given.

Put those brain waves to work for you!

- Put on something that utilizes alpha waves to visualize, or work a ritual!
- Study the material in this book or write while playing a beta waves piece.
- Use theta wave music to meditate on a problem.
- Make a playlist of delta wave music to sleep by.
- Use gamma waves to create art or seek divine inspiration or communion.

Exercise 29: Balancing Frequency (Groups Only)

Have your group all join hands. Beginning with the ritual leader, direct energy from your right hand into the left hand of the person next to you, and run it around the circle in an electric circuit. You will feel it naturally growing and increasing as it spins.

If you like, you can start toning together as well. One person begins making a droning noise or singing an *aaahhhhh* sound, and everyone else joins in with long, continuous noises. You can harmonize or be at entirely different pitches, creating a discordant sound like a wolf pack howling together. You can even howl if you want! If you are using this to balance the frequency of your energies, taper off naturally once you feel all is in accord; or, you can use this energy to build a cone of power, which spirals around the circle up into a point in the circle's center as the toning gets louder and louder. When the cone is ready, the ritual leader directs everyone to release the energy toward your purpose, either by crying "Now!" or raising her arms suddenly, or yelling wordlessly. The energy goes to its purpose and everyone centers and grounds.

KINESTHETIC DRIVING

Kinesthetic driving is anything that induces a trance through movement, which is usually rhythmic and repetitive. You have already touched on this in Exercise 27: Drumming Circle (Rhythmic Driving), which also becomes a repetitious physical task that you lose yourself in the rhythm of doing (drumming, rattling, etc.). Here are a couple simple ways to put the technique to work for you.

Exercise 30: Walking Meditation

Pick a repetitious physical task that you do on a daily basis. Perhaps you walk along a specific route from the office, or maybe you use an exercise bike while watching TV in the evening. It doesn't need to be that physical, either. I like to do this while doing the dishes, because that is a very dull repetitive task that I dislike!

Concentrate on the way your body moves. If you are walking, pay attention to the way your foot makes contact with the ground. What part of your foot touches the ground first? What follows? If you are doing dishes, how do your hands move? What direction do you wash the plates in? How does the glass surface feel on your fingers? Just be mindfully aware of this sensation and pattern, without overanalyzing it.

Allow yourself to drift into that "unfocused focus" state. Let thoughts come and go. Do not fixate on any one daydream, or allow a thought to become distracting. Try expanding your awareness to be open to receiving impressions or visions of what the following day will bring you. Ask for them! With practice, you will soon become accustomed to receiving such insights. Write them down as soon as you become aware of them.

Exercise 31: Take a Ritual Bath

Run a bath at a temperature you prefer. Add some salt and scented oils you like, or perhaps some herbs (suggestions in chapter 4). Perhaps light a candle and turn off the lights, and sit in the bath for some time, being aware of the feel of the water on your body and changes of temperature. Wash yourself gently and take time to enjoy the experience. Add more water when it gets cold if you like. When you are finished, allow all the water to run down the drain before you get out of the tub, visualizing all negativity and distractions draining with it. This purification practice is a good habit to get into before doing magick or ritual.

Exercise 32: Go for a Country Drive

Driving a vehicle brings many different factors together at once to induce a trance—the rote physicality (especially on a long drive) of keeping the wheel straight, checking your mirrors, and correcting your slouching back; the vibration of the tires on the road; the hum of the engine and the stereo; the blinking traffic lights and dotted yellow lines whirring by. This is not a bad thing! Remember, any effective change in consciousness can be considered a trance; it's just a matter of not falling into a deep enough trance that you fall asleep.

For this exercise, take yourself for a relaxing country drive. Feel free to use whatever music you wish, especially if it encourages your imagination. Try to induce a low-level alpha trance, encouraging daydreaming and visualization. Consider something that has been on your mind without making a huge effort to concentrate on it. See if the solution just naturally comes to you! Don't be too worried if you fall into a light theta state, so that you don't remember driving the last ten miles. You may even find this helpful when driving; I've been known to get intuitive flashes to suddenly slow down, for example, to find a deer wandering out in the middle of my path as I round a sharp corner. Just don't fall asleep!

People have been using this method to consider their problems since cars were invented. Often, artists will take a drive to focus and gain clarity. I do some of my best writing and imagining this way. Two or three gifted psychics I know claim that they do their best channeling while behind the wheel as well.

Olfactory and Gustatory Driving

Olfactory driving is using your sense of smell, or pheromones, to induce a trance. Many things can accomplish this; incense, aromatherapy, perfume, foods, or any smells that have memories associated with them.

Gustatory driving is using anything that you swallow or ingest (or don't, such as in the case of starvation) to induce a trance. This includes oils, herbs, overeating a turkey dinner, fasting, and, of course, drugs of various stripes.

We'll be spotlighting these two methods of trance induction in chapter 4, but for now I would like to give you a little taste of how they work.

Exercise 33: A Cup of Tea

Make yourself a cup of tea. Choose your tea based on the effect you're intending to induce.

TABLE 2: Simple Psychoactive Teas

Intended Effect	Brain Wave State	Best Kinds of Tea to Use
Increase focus, good mood, and concentration	Beta or even gamma waves in a high enough dose	Earl Grey, ginger, or orange pekoe
Achieve a state of relaxation	Alpha or theta	Lavender or mint
Achieve a deep state of relaxation or relieve anxiety	Theta or delta	"Sleepytime" blend, especially one that contains catnip or valerian

Make sure that you thoroughly enjoy your tea by holding the cup in your hands, smelling it, relaxing while you're enjoying it, and perhaps dressing it up in a fancy teacup. Drink it slowly, keep it covered between sips to preserve its flavor, and record your results in your magickal journal. How does it make you feel? Does it force a more dramatic change of consciousness than other techniques you have experimented with thus far?

TRAUMATIC DRIVING

Some trances are driven entirely by traumas or suffering. Pain has its own rhythm and consciousness-changing effects. We'll be revisiting this in chapter 7.

Exercise 34: Breathe Through the Pain

I would not advocate deliberately causing yourself pain, but the next time you experience a significant pain, rather than reaching for the nearest painkiller, try "breathing through the pain." This will look and feel a lot like Lamaze techniques. What is the anatomy of your pain? Throbbing, burning, or aching? Be aware of the cycles of pain. Find a rhythm. After a while, do you feel how your consciousness shifts? Record your results.

When you have a free long weekend and don't have to function and work for a few days, you can use one of the most ancient and most effective techniques we have for changing consciousness: depriving yourself of sleep. Deliberately see how long you can go without sleeping, and use the opportunity to meditate and seek insight. Alternatively, try seeing how long you can go while getting sleep in tiny short bursts. Mothers of young children understand this practice well, and so do people who work on-call jobs or split shifts!

Warning: Do not do anything that requires your full attention at this time, such as operating a vehicle or heavy machinery. Also do not use this exercise if you suffer from any sleep disorders, are taking medication that affects your sleep, or suffer from anxiety disorders of any kind, including PTSD.

Be aware that you may be irritable and difficult to live with during this experiment, and warn your loved ones.

TRANCEWORK

Well, now that you know how to induce trances, how does this apply to magick?

Dion Fortune tells us "Magick is the art of changing consciousness according to Will." Every act of magick involves a change of consciousness. That is the only thing that makes it possible. Beta consciousness is not capable of magickal thinking on its own.

Olympic athletes use creative visualization in their training programs. They consciously take themselves through an alpha or theta visualization process where they actually see, and *experience*, themselves running the race, or skating the routine, or skiing a perfect run. By visualizing this, they experience the whole process *as if it has already happened*. And do you know what? Since our subconscious responds to symbols, metaphors, and feelings, it has no sense of time, and no way to differentiate an intense visualization or dream from what we call "reality." Therefore, to visualize such a thing so clearly, and to believe it, essentially tells your subconscious that *this has already been done*. If you could do it once, why not again?

Dreaming lends itself very well to psychic work with some conscious effort. My first psychic experiences were dreams that came true. I started having them about the time puberty hit. Parapsychologists have noted that puberty is often a time when such things begin to manifest, so there is likely a hormonal component to the necessary altered state.

Sleep deprivation also lends itself well to shifting consciousness. The reason is that the body tries to force the mind into the appropriate states for healing and regeneration when we are still awake! This makes it easier to consciously direct and work with theta and delta states. Significant hormonal changes have similar effects on consciousness to sleep deprivation. You can make these changes of life work for you in accessing altered states; and you can make sleep work for you as well. Most women have a special blessing in that they may also make use of their natural monthly cycles in this way. Perhaps this is the source of "women's intuition."

Exercise 36: Dream Incubation

In order to make best use of this exercise, you will need to have found some success with Exercise 23: Dream Recollection.

While in the process of falling asleep, determine what you would like to dream about! Just as you have decided to recall your dreams, focus meditatively on your chosen dream subject as you drift off. You might seek information on how to solve a problem, or gain flashes of psychic insight.

If this doesn't work right away, keep at it! Practice makes perfect. Journal your results.

Exercise 37: Lucid Dreaming

Successful use of Exercise 36: Dream Incubation is a prerequisite for this exercise.

Lucid dreaming is the ability to consciously direct your dreams and affect their course and outcome. It's not nearly as difficult as it sounds! The ability to consciously recall your dreams is the first step. Don't forget to journal everything! It is important to keep track of even your smallest successes in order to be good at this. Because we have been led to believe for so long that controlling dreams isn't possible, your subconscious needs a little persuasion to see that it's working.

Just as you established a practice of remembering your dreams, focus on a conscious thought just before you fall asleep. Say to yourself, "I can control the course of my dreams." Then go to sleep normally.

Start by directing small things. For instance, if your shoes are blue, try making them red. Try turning water into wine! (It's not hard in a dream, really.)

When you can achieve this on a fairly regular basis, try larger changes. For example, if you're cold in the dream and it's snowing, make it rain instead. You might even be able to change winter to summer, or make the sky purple.

Once you are accomplished with those sorts of shifts, begin to work at altering events. This is really the key stage. It's very handy for dealing with reoccurring nightmares or, better yet, for recollection of traumatic life events. Very effective soul-healing work can be done in this way, giving you control of a situation when you once felt very much out of control, and achieving similar results to years of therapy.

WISDOM OF THE ORACLE

I have mentioned several times that shifting consciousness is the way by which you access your psychic abilities. Now we're going to practice some of that! Let me begin by reassuring you that this is not as hard as it sounds. Some of you will struggle at it more than others, but I can tell you that with persistence, anybody is capable of using this skill.

Exercise 38: Psychic Card Tricks

Get a deck of regular playing cards, or, if you prefer, you can find ESP cards at your local metaphysical store. ESP cards are based on Zener cards (developed by psychologist Karl Zener), and they use a five-suit system instead of a four-suit system for greater clarity and accuracy. They are designed to test the existence of ESP through statistics, and those statistics are useful to us as a guide to indicate how we are doing. Let me explain how it works.

Let's say you are trying to guess what card your friend is holding by suit. If you're using a typical playing card deck, you would be trying to guess whether the card in question is a spade, a diamond, a heart, or a club. You should expect to accurately guess the suit 25 percent of the time by random chance (20 percent with Zener cards). Parapsychologists say a person shows psychic ability if they routinely guess more accurately than this by a "significant margin," which would be 40–50 percent accuracy or greater. Conversely, a person might show repressed psychic ability if he or she routinely guesses abysmally!

In order for these tests to be considered scientifically accurate, you have to repeat them hundreds of times. But they also work as a tool to test yourself for, and improve, your psychic ability.

Telepathy

You'll need a deck of cards and a partner for this exercise.

Remove the jokers from the deck of cards and arrange them in a stack. Ask your partner to pick up the card on the top of the deck and concentrate on what suit it shows. Write down what suit you think it is. Discard the first card and pick up the next. Guess the suit again on paper. Continue this until the deck is completed.

Turn over the discard pile and record how many of your guesses were correct and incorrect. Divide the number of accurate guesses by the total number of cards (which should typically be fifty-two) in order to get your percentage of accurate responses.

You may also wish to note what the symbol/suit actually was in case of similarities. For example, a color-oriented person might routinely get diamonds instead of hearts, while a more structure-oriented person might get spades.

Because there are two types of telepathy (projective and receptive), you may wish to switch places with your partner and do it again. You may find that you are much more on target with one person in the receptive role and the other in the projective role. Just like anything else, some people will be naturally more apt at some psychic skills than others, but with practice, you will find that anyone can improve!

You can up the stakes by performing this exercise from different rooms or even on the phone. Most of the experiments in parapsychology that were popular in the fifties and sixties were conducted in similar conditions.

To adapt this exercise for a group, simply divide into partners. You can even get a better feel for who is a more projective psychic than receptive in this way by changing partners!

Clairvoyance

Conduct this practice just like the telepathy practice, except that your partner should never once look at the card until the deck is finished. Instead, have your partner touch the card that you are supposed to be tuning into before discarding it in the discard stack, and double-check it against your answers.

Precognition

Stack a shuffled deck in a pile. See if you can visualize what the next card is going to be without touching it. Record your guess. Then pick up the card and stack it in a discard pile. Do not look to check whether your guess was right or wrong until you have finished going through the whole deck! Having an emotional response of either excitement or discouragement as you are in the process of making your guesses may affect the psychic information you receive. When you have finished going through the deck, double-check it against your guesses to see how accurate you were.

If you want to adapt this exercise to a group, just have a partner turn over the cards for you after you have made your guess. This way, you have no contact with the card yourself and can have no influence on it. Your partner can record the results as you go, or double-check it against the deck afterward just as you would have done working on your own.

Psychometry

Just like the precognition exercise, except that you should touch the top card without looking at it before or while making your response. (To differentiate between psychometry and precognition is why it is important that you not touch the cards in the precognition practice.)

Exercise 39: Psychic Dice Games

Sometimes more than random chance affects the throw of a die. You can sometimes predict the way a die will roll, and sometimes, you can even influence how it will roll. I hope I don't have to warn you against misusing this!

Precognition

Get a normal six-sided die. Predict what number will come up, then ask a friend to roll the die for you. This will prevent you from subconsciously influencing the roll in any way. Record your results.

When I did this exercise with my brother, I only did it three times. Having been accurate on the first two guesses, in the third, the image of both a one and a two flashed intermittently behind my closed eyelids. After some hesitation, I chose two. He rolled; the die landed in a groove on the carpet, exposing the "one" and the "two" on a perfect diagonal. I quit at that point. I was convinced.

Telekinesis

Those of you with visions of dice floating across tables into your hand or pelting people in the forehead, calm down! The truth is, nothing in magick contradicts the laws of physics.

Get your die again, and try to roll a certain number. You can either roll it yourself or get a friend to roll it for you if you are worried about influencing it with subconscious tiny twitches of your muscles. Record what number you are trying for and what number actually comes up, or tell your friend before he or she rolls what you are trying to achieve.

Exercise 40: Scrying

Find a reflective surface, ideally something dark and reflective, such as a puddle, a deep pool of water, or even your blank TV or computer screen. Witches have also used darkened mirrors or lenses, crystal balls, flat reflective stones, and cauldrons filled with water. This is your scrying surface. Try to position things in such a way that you minimize the reflections shown in the surface (so no overhead lights or backlighting).

Gaze into the surface until it seems to blur and blend. You can even close your eyes, once the proper state of mind has been achieved (relaxed, visualizing, and open to suggestion). Do this until it becomes boring, and then do it some more.

Eventually, feelings and images will come to you. Do not censor or judge them. Simply allow them to come and record them. You could get a friend to write them down, recite the information in a flow-of-consciousness on your computer, video yourself with your webcam, or use an old-fashioned tape recorder.

It may help to have a specific matter you would like information on when you begin, but even if you don't, the information will be relevant, though you may not recognize the symbolism right away. I illustrate how this might look and sound in my YouTube video "Sit for a Spell Episode 7: Scrying and Divination."

What you're trying to achieve is a medium alpha to light theta trance (theta being preferable in the scrying exercise). If you're having trouble reaching that, the reason is usually one of the factors that interfere with meditation. Are you comfortable? Are you stressed and having difficulty relaxing? Are you trying too hard? Relax and open your thoughts without attaching too much emotion to any potential outcome. Above all, trust your instincts, and don't second-guess yourself, or you will lose the ability to listen to that internal voice. After a while, you will begin to develop your own internal dictionary of symbols (or, if you study the symbols of other cultures or the Western magickal tradition, you will start to interpret things in those symbols as well).

Seeing Dead People

Most Witches believe not all sentient beings that exist in the Universe are physical; many of them exist only in spirit, which is to say they are beings of pure consciousness. Some of these beings were once physical, like ghosts; but others, like many of the Fair Folk (fairies), never were. Some do have physical forms, but their connection with that form presents in a way that makes beta-level communication difficult or impossible (like elementals). Some of them represent the consciousness of ideas (such as totems). Some of them, such as angels, are friendly, while others, such as demons, are hostile. As you develop your psychic abilities, you will likely become more aware of them and begin to interact with them.

My first piece of advice is this: don't be afraid! I've had many people come into my shop terrified of the ghost haunting their house. My usual response is, "What do you have against dead people? You're going to be dead someday too!" Ghosts were all once people. Treat them just as you would anyone else! That also means that just like anyone else, some ghosts are helpful and some are jerks. Some are interesting and some are as dull as an overcast day. Some are mostly fun but can be irritating on occasion. React accordingly.

You don't have to immediately come to their beck and call just because they're dead. If anything, they have more time than you do. If you do feel a call to help them out, define boundaries. My medium friend Lois has certain times that she is available to them throughout the week, and she will not deal with them outside of that unless it is a genuine emergency. Kick them out when the party is over, just like anyone else.

Another thing you'll learn as you go is that most of the so-called "ghosts" that people see are actually not spirits at all! Especially if some particular event seems to repeat itself over and over, that's just psychic resonance. The more emotionally charged an event, the more likely it is to leave an imprint of itself behind that the psychically aware will pick up on; that's why so many of these types of manifestations are so frightening.

Nor are all of them "stuck" here, either! Some of them are, it's true, but usually because they have died in a traumatic and sudden way and they don't realize that they are dead. But many stay because they aren't quite finished yet. They may have spouses they are waiting for; they might have descendants they are looking after; and maybe they are here to guide future generations. Not everyone who dies instantly becomes an enlightened being, but some do, and a nonphysical being certainly often knows a few things we don't. Don't be so arrogant as to "guide them into the light" without their permission. How do you know what's good for them?

Some of the things you will see and deal with will be creations of your own subconscious. I used to call these things "shadow-creatures." You might see them out of the corner of your eye, but then you look right at them and they disappear. They are especially drawn to newly expressed psychic power. Don't pay them much mind; they are likely manifestations of the repressed parts of your subconscious, and we'll work on those in chapter 7.

My other piece of advice is to exercise caution when dealing with nonhuman entities. Even angels don't understand human frailties and vulnerabilities very well, and they can often ask more of us than we are capable of giving. Fair Folk are notoriously capricious, have not much more understanding for human limitations, and not all of them are sweet little pixies making flowers grow. However, not even the most nasty and malicious of spirit forms, commonly known as demons, can bring us harm or do anything to us without our permission. On some level—maybe the desire for more personal control in our own lives, maybe out of self-pity—whatever it may be, we give them an in. If you're feeling intimidated and scared, practice your bubble of protection and tree meditations. Don't let them scare you.

Exercise 41: Spirit Communication

There are several different methods of communicating with spirits if that's something you would like to do. Here are some of the simplest.

Scrying Mirror

The same sorts of surfaces which are effective for scrying are also effective in communicating with spirits. Make sure that you bless them first and set your Intent; only beings with positive intentions are welcome. This prevents those negative entities I've mentioned from messing with you. Gaze into the mirror just as you did before, but this time with a desire to communicate with other-worldly beings. It may help to have specific entities in mind.

Pendulums

A pendulum is a device that swings in perfect balance. You can use a balanced pendant on a chain, a ring suspended on a string, or you can find a version at your local metaphysical store. When choosing a pendulum, ask it to show you what yes and no responses look like for you (mine happens to swing clockwise for yes and counterclockwise for no), and select one that reacts in a way that you just can't mistake for anything else. Say a quick blessing over it and do an energetic cleansing. You are now ready to work.

There are many uses for a pendulum in magick. One use is divination. Ask it yes or no questions, hold the small end between your thumb and forefinger steadily but loosely enough that it can move, and wait for the response. My pendulum has never been wrong, though sometimes I haven't thought to ask the right questions!

For spirit communication, define your conditions and parameters just as you did for the scrying exercise. You can ask yes or no questions, or you can use an answer board (often called a Ouija board) which, paradoxically, is often available through games and toy stores but not metaphysical stores due to fear and superstition! I imagine that a computer keyboard would work just as well, however.

Hold the pendulum steady and ask your questions. You will feel it pull toward particular letters in order to make the spirit's response and then hover over the appropriate one until you acknowledge it. Writing the letters down as you go may make it easier to keep things clear. Don't be too picky; some spirits can't spell any better than the rest of us can!

Exercise 42: Automatic Writing

Take a pen and paper or a computer. Decide what sort of entity you might wish to reach. Create a sacred space by forming the white bubble of light and the blue pentagrams of Exercise 3: Visualizing Symbols. This, again, will prevent interference from hostile or negative entities. Unfocus your thoughts and allow yourself, by whatever method you prefer, to slip into a deep alpha or light theta state. Invite your chosen entity to use your hand(s) to write whatever it wishes to say.

Nothing might come to you at first, and that's okay. Try it again another time. Some people find it helpful to use their nondominant hand to do the writing.

When you do start writing, allow it to flow through you like a stream. Do not censor yourself or overthink it. Don't worry about spelling or the quality of your printing. Remember, you are merely the vessel. You can worry about all that when the message has been delivered.

When you are done, thank the spirit or deity you have been working with. I have developed a ritual of clasping my hands together in a gesture of prayer. Then read over what you have written and edit accordingly.

HEALING WISDOM

Trance states are also used for healing. There have been numerous studies that substantiate the effects of psychic healing, either through prayer or touch. Lawrence LeShan's *The Medium, the Mystic, and the Physicist: Toward a General Theory of the Paranormal* is an excellent book on this subject.

One form of energetic healing that has gained popular acceptance from more mainstream medical environments like palliative care facilities and cancer clinics is Reiki, a form of energetic touch healing originating from Japan that relies on attunements to link the practitioner to its energies. There's really not much difference between Reiki and other forms of energy healing, except that Reiki draws upon energy that does not come from you, and it accesses specific spirit guides to aid you.

Exercise 43: Aura Sight

This exercise requires the assistance of a partner. Ask your assistant to stand against a white or light-colored wall. Dim the lights. Unfocus your gaze and aim for a middle alpha state. Close your eyes. When you feel you have achieved a relaxed alpha trance, open them again and look directly at your friend, but pay attention to the area directly around his or her body out of the corner of your eye. At first, you might just see a faint glow or mirage-like shimmer, but with practice you will notice colors, changes in brightness, fluctuations, holes, and shadows. Over time, you will be able to do this under any conditions of lighting or background.

An alternative way to practice this exercise for the more kinesthetically oriented is to ask your partner to lie down. Close your eyes and hold the palms of your hands just above his or her body. You will feel something like a faint static charge. Run your hands down your friend's body, almost but not quite touching. Do you sense any areas where the energy flow changes, either increasing or decreasing in intensity? Does it feel like heat, static electricity, or just a tingling sensation? Over time you will discover what different sensations mean to you. I sense a decrease of energy, like a dead zone, where there are injuries or health problems. I sense resistance or blockages where there is tension or an emotional issue.

Don't worry if you feel things rather than see them. To this day I get clearer tactile sensations than visuals, but it is an essential part of my healing practice and I am very accurate.

Sometimes psychic information comes to you as well. For instance, you might sense a trouble spot at a client's ankle, and an image might come to you of your client as a child falling off a bicycle. This gives you information about where the injury may have come from when your client might not even be aware.

ASTRAL PROJECTION

Shamans have utilized the art of astral projection, or "journeyworking," to travel to other worlds and deal with the spirits on behalf of the people they help. This ancient practice has been used for millennia to heal mind, body, and spirit, and trance is the only intentional way to get there. I'm afraid the scope of this book will only permit the most basic introduction to this interesting field of magickal practice, but I encourage you to explore!

Taking a walk away from your body is a perfectly natural human experience. We often do it when we are dreaming. It rarely happens when we are awake, but there are thousands of people who have suffered a close brush with death who can describe out-of-body experiences. People who have been in comas also describe astral travel; and oftentimes people with severe mobility difficulties are very good at it.

I had real difficulty with astral projection at first, probably because I enjoy being physical so much. But there is such a wide scope of things you can achieve by releasing firm attachment to your body that I believe it's worth being persistent! Here are some techniques that can improve your practice.

Exercise 44: Astral Projection for Beginners

Get comfortable and begin your basic meditation practice. Aim for a high theta trance (shamanic consciousness 4.5–6 Hz). When you have reached the desired state, try to see your body from the outside. Look down at yourself lying where you are. How are your hands positioned? What is the expression on your face like?

Look down at your spirit body. Are you glowing? Do you appear as your physical body does, or do you have a totally different image of yourself in the spirit world?

Do you see a silver cord that connects you to your physical body at the navel? It's all right if you don't; I believe this to be an ancient convention to assure people that they are still attached to their bodies, and in the age of wireless Internet and cell phones, I'm not sure it's necessary any longer. If you do see it, be aware of it. You may have heard that cutting your silver cord will send you spiraling into the astral plane forever, but don't worry; it's much more resilient than you might think!

Wander around a bit and experiment with the way things look and feel. I find that I hear vibrations of objects more clearly in this plane and living beings have brighter colors. You may have your own experiences with this.

Do you feel up to wandering around your house? If so, check things out! Maybe check up on family members and see what they are up to. You'll be amazed when you confront them later and they confirm your observations! (Don't spy on people, though; that's just rude.)

You may find that at first you keep snapping back into your body. Don't worry, just keep at it.

When you are ready, return to your body and bring yourself back to a conscious beta state.

Exercise 45: Visiting Friends

The next step in astral travel is to try to visit a friend. This works especially well between covenmates. Tell a friend about what you are doing and seek his or her permission to drop in sometime while you are sleeping. If you want to test your abilities, don't tell your friend precisely when you will show up. Observe what he or she is doing when you arrive, notice details about their home, what kind of music they might be listening to, etc. You might find that some things appear to you that might not in the physical world. For instance, when I tried this at our covenstead, their household ghost met me at the door. Discuss the details afterward to substantiate your experience.

When you become more advanced, especially if you have already been working on telekinesis, try to alter the environment and see if your friend notices! Move something on the kitchen table, or leave a psychic message as a symbol in the air, or maybe sing a song and see if your friend is humming it the next morning! Have fun!

Exercise 46: Time Travel

Time and space are irrelevant when you are not in physical form, so one of the most effective uses for astral projection is time travel. You can glean glimpses of the future and set things up to put yourself in a better position when the situation you've foreseen happens, or you can heal events from your past. Exercise 37: Lucid Dreaming is a prerequisite for this exercise.

Begin by practicing Exercise 26: Your Safe Place. Then continue with the following meditation:

Near to your safe place, visualize a river. In the direction of the river's source you can see images, mirages almost, of scenes from your life floating above it. The things that you feel have made the greatest impact on you are the most clearly visible, with other memorable, but less significant events appearing as ghostly holograms. Do any of those events draw you?

Reach out to an event that was traumatic for you. What if things had happened differently?

Stick your head into the hologram of the event and consider it again from your current perspective. You can watch it as if it is happening to you, or watch it from the position of an observer, always remembering that it has already passed and cannot truly hurt you. Allow yourself about five minutes to witness the event.

Now, just as you have done in your work with lucid dreaming, alter the environment and change that event. How do things unfold now? Do you feel better or worse about the situation?

If you find that you cannot—or will not—change the event, then send healing to yourself in that time period. Forgive yourself for your mistakes, and send love and healing to the self you used to be. You may also have left a part of yourself behind at this point in time. Can you reintegrate that piece of yourself without harm?

When you are finished with your work, remove your face from the event. In your own time, return to your safe place. As you begin to return to conscious awareness, consider how you currently feel about this happening in your past. Hopefully you will have some sense of peace and resolution.

Exercise 47: Astral Temple

This exercise can be performed alone or with a group.

Cast a circle. Then enter a shamanic trance and build a temple in the astral plane. What does it look like when you enter? Is it a pyramid, a cathedral, a henge of stone, or maybe just a cave? What are the doors like and what are they made of? How is it guarded and protected?

What is the interior like? Is there an altar? A skylight? An atrium? A fountain? Are there big comfy chairs, pillows, or mats, or nothing at all? Is the floor made of wood, marble, stone, crystal, earth, perhaps leaves or fern fronds, or even cushions of air?

Are there private rooms, or one communal area? Do you have daybeds, furs, or maybe hammocks for resting? What symbols are around you? Are they carved into the walls or glowing in midair like neon signs? Are there statues?

When you arc finished, return to your body. Over the next couple weeks, make plans to travel to the astral temple to relax or simply hang out. If you are working in a group, test each other to see if you remember the same experiences!

SELF-EVALUATION

Though there's still lots of room to explore the realms of trance, this material should equip you with the basic tools. Take a moment now to review what you've learned.

These two chapters are the foundation for the rest of this book. The better you have absorbed them, the easier your magickal practice will be. Remember, there is always room for improvement! With every word I write, and every workshop I teach, I learn something new.

chapter three

THE CRAFT

3) Rites, Chants, Spells, Runes, Charms, etc.
—Gerald Gardner, *The Gardnerian Book of Shadows*

Darksome night and shining moon,
East and South and West and North,
Hearken to the Witches' Rune,
Here we come to call ye forth!
—Doreen Valiente, *The Ancient Call*

The use of language, sound, and ritual is the most familiar form of Witch's magick; it's what people usually think of when they hear the word "Witchcraft." Rites, chants, spells, runes, and charms speak directly to your conscious mind to formulate your Intent, and if well written, they also utilize symbols, archetypes, correspondences, and mythology to speak to your unconscious mind. Most Witchcraft books focus on this Third Path. My intention with this chapter, then, is to teach you about the theory rather than specifics. Hopefully you will never need to consult a magickal recipe book ever again, and will instead have the practical tools at your disposal to make the best kinds of spells, rituals, chants, charms, and runes; the ones you write for yourself.

These methods all use a language of symbols and art to speak to the subconscious mind, and through that, the Universe, to communicate a specific desire. Learning the Witch's language of symbolism is like learning the language of manifestation. Using it makes it easier to communicate to the Universe what you want. The study and practice of this symbolic language is called "the art" or "the craft" for a reason.

Charles Poncé proposed the idea that magick is simply a way of mapping the complex psyche of the human mind. If that's true, the symbolism used in magick could have a universal application.

In her groundbreaking sociological work *Persuasions of the Witch's Craft*, T. M. Luhrmann writes of a field study she conducted of England's occult community. In it, she noticed that a Witch's perceptions slowly shift during the course of her studies in magick to see different symbols and meanings in events, experiences, and responses to the world. Prior to occult study, these connections and interpretations would not have been made. Luhrmann called this "interpretative drift," and she viewed it as the process of overcoming skepticism. She ultimately found it impossible to maintain the detached perspective of the anthropologist and continue occult studies. Eleven years later, anthropologist Susan Greenwood published *Magic, Witchcraft, and the Otherworld: An Anthropology*. Greenwood undertook the study of occultism in earnest in her field research, rather than approaching it as an outsider, and treated it like "learning the language" of another culture, complete with that culture's framework and comprehension. She saw the occult community's view of the otherworld, which coexists with the rational world of science, as another form of "knowing," and one did not have to be rejected to embrace the other. This view was also shared by Carlos Castaneda, and it is beginning to gain more common acceptance in the field of psychology, where tools such as guided meditation and visualization are being incorporated into mainstream psychological and therapeutic practice.

"Interpretative drift" is exactly what you want to achieve in the study of Witchcraft. When you learn to speak the language, and when understanding the language becomes second nature and you begin to see its symbolism in everyday life, you will be able to work your magick, and thus create change in the world according to your Will, more effectively.

THE POWER OF WORDS

Language is a series of symbols representing ideas, and it is our primary method of communication. This is important to understand. We are not used to thinking of language as symbolism, but it is. The words themselves don't really mean anything; they represent what it is that we mean. We simplify a big concept into a short sound that we collectively agree represents that particular idea.

The human brain is geared to comprehend symbols. It is really quite brilliant at it! I suppose that is probably the element that gives us language in the first place. Understanding that is key to magick, because magick is using your consciousness to create effects in your reality. Would it not help you to have a clear, simple idea of what you intend to focus on in order to make it happen?

So, my first cautionary note to you when creating a spell is to choose your wording carefully! Magick is like the genie who grants wishes. If you phrase your request poorly, the genie will give you exactly what you have asked for! Why? Because in your subconscious, you have feelings about every word that you know that influence you. Consequently, when using a symbol as your focus, even a word, you bring about all aspects of the symbol you have chosen.

Let me show you.

Exercise 48: Anatomy of a Word

Write the following word on a blank piece of paper: power.

Look at that word for about thirty seconds. When you are finished, scratch down any word that comes to mind when you look at the word "power."

When you have completed that exercise, take a close look at the words you have written. Some of them, I am sure, are positive. Some of them may also be quite negative. Do you have more negative associations than positive ones? If the answer is yes, then why would you ever ask for power? Do you not know that you will acquire all the negative aspects of the word as well as the positive ones?

Look up the definition of "power" in the dictionary. Subconsciously, you likely know all these definitions already, and so subconsciously you would be asking for all these things if you asked for more power in your life. So, what *kind* of power, would you like? Many Witches clarify that they are looking for personal power, or magickal power, as opposed to "power over," when they dare to ask for power.

THE IRON PENTACLE

The Iron Pentacle comes from the Feri tradition, which influenced the Reclaiming tradition and thus, mine (Star Sapphire). It is a tool of transformation that involves reclaiming ideas that we are often taught are negative, which diminishes our personal power.

Figure 3: Iron Pentacle

Take a look at the five words in figure 3: power, sex, self, passion, and pride. These are words that we are usually not comfortable with in our society. But as Witches, we must not only become comfortable with these words, we must also accept them as necessary facets of ourselves. We are going to use the ancient symbol of the pentacle—a perfect five-pointed star contained within a circle—to focus our intentions. We are going to draw an invoking pentagram on our bodies, and work with the energies we are calling.

The location of these points is no accident. Consider it: *Pride* and *passion,* like your feet, are foundational concepts to healthy boundaries. *Self* and *power* are active qualities that require action and "reaching out" into the world. And *sex,* which is a relationship with the source of creative life energy, is about interacting with things using the senses.

Exercise 49: The Iron Pentacle

This exercise is adapted and expanded from T. Thorn Coyle's meditation "Calling Back the Points" in her excellent book, *Evolutionary Witchcraft.* You may find it effective to read the following as a guided meditation.

To start, get into a comfortable position. Standing or lying down, form a pentagram with your body. Relax, breathe deeply and slowly, and go within.

Reach deep down into the core of the Earth. Feel its heat and its strength. Reach out with the palms of your hands and draw that molten earth energy into them.

Bring your arms up along your sides, inhaling as you do so. Bring your hands together over the top of your head. When you exhale, push that earth energy gently into your crown chakra. Now allow that energy to pool in your head behind your forehead or your third eye. Feel this energy building, not in a painful way, but in a revitalizing way, until it glows like a small star. Give this energy a name: it is called *sex*.

Think about the word sex. What does it mean to you? What have your experiences been with that word? Do you regard it with fear? With hope? With excitement? With shame?

Consider all the negative experiences you have had with sex. Getting caught masturbating and being shamed by your parents; hiding your period from your family; former lovers, unrequited lovers; pressure to perform when you had no interest; anything abusive. A piece of you was left in each of those sorrowful experiences. Call them back! Allow yourself to embrace this powerful life force energy. Consider yourself as a sexual being. Sex is raw life force. Why fear it? Embrace it and make it your own again!

Recall any good experiences you have had with sex; the first time you made love to someone you really cared about; the first time you shaved your legs; dressing to impress and attract; discovering masturbation and your own private joy in sex; being attracted to someone and knowing that your quarry was responding to your flirtations; smelling flowers; the feel of silk against your skin; dancing. These experiences are yours and you have a right to take pleasure in them!

Pride

Run that red iron earth energy now from your head down into your right foot in a glowing laser beam line, pooling there and creating another bright star. Here is where you find *pride*. Do you feel how sex and pride are connected? Does this line feel clear and strong, or thick and sluggish? How can you awaken it?

Reclaim your pride! Take it back from all the times someone cut you down; from every time you were dumped; from the times you weren't picked for the softball team; from the times you received poor grades in school; from being passed over for that promotion; from the times you told yourself you couldn't do something; from the many times you have insulted yourself and said that you were "lazy" or "stupid" or "stubborn"; from the times you were arrogant; from the times you felt unworthy or embarrassed; from the times you were ashamed.

Celebrate the times you accomplished something you didn't think you could do; the time you received that promotion; the times you realized that you were naturally talented at something; the times you claimed your worth; the times you stood up for yourself; the times you remained strong in crises when everyone else came apart.

We are taught that pride is wrong, that we should always be humble, but to claim that you are not good at something when everyone knows that you are is false humility, and it demeans the accomplishments of others who struggle. Allow your ego to be right-sized! Admit your pride and claim it as your own! This is your energy!

Self

Now, run that laser beam of red life-giving light from your right foot, up your body, and into your left hand, glowing and pooling into a bright star. Name that star *self*. Again, check the line that connects pride to self, and be sure it is clear and direct. Do you see how sex feeds the energy of pride, and then self?

Now, take yourself back from all the times someone told you that you had to look or act a certain way; the times you pretended to be someone else to fit in; the times you concealed part of your personality because you were afraid you would hurt someone you cared about; the roles you have played in life out of necessity; the times you've lied to yourself.

Then, celebrate a time when you stood up for your beliefs, even in the face of adversity; when you wore an unpopular style because you really liked it; when you decided that you are beautiful just the way you are; when you told your spouse how you really felt about something; when you told your mother that no, you weren't going to cut your hair, or yes, you were going to get that piercing or tattoo; when you took time for you, no matter how many things you had to do that day. Be fully, completely, and in all ways, yourself!

Power

Next, shoot that red laser beam across your heart and into your right hand. This star's name is *power*. Do you feel how power can only be sustained by generating from pride and self?

Reclaim your power from all the times someone exercised power over you; all the times you exercised power over others; all the times you felt disempowered, victimized, used, or abused; all the times you felt that you couldn't do something; and all the times that you felt there was nothing you could do.

Recall those times when you were strong when others might have crumpled; when you asserted yourself; when you did something amazing that you weren't sure you were capable of. Consider all the different types of power: physical, mental, emotional, and spiritual. Are you physically strong or attractive? Mentally enduring, wise, artistic, or good at math? Are you emotionally sturdy, or spiritually inspiring? These are all forms of power, which is simply the ability to make what you want happen. Be empowered!

Passion

Draw that laser beam of fiery light from your right hand to your left foot. This star is named *passion*. Feel, for a moment, how power feeds passion and self feeds power.

Reclaim your passions from the graves you buried them in; from every dream you surrendered rather than pursued; from every unfinished painting, garden, craft project, or novel.

Now, think about the times you pursued your passion; about the business or charity you started, the garden you grew, the incredible painting you finished, or the sports event that you won because you practiced each and every day as hard as you could. Think of that spectacular science project you finished in the fifth grade, or the school play when you were absolutely stunning in the lead role. People told you that your idea was foolish, or too big, or out of your league, but you did it anyway, and you were amazing! Don't be afraid to embrace your passions! They are the things that drive you to make a difference in this world! They matter!

Coming Full Circle

Draw that laser beam back, now, connecting your left foot to your head again. Feel how passion feeds sex (and not the other way around!). Trace the line of energy, being comfortable with your sexuality. Your creative soul feeds your pride in yourself; and having pride enhances your self-confidence; being grounded in yourself empowers you; having power within fuels your passions; and embracing your passions feeds your sexual energy.

Last, call upon the Divine to draw the circle of protection around you in a sunwise sweep; from sex to power to pride to passion to self and back to sex, sealing those strengths within. You have reclaimed the forbidden powers of the Iron Pentacle. You are whole and complete. Blessed be!

Magickal Words and Languages

With such powerful associations hidden in the words we choose, why do Witches and magicians use words that have no meaning in the language they speak, or even words that have no true meaning at all?

Using a different language signals to our subconscious that we are now entering the realm of the sacred and the magickal, and in that frame of mind we can accomplish things that we do not normally believe we are capable of. Modern Celtic Reconstructionists use Gaelic phrases in their workings, because they believe it establishes a connection with the Druids and the Celts. Christians repeat the Hebrew word "amen" after a prayer to reinforce their belief that the words they have just said will manifest. "Amen" really means "the end," like a period at the end of a sentence. But I am sure that if you spent any time in a church as a child, saying "amen" after anything seems to give it a little more oomph, doesn't it? Catholic and Anglican churches continued to say Mass in Latin for centuries, even after Latin became a completely dead language. Why? Because when the tradition was established, Latin was only spoken by great scholars; continuing this practice gave the service a little more authority. Later on, there was magick in the words and the tradition, even though nobody could understand it in direct translation any longer. There are even languages created entirely for magickal purposes, such as Enochian, the language of the angels.

One of the most ancient magickal words that we are familiar with is *abracadabra,* which comes from the Aramaic Ahbra Kedahbra, which loosely translates to "I create as I speak." It was used in a poem in the second century CE by a Roman physician named Serenus Sammonicus, who prescribed that writing the word on an amulet in a diminishing triangle to be worn by a patient would diminish the hold of an illness. To the modern occult student, this is clearly a use of sympathetic magick to reduce an illness as the word reduces:

```
ABRACADABRA
 ABRACADABR
  ABRACADAB
   ABRACADA
    ABRACAD
     ABRACA
      ABRAC
       ABRA
        ABR
         AB
          A
```

Figure 4: Abracadabra

NAMING

Names are special words of power. They define a person, item, or being. They become a short sound that encompasses all that a given being is. Adam's primary power in the Bible was being given the right to name all living things, and the Druids also traditionally had the power of naming. In most indigenous traditions, knowing the name of a thing gave you power over it. In ceremonial magick, the names of angels and demons can be used to issue a summons they cannot deny and bind their actions to your Will. If you consider that much of our reality, if not all of it, is defined strictly by our perceptions, naming is an incredible power!

Exercise 50: Your Craft Name

Have you chosen a Craft name yet? Many Witches choose a name to define themselves among other Witches. Some of them are inspired by nature, some by deities, and some just seem right. My only cautionary note to you is that if you do choose a deity to name yourself after, alter it in some way. It's a little presumptuous to claim that you are a deity, and by taking that name and no other, you are claiming it for yourself, rather than showing how it inspires you.

My Craft name is Sable Aradia. Sable was the name I began calling myself when I became involved in a medieval reenactment group. Because many of the first Pagans I met were involved in the same group, and because we primarily communicated online, Sable was how they knew me. When I received my Third Degree initiation (a rite in initiatory traditions of witchcraft that acknowledges a High Priestess or Priest), I chose to keep the name Sable in recognition of that identity. Aradia was my acknowledgment of my goddess Diana, and the purpose I believe she has asked me to take on in this life—to teach Witchcraft to the masses, to empower people through the practice of magick, and to liberate the oppressed as Aradia, Diana's daughter, did. There are many different methods of finding a Craft name; the key is choosing something that resonates strongly with you and that feels like "you" when you hear it.

Your assignment is to choose a Craft name by which you will be called in the Pagan community. Take your time and think about it. You can progress to other exercises in the book before you come up with your final decision.

Exercise 51: Your True Name

For the second part of your assignment, find your secret magickal name, your True Name. This is something different; you will not invent this name, but it will find you instead. It will likely be in a language you do not understand, or maybe no language at all. It will sound right to you when you say it, and it will resonate in your body when it rolls off your tongue. Do not share this name with anyone, just find it and know what it is. You will be guided by intuition and dreaming, and it will likely not have any logical rhyme or reason to it, but you will know that it is right.

The ability to know your own True Name gives you the power to make changes to yourself and your life like nothing else can. Just be careful how you use that power!

Magickal Alphabets

Some alphabets are designed specifically for magickal use, but there are also alphabets that have magickal associations because the cultures that created them recognized the power of the collective symbolism that forms language and writing, which fixes concepts and ideas in physical form.

The Norse runes and Celtic ogham were used primarily for religious purposes and for keeping track of trade. This was because in cultures that had strong oral traditions, writing was a carefully guarded secret, used rarely or not at all.

The Norse runes each have a letter sound that they correspond to, and a meaning far beyond that simple letter.

(F) FEHU "Cattle"
Wealth, stability, security, fertility

(U, V) URUZ "Auroch"
Creativity, sexual energy, end of a cycle, change with challenge

(TH) THURISAZ "Thorn"
Conflict, challenge, protection, inner strength, struggle

(A) ANSUZ "Mouth"
Advice, communication, omens, guidance, psychic power

(R) RAIDHO "Cartwheel"
Travel, transformation, quests, movement

(C,K) KENAZ "Torch"
Light, danger, fire, fever, hope, passion, inspiration

(G) GIFU, GEBO "Gift"
Receiving gifts, relationships, partnerships, love, peace, duty

(W) WUNJO "Joy"
Happiness, fulfillment, success

(H) HAGAL(AZ) "Hail"
Setbacks, discord, limitations, bad luck

(N) NIED, NAUDIZ "Need"
Hardship, struggle, strife, patience, acceptance

(I) ISA "Ice"
Obstacles, caution, patience, warning, coldness, death, end

(J) JERA "Harvest"
Resolution, justice, reckoning, prosperity

(E) EIWAZ, YR "Yew Tree"
Death/rebirth, resurrection, renewal, spiritual strength

(P) PERDHO, PERTH "Dice Cup"
Possibility, luck, future revelation, womb, mystery, female fertility

(Z) ALGIZ, EOLH "Elkhorn"
Protection, defense, shelter, friendship, warding

(S) SIGEL, SOWILO "Sun"
Guiding light, regeneration, renewal, beneficial magick, health, happiness

(T) TYR, TIWAZ "Justice"
Justice, vigor, victory, success, protection, strength

(B) BEORC, BERKANA "Birth"
Birth, fertility, growth, creativity, prosperity, new beginnings

(E) EHWAZ "Horse"
Travel, change, promotion, progress

(M) MANNAZ "Man"
Family, memory, culture, duty, wisdom, community

(L) LAGAZ "Water"
Intuition, mystery, ebb and flow, gain for a price

(NG) ING, INGWAZ "Fertility"
Fruition, achievement, male potency

(D) DAGAZ "Day"
Unexpected success, growth, beginnings, optimism

(O) OTHEL, OTHALA "Home"
Legacy, inheritance, prosperity, moving forward, new ways

( ) WYRD "Fate"
Inevitable destiny, the unknown

Figure 5: Elder Futhark

This set of runes in figure 5 is known as the Elder Futhark because it is the earliest recorded rune set, and the first six characters form the sound *F–U–TH–A–R–K.* There is no *C* in the Elder Futhark. It is written either as the hard *K* or the soft *S,* depending on the intended sound.

Runes were often used in divination as well as writing, and you can join several runes together to form something called a *bindrune,* which can then be made into magickal talismans (physical objects that hold ongoing charms or spells). A point to note is that while the blank rune, Wyrd, representing Fate, has become fairly accepted as part of a runeset, it is strictly a modern invention and the Norse did not actually use it.

Oghams, or Celtic tree runes, were not really writing at all, but a system of recording records or making talismans that had associations with different sacred woods and the associated magickal properties of each. Modern Celtic occultists assign letter equivalents to them:

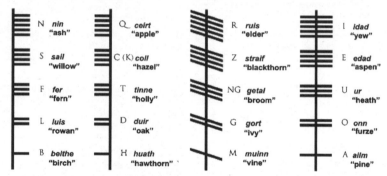

ENGLISH SUBSTITUTIONS: There is no "J," "P," "V," or "W" in Celtic languages, and there is no soft "C" sound. To substitute those letters, try using other letters which sound close (such as Beithe for a "P" sound,) or that have alternate pronunciations (such as Idad, the "I" sound, for a "J." You can use a single "F" or Fer to represent a "V" sound and double "Fs" or Fer twice to represent an "F" sound, as Welsh, which is a Celtic language, is written. A doubled "U" character at the beginning of a word is often used for a "W" (that's actually the origin of the letter's name,) and when a "C" would be called for in English, use the Sail (S) or the Coll (K) sound that you would pronounce instead.

Figure 6: Celtic Ogham

This set is known as Theban script or the Witches' Alphabet.[2] It has only ever been used in magick. For that reason it is not considered to be a "runic alphabet" by scholars, but for our purpose it is the same sort of idea: a magickal substitution cipher. The modern letters *J, U,* and *W* are not utilized traditionally, so in modern usage these are transliterated using the Theban characters for *I, V* and *V V.*

---

2. First published in Johannes Trithemius' *Polygraphia* (1518), in which it was attributed to Honorius of Thebes, then later attributed to Pietro d'Abano (1250–16) by Trithemius' student Heinrich Cornelius Agrippa in *Three Books of Occult Philosophy,* 1531.

Figure 7: Theban Script "The Witches' Alphabet"

Other alphabets commonly used in magick include the Hebrew script, used by Kaballists and ritual magicians, and Enochian or angelic script, which was invented by John Dee and Edward Kelly (or revealed to them by angels) in the late sixteenth century.

Exercise 52: Crafting a Runeset

In this exercise, I would like you to make a set of either the Elder Futhark runes or the Celtic oghams. Traditionally, the oghams were made from sticks of a sacred wood with the symbols scratched on, but you can make them from any material you wish—wood, stone, antler, clay, little bits of colored glass designed for fishbowls, or whatever else you desire. You can paint them, carve them, inscribe them, tool them in leather, or form them with a wood burner. If you are painting on a smooth surface such as glass, you may wish to use enamel paint or spray them with acrylic lacquer to protect them from being scratched off through wear. They do not have to be artist quality; they just have to be useable in divination. If you are making runes, you can choose to include Wyrd if you wish, or skip it if you like.

Exercise 53: Runic Communication

Get together in your coven, or find a partner to work with, and write each other messages in the Runic language you have chosen to study, just like when you were a child making up your own secret language. If you are working alone, start writing in your Book of Shadows in this alphabet. This will give you practice in using this alphabet until it becomes second nature, and you can call upon it at the drop of a hat. Because I practiced this when I first began studying magick as a teenager, I can now write fluently in the Elder Futhark, and so I can make effective talismans without consulting any sort of book; a useful skill!

RUNES AND CHARMS

To bind the spell well every time, let the spell be spake in rhyme.
—DOREEN VALIENTE, "THE REDE OF THE WICCAE"

Traditionally, spells were composed as rhyming verses. Rhymes are easy for us to remember and have the added benefit of creating links in your subconscious that have more impact than essays to its childlike intelligence.

RUNES AS POETIC VERSE

A *rune* is either: a) a character used in the Old Norse alphabet, b) a similar character in another symbolic alphabet believed to have magickal powers, or c) a poem or incantation. We have already dealt with Norse runes and other magickal scripts. Now, I am concerned with the third meaning. This name for poetic verses with magickal intent likely derived from the Norse Rune Poems, which delineate the secrets of the runic alphabet, and were written in this style.

The Witches' Rune and The Ancient Call

"The Witches' Rune," written by Doreen Valiente, is a spell-poem designed to produce a magickal effect through the power of its language.

Doreen Valiente (1922–99) wrote a wealth of literature for the craft in her lifetime. This was one of her best-known works. If you are ever stuck for something to say to invoke magickal power into your work, "The Witches' Rune" is a great default.

There is also a second, alternate version known as "The Ancient Call." This is the one that I originally learned, and I still prefer it.

The Witches' Rune

Darksome night and shining moon
Hearken to the Witches' Rune.
East then South, West then
   North
Hear! Come! I call thee forth!
By all the powers of land and sea
Be obedient unto me.
Wand, pentacle, and the sword
Hearken ye unto my word.
Cords and censer, scourge and knife
Waken all ye into life.
Powers of the Witches' blade
Come ye as the charge is made.
Queen of heaven, queen of hell,
Send your aid into the spell.
Horned Hunter of the night
Work my will by magick rite.
By the powers of land and sea
As I do say, "So mote it be!"
By all the might of moon and sun
As I do will, it shall be done!
Eko Eko, Azarak
Eko Eko, Zomilarak
Eko Eko, Cernunnos
Eko Eko, Aradia.

The Ancient Call

Darksome night and shining moon,
East, then South, then West, then
   North,
Hearken to the Wiccan Rune.
Here we come to call you forth!
Earth and water, air and fire,
Wand, and pentacle and sword
Work ye unto our desire,
Hearken ye unto our word!
Cords and censer, scourge and knife,
Powers of the Witches' blade.
Waken all ye unto life,
Come ye as the charm is made!
Queen of heaven, Queen of hell,
Horned hunter of the night.
Lend your power unto our spell,
And work our will by magick rite.
In the earth and air and sea,
By the light of moon and sun.
As our will, so mote it be,
As it is said, so be it done!
Eko, Eko, Azarak,
Eko, Eko, Zomelak.
Eko, Eko, Pan,
Eko, Eko, Diana!

Traditionally, "Eko eko" is supposed to have been an invocation meaning "Hail!" or "Hail and come forth!", and Azarak and Zomilarak are supposed to be brother and sister angels that represent fire and water. But it has also been argued that these lines are meaningless, and are only "a sorcerer's cry in the Middle Ages."

Whatever its origin, repeating those lines gives the experience more power and energy, exactly as a magickal incantation ought to.

Exercise 54: Hearken to "The Witches' Rune"

Memorize either "The Witches' Rune" or "The Ancient Call" so that you can use it at will for any spell you might require! You could do this by writing it out repeatedly, or by drawing mnemonic pictures. Keep in mind your learning style! There are several versions that have been recorded as music that you can learn to sing; that's what I did.

Exercise 55: Let the Spell Be Spake in Rhyme

Why not try your hand at creating your own rune?

Begin by considering what it is that you'd like to accomplish. Make it something relatively simple to maximize your chances of success. Let's say that you want to improve your finances. (Who doesn't?)

Now that you have defined your purpose, boil that purpose down into a single word of no more than two or three syllables. In the case of a finances spell, perhaps I would distill it down to the word "money."

Then, play a little game with yourself. Get a piece of paper and a pen (or your laptop). Start at the beginning of the alphabet, and see how many words you can come up with that rhyme with your chosen word by replacing the first letters! Change spellings when necessary.

Consider how any one of those words might be used in a two-line rhyme with your original word, and also how you might incorporate that into an action or incantation that would make sense for a spell.

With my example I might say:

Ostara, goddess of egg and bunny,
Bring me abundance! Bring me money!

Or:

THE WITCH'S EIGHT PATHS OF POWER

Cinnamon, ginger, clove, and honey,
Bind ye well and bring me money!

Or:

Money money money, must be funny, in my rich man's world!

Well, okay, so it does not have to be boring and serious! Go to it, have fun with it, and then use it. Use it with the actions you have envisioned, or use it like an affirmation to bring you what you want. Try it!

SPELLS

Like creating a new recipe, making your own spell involves mixing ingredients in a pleasing way. These symbols can be inscribed on paper, amulets, statues, magickal tools, or pretty much whatever is desired. There are a few simple principles behind the creation of an effective spell:

USE SYMPATHETIC MAGICK

In magnetism, opposites attract. But in magick, like attracts like. Thinking positively attracts positivity, but having a negative attitude is sure to bring negativity. This also encompasses an assumed similarity of function. For example, pointy herbs and thorns are associated with psychic protection. Think of them as forming a briar barrier between you and the world, like in the tale of Sleeping Beauty. Mistletoe, because it flourishes even in the dead of winter, is associated with healing, life, and even resurrection. Bloodstones are supposed to be good for blood disorders and the circulatory system. Mandrake resembles a human body when pulled out of the ground, and often it has an extra root that looks like an oversized penis, so it is associated with healing and fertility. This is the point of making *poppets,* sometimes known as voodoo dolls. They represent the body of a person you are doing magick for, which can just as easily heal as harm. As long as you understand the connection it will work for you.

In his classic *Real Magic,* the late Isaac Bonewits refers to this as the Law of Similarity and the Law of Contagion. This is also the same principle that explains why many traditional systems of folk magick make use of parts of a person's body, such as fingernails, hair, sweat, urine, or blood. Anything in contact with a person's body still contains their essence (DNA), and it can be used to reach that person energetically. But, by this same principle, the blessing given to holy water can be given to more water simply by pouring some of the original holy water into it. You might be interested to know that quantum physics also bears up the idea that any object that was once in contact with another can continue to affect each other when separated by distance; this is known as Bell's theorem.

Maintain the Balance

Bonewits' Law of Polarity states that everything contains its opposite. The *anima* is the female aspect that lives at the heart of every male; the *animus* is the male aspect that lives at the heart of every female. Think of it like a *taijitu* (the yin-yang symbol). Each side contains a seed of the other, and both aspects flow into one another and exist in balance. Or at least, this is the ideal. For most of us, the other is a subject of discomfort and fear. In our culture especially, men are taught to eschew the anima as a weakness (which by itself is an argument for the continued relevance and importance of feminism).

It is important to maintain a balance of forces in your workings. If you bring it out to play with, put it away. If you invoke Fire, make sure to call upon Water as well. (A balance of all four elements is preferable.) Respect ebb as well as flow.

Engage the Five Senses

Spells that engage all five senses are more effective. The reason why is because we all learn differently. If you put all elements to work on the same purpose, it is communicated more effectively to your subconscious. Consider all the different methods of driving a trance, and try to put as many of them to work as possible.

Keep It Simple

If you make something too complicated, your subconscious will just get confused. This is why we kept things to a basic statement or picture in chapter 1. Use things that speak to you on a primal level as your focus; or practice a particular method until you can do it in your sleep.

Give Back

Whether or not you believe in any sort of divine power, you likely believe in physics. Physics tells us that energy is neither created nor destroyed; it just changes form. Even quantum physics tells us that matter or energy that seemingly appears out of nothing is actually "borrowed" from the future![3] So if you take energy from the Universe to create your spell, you must give it back. This can take the form of redirection from one elemental force into another, transmutation, an offering to the Divine, a ritual of thanks and gratitude, a simple "Namaste" to the Source of All, or that subject of so many horror stories, a trade. Failing to do these in some way will depower your spell and it just won't work.

Magickal Symbolism

There are two kinds of symbols: personal symbolism, which is organized by our subconscious minds; and group symbolism, which is widely recognized by a large number of people.

When a group decides on the meaning of a symbol, they give it a semblance of consciousness. We call that consciousness an *egregor* in magick. Deities are, by nature, egregors. They are personifications of concepts that a large group of people have mutually agreed, either consciously or subconsciously, have certain traits. Just like with words, when you connect to a deity, you connect to all those energies, both positive and negative.

Other egregors exist as well. There are egregors for covens, traditions, religions, nations, and social clubs. Our modern mind understands this easily; they are "ghosts in the machine," artificial intelligences of a sort which have acquired a degree of sentience. Sometimes egregors take on a life of their own and people get carried away with them; which is how mob mentality works.

The Christian egregor, for example, is a very strong one in our culture because so many people believe in it, and even though the overall population of Christians appears to be on the decline, it continues to affect us.

There are two ways to enact your Will in the world. The first is to hone your own Will to be strong and precise, like a diamond-tipped drill bit. The second is to get other people to want what you want and believe what you

---

3. A simplistic understanding of "The Uncertainty Principle" and "Virtual Particles." Dr. Stephen Hawking has an excellent essay on these subjects on his website *www.hawking.org.uk* called "Godel and the End of the Universe": *www.hawking.org.uk/godel-and-the-end-of-physics.html*, accessed September 7, 2012.

believe, and the more that do so, the more effective you will be at manifesting your Will.

The purpose, then, of using symbols that have time-honored meanings is to invoke an existing egregor, and give magick some less resistant paths to travel. For reference I have provided some of the more basic and time-honored magickal symbols here and in the appendixes of this book. If you want more I recommend Crowley's classic *777* or Bill Whitcomb's *The Magician's Companion*.

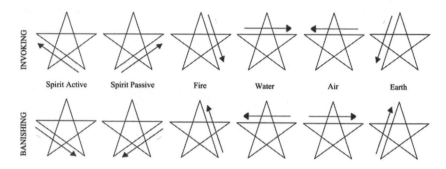

Figure 8: Invoking and Banishing Pentagrams

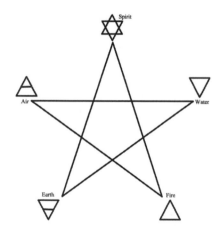

Figure 9: Elemental Symbols and the Pentagram

THE WITCH'S EIGHT PATHS OF POWER

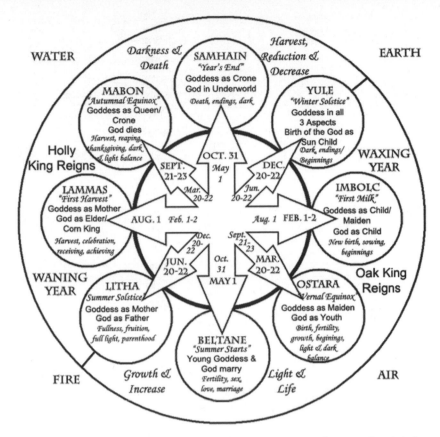

WATER

EARTH

Darkness &
Death

Harvest,
Reduction &
Decrease

SAMHAIN
"Year's End"
Goddess as Crone
God in Underworld
Death, endings, dark

MABON
"Autumnal Equinox"
Goddess as Queen/
Crone
God dies
Harvest, reaping,
thanksgiving, dark
& light balance

YULE
"Winter Solstice"
Goddess in all
3 Aspects
Birth of the God as
Sun Child
Dark, endings/
Beginnings

Holly
King Reigns

WAXING
YEAR

OCT. 31
May
1

SEPT.
21-23

DEC.
20-22

Mar.
20-22

Jun.
20-22

LAMMAS
"First Harvest"
Goddess as Mother
God as Elder/
Corn King
Harvest, celebration,
receiving, achieving

IMBOLC
"First Milk"
Goddess as Child/
Maiden
God as Child
New birth, sowing,
beginnings

AUG. 1 *Feb. 1-2*

Aug. 1 FEB. 1-2

Dec.
20-
22

Sept.
21-
23

JUN.
20-22

Oct.
31

MAR.
20-22

WANING
YEAR

MAY 1

Oak King
Reigns

LITHA
Summer Solstice
Goddess as Mother
God as Father
Fullness, fruition,
full light, parenthood

OSTARA
Vernal Equinox
Goddess as Maiden
God as Youth
Birth, fertility,
growth, beginnings,
light & dark
balance

FIRE

Growth &
Increase

BELTANE
"Summer Starts"
Young Goddess &
God marry
Fertility, sex,
love, marriage

Light &
Life

AIR

DATES IN LARGER TYPE: NORTHERN HEMISPHERE   *Dates in smaller type: Southern Hemisphere*

Figure 10: Wheel of the Year

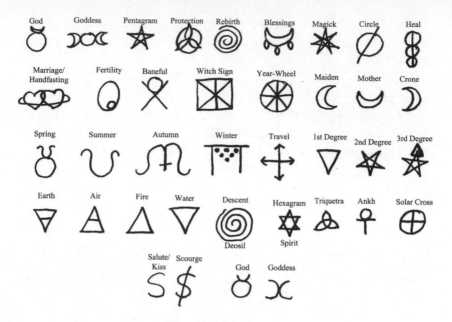

Figure 11: Wiccan Symbols

Exercise 56: Candle Magick

Consider a spell you would like to do. Don't do something you have already done; remember what I said about trusting the Universe?

Figure out which color would be the most appropriate to your purpose (see appendixes B and E). For example, if you were to do a spell to bring you success in a custody dispute, you might choose orange for legal success, green for new beginnings, purple for responsibility for others, white for protection, or pink for children.

Next, consult the appendixes to decide on a magickally appropriate time to do your spell. It is rare to be able to wait until the most magickally appropriate moment to do a spell, but do the best you can. Be creative and do what feels right. Ultimately, if you must choose between ideal times, try to make sure that the moon is waxing if growth and increase are needed or waning if reduction, banishing, or endings are needed, and go for the appropriate day of the week. Then, at least none of the major energies are working against you!

THE WITCH'S EIGHT PATHS OF POWER

At the time you have selected, center and ground and invoke your circle and pentagrams of protection. Do the remainder of this exercise within the confines of your circle.

Select some appropriate symbols from the other correspondence tables. You might want to use the symbol of Mercury, which is the planet that helps to deal with bureaucracies, and the sun, which is protective. You might also want Libra for balance and justice. Whatever you choose, carve those symbols on the candle you have chosen with a pin or a pocketknife.

Next, write a word in any one of the magickal scripts on the candle with the same tool. Choose something that focuses your Intent. You might wish to use a single word, or you could even use a phrase, such as "justice for *X*," or "protection for *X*."

Then, anoint the candle with your finger. Direction matters. Choose something with a scent that you enjoy, or any of the following multipurpose magickal oils: olive, rosemary, frankincense, or High John the Conqueror. If you are bringing something toward you, start at the top of the candle where the wick is, and run your oil-dipped finger down toward the middle; then stop, begin again at the base of the candle, and meet the point in the center where you stopped coming down. If you are banishing something, start with the middle of the candle and run your finger out to the top and the bottom. Do this a number of times that suits your purpose according to basic numerology (appendix E). If you don't know what number to use, use three.

As you are carving and anointing the candle, visualize the results you are trying to achieve, as explained in chapter 1. Bring all your senses into play!

When you feel that you have a clear visualization of your Intent, gather energy in your hands just like in Exercise 6: Visualizing Energy, and direct it into the candle! Complete the transfer with a statement such as the Witches' Rune, "so it is," "amen," or "so mote it be!"

Burn the candle until it burns out, or light it and burn it over the course of a numerologically appropriate number of days, timing it so that it will finish when the required number of days have passed, when the moon phase changes, or when the day of the event in question is scheduled to happen. Give no more thought to it and trust that the Universe will fulfill your desire.

Exercise 57: Spellcrafting

Using the correspondence tables in the appendixes, create your own spell!
Keep in mind that in order to engage all five senses you will need:

- Something to look at (colors, symbols, pictures, tools, etc.)
- Something to hear (a song, a rune, a word of power, drumming, etc.)
- Something to feel (touching or handling something)
- Some action to take (burning a candle, washing a tool in water, waving a wand, lighting incense, drinking tea, burning a piece of paper, etc.)
- Something to taste and/or smell (incense, scented oils, wine, water, fruit, sage, etc.)

Record your spell and its results in your Book of Shadows!

CHANTS AND MUSIC

Chants create a trance state through repetition and simplicity of sound. The creative Pagan tradition offers hundreds in books or online, or you can write your own! Music and drumming can be used for dancing, creating an emotion, setting a scene, or as an offering to the Divine. I have recorded a few of the more well known chants in the Pagan community in a video on my YouTube channel for you to use: search "Witch's Eight Paths of Power: Basic Chants."

Exercise 58: Chanting

There are hundreds of Pagan chants out there. Your assignment is to find one that you enjoy and practice it until you know it by heart. Then apply it to a spell or ritual. Chant to boredom, and chant some more if you wish to reach the necessary trance state.

SOUND HEALING

Sound healing works on the theory that we are all formed of vibration, and so creating particular harmonious vibrations will synchronize our bodies and spirits to a state of health.

The Musical Scale

Like much of modern mathematics and the Western occult traditions, our musical scale was first invented by Pythagoras in his efforts to explain the Universe through harmonious mathematical equations. Each astrological sign and planet has a note associated with it (see appendixes A and F), and each chakra also has a musical note associated with it (see appendix B). The vibration of sound created by the note has healing properties that invoke and attune those energies.

Exercise 59: Musical Healing

Select or compose a piece of music to aid in a spell or in healing work, and put it to work!

TOOLS OF THE ART

Wicca utilizes some traditional tools, also known as "weapons," in ritual. Each of these tools has a symbolic meaning and is associated with specific magickal work. I'll assume you are at least familiar with the four Elemental Tools: the athame, the wand, the chalice, and the pentacle, because every Wiccan how-to book out there tells you that you need them. I recommend *Buckland's Complete Book of Witchcraft* for an excellent description of how to make or acquire them.

ELEMENTAL TOOLS

These four tools have their origins in ritual magick. I believe it's very important for Witches to acquire these basic weapons. Notice that these comprise the four suits of the Tarot. In my own practice I will not personally initiate anyone to the Second Degree (the teaching degree) without them, and I won't initiate anyone to First Degree without at least an athame. Gardner's Book of Shadows says that there are eight, but which of the other tools he considered to be associated with what element is unclear.

TABLE 3: Elemental Tools

Tool or Weapon	Element and Gender[1]	Description	Purpose	Equivalents
Athame	Air (Alexandrian), Fire (Gardnerian); Masculine	Black-handled, double-edged knife; sometimes single-edged or wood-handled (kitchen Witches); may have mystical symbols on hilt	Casting the circle; drawing symbols and barriers of protection; blessing and consecration; the "first forged" of the magickal tools	Sword, spear, lance
Wand	Fire (Alexandrian), Air (Gardnerian); Masculine	Wooden stick, perhaps with carving, or decorations such as crystals, feathers, or symbols; sometimes a long crystal or tube of conductive metal such as copper	Casting circles dealing with the Fair Folk and other nature spirits; blessing and consecration; forming a conduit between Heaven and Earth; journeyworking	Staff, stang, spear, dorje
Pentacle	Earth; Feminine	Round disk with pentagram, sometimes with other symbols or stones	Blessing/holding ritual food; consecration; protection against harmful magick	Disk, coin, shield, dish
Chalice	Water; Feminine	Round bowled glass with a stem, traditionally of silver, sometimes with symbols or gems	Blessing/holding ritual wine or drink; purification; creation	Cup, cauldron, bowl

1. Gender associations are traditional but optional.

A Few Notes about the Elemental Tools

All other tools can be consecrated by the athame, the "first forged" tool. In British Traditional Witchcraft an athame can be consecrated by placing it between the naked bodies of the priestess and priest of the coven. The sword is essentially a big athame used by groups for the same purposes. When the high priestess of the coven straps on the sword, she may act in place of the high priest. In many traditions the sword cuts nothing but air.

The wand is used "when dealing with certain spirits with whom it would not be meet to use the athame." In practice, that usually means the Fair Folk (fairies), since they don't like cold iron. Variations are used all over the world to create a channel between the Divine and the material, whether that's in prayer, magick, or astral travel. A special kind of staff used in witchcraft is topped with antlers and is called a *stang*. It represents the power of the Horned God (and makes handy hooks to hang things on).

Traditionally a wand is made from a Celtic sacred wood or a fruit tree, each of which has its own symbolism and meaning. I recommend some books in the bibliography that may help you to select the appropriate wood based on its magickal properties. This list includes the Druid sacred trees that could be easily made into wands, a handful of fruit trees, and other sacred trees. It is very simplified and by no means exhaustive, so you may wish to do your own research.

TABLE 4: Sacred Woods

Wood	Meaning and Usage
Alder	Confidence, diagnostics, divination, men's rites of passage, shielding, war
Apple	Fertility, healing, journeyworking, knowledge, love, otherworld, prosperity, tree of life
Ash	Banishing, initiation, healing, power, protection, tree of life
Aspen	Astral travel, communication, protection
Beech	Invocation, knowledge, preservation, understanding
Birch	Clearing, exorcism, protection, renewal, purification, warding
Blackthorn	Destruction, entropy, exorcism, hexing, protection, revenge
Broom	Banishing, divination, purification, spells, weather magick
Cedar	Divine communication, journeyworking, protection, wealth, tree of life
Cherry	Divination, love
Chestnut and Horse Chestnut	Love, protection, banishing hexes, healing, wealth
Elder	Banishing, crossing thresholds, death and rebirth, exorcism, fate, judgment, rites of passage, sleep, transformation, "the Lady's tree" (not to be burnt)
Elm	Attracting fairies, communication, love, protection of the dead and of spirits, psychic powers, relationships
Eucalyptus	Healing, protection, tree of life

continued on the next page

continued from the previous page

Gorse (Furze, Silver Fir)	Protection, warding, wealth
Hawthorn	Banishing, fairies, fertility, the Goddess power, happiness, love, sacred marriage
Hazel	Awen, divination, enchantment, healing, psychic power, wisdom, wishes
Holly	Dream magick, reincarnation, sacrifice, protection vs. lightning, bad luck and evil
Juniper	Exorcism, health, love, protection against accidents, theft and wild creatures
Lilac	Exorcism, protection
Maple	Longevity, love, wealth
Oak	Awen, courage, endurance, fertility, good luck, justice, power, sovereignty, strength, tree of life
Peach	Exorcism, fertility, longevity, love, wishes
Pear	Love, lust
Pine	Abundance, good luck, health, love, prosperity, purification, wealth
Plum	Love, protection
Poplar	See Aspen
Rose	Divination, healing, love, luck, protection, psychic powers
Rowan	Awen, divination, hex-breaking, inspiration, protection, psychic powers
Walnut	Health, hexing, mental powers, wishes
Willow	Binding, blessing, enchantment, healing, protection, women's rites of passage
Yew	Ancestor magick, death rites, immortality, journeyworking, shamanism, protection vs. evil, transformation

The First Degree initiation is typically offered in Witchcraft when a Witch has been practicing for a year and a day. It is a statement to the Lady and the Lord that Wicca is your chosen path and you are willing to follow where it leads. It is a commitment not unlike that of a baptism in Christian faiths that have voluntary baptism rites. It means you are willing to accept responsibility for your actions under the Rede.

You are presented to the Four Directions at your First Degree and instructed in the use of the basic tools.

Exercise 60: Acquiring Your Tools

Set yourself a time limit of one lunar cycle in which to find each of the four elemental tools. Start by acquiring a knife that will serve as your athame, then find or make a wand in the second month, a pentacle in the third month, and a chalice in the last month. Some possible sources include online Wiccan businesses, metaphysical stores, pawnshops, thrift stores, Asian shops, kitchen supply stores, and specialty shops. When acquiring the materials to make your tools, do no harm if you harvest things from nature and make sure you leave an offering. Select a knife or dagger that resonates with you and "feels right." Or you can make your own!

When you find (or make) the right piece, it is traditional not to barter or bargain for it. If it is meant to be yours, you can find a way, and it is human nature not to value anything that we didn't have to work for anyway. Pay what the seller is asking for it. (I hope I don't have to emphasize how inappropriate—and karmically bad!—it would be to steal your ritual tools! They would never work in the right way for you, and may very well be cursed.)

If you have acquired your tools second hand, make sure to cleanse them of all influences from the past, be they good or bad, except if you have inherited it as part of a magickal tradition. There are many ways to do that; choose a method that's appropriate for the materials. Don't use any method that would cause damage. I offer some suggestions for cleansing and consecration later.

Be aware of the laws in your area regarding weapons. If you are buying online, there may be rules about shipping across borders, and you could get into a lot of trouble!

Second Degree

The Second Degree is usually offered after a Witch has been practicing for a few years. It means you understand all the essentials of Wicca (Sabbats, Esbats, elements, tools, etc.), you have developed a personal relationship with your deities (more on how to do that in Chapter 8) and that you are now ready to be a teacher of the craft in your own right. You should probably have your own tools at this point, because you will not want to keep using the tools of your coven leaders!

Other Traditional Tools

There are many other tools used in witchcraft and magick. Most are traditional but all are optional. You can acquire them in similar places. All should be consecrated if they are to be used in the magick circle.

TABLE 5: Tools of the Art

Tool	Element and Gender[2]	Description	Purpose
Besom	Masculine and feminine conjoined	Broom	Clearing negativity in ritual space; fertility symbol; creating a threshold
Boline	Earth; Feminine	White handled knife with curved blade	Harvesting ritual herbs; cutting and carving things; lunar magick
Book of Shadows	Air; Masculine	Book with blank pages	Recording magickal experiences and information
Candle	Fire; Masculine	Colors used to represent directions and elements	Symbolizing spirit, the element of fire, the Watchtowers, or the deities
Cauldron	Water and/or Fire; Feminine	Round metal pot with handle and often three legs	Burning things to banish; scrying (with water); cooking magickal recipes; symbolizes womb of the Goddess
Censer	Air; or conjoined Air-Fire; Masculine	Metal container on chain; dish of sand; stick or cone incense holder	Consecrating circle, tools or spells

Tool	Element and Gender[2]	Description	Purpose
Cingulum or Cords		Colored cords sometimes worn around waist	Symbolizes degree; cord magick and binding; outlines the circle; special cingulum called "the Measure" (see below)
Dish of Salt	Earth; Feminine	Dish with salt in it	Mixed with water to consecrate circle, tools, or spells; purifies anything it contacts
Icons	Feminine (goddess); Masculine (god)	Images or statues of a goddess and/or a god of your choice	Focal points for working with deities
Offering Dishes	Earth or Water; Feminine	Dishes used to hold water, ritual food, or offerings	Making offerings; holding blessed food; water mixed with salt to consecrate circle, tools or spells
Scourge	Fire; Masculine	Flogger or cat-o-nine-tails	Purification, trance induction; represents pains of life

2. Gender associations are traditional but optional.

Notes About Other Traditional Tools

A cingulum is a length of cord worn around a Witch's waist or hips. Different traditions will use different colors to signify levels of understanding, otherwise known as degrees. A special kind of cingulum is one's *measure*. A length of cord is taken and tied at specific spots during a First Degree initiation, and some traditions will also put a few drops of the new Witch's blood on it. It is symbolic of a person's spirit, and suggests a rebirth (like an umbilical cord). It is usually given to the initiate during the ceremony as a symbol of love and trust. Magick can be done by tying knots in the cords in specific patterns, and a Witch used to carry a nine-foot cingulum to delineate the boundaries of the circle. Cords can also be woven together or tied in nine places to fix a spell, which are then untied when the spell is completed.

A besom (Witch's broom) is used to sweep away negative energy before casting circle. Because its imagery is a stick thrust into a fuzzy triangle, it is also a fertility symbol, which is why a couple jumps over it in a handfasting (wedding) ceremony.

Jewelry and Clothing

Some traditions work "skyclad" (nude) and others use robes. Shedding your workday clothing symbolically sheds the concerns of the day, and donning a robe or just a cingulum instantly focuses your consciousness toward ritual. Jewelry can also be used for this. Traditionally, high priestesses wear beaded necklaces, and in some traditions, those beads are of amber and jet. Amber (made of fossilized tree sap) symbolizes life, and jet (fossilized charcoal) symbolizes death. A priestess may also wear a special tiara called a *moon crown*, and a priest may wear a *horned crown* (topped with antlers, goat, or even bull horns like a Viking helmet). There are thousands of pendants, earrings, and rings available with Wiccan symbols as well. I always wear a piece of jewelry with a pentagram or a goddess no matter what I am doing, which is my way of letting people know that I am a priestess of the craft, available to answer their questions.

Other Tools

There are many other tools used in Witchcraft, including but not limited to: crystals, feathers, offering bowls, oil diffusers, mortar and pestle, musical instruments, Tarot cards . . . the choices really are limitless and come from desire or need.

Essential Altar Layout

There are many different ways to set up your altar. You probably already have your preferences. There are two keys: practicality (How are you going to use your tools?) and aesthetics (What does the symbolism of your tools' positioning mean to you?). Each tradition has its own beliefs. Here's how mine does it:

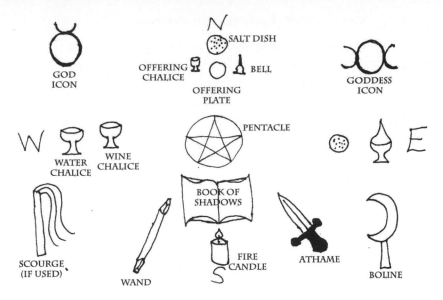

Figure 12: Star Sapphire Altar Layout

Exercise 61: Consecrating Your Tools

I am going to offer a short ritual to consecrate (bless) your tools. Here are some options:

Invoke your bubble of protection and draw the protective pentagrams illustrated in Exercise 3: Visualizing Symbols. Call upon the four directions or elements and the Divine as you understand it.

Make a Statement of Intent. For example: "I call upon the directions and the Lady and Lord to consecrate this athame and charge it to its purpose: to serve me well in the magick circle."

Bless and cleanse your tool to remove previous influences (choose whichever one works):

- Cleanse it in saltwater
- Thrust it into the ground
- Place it in direct sunlight for one full day
- Smudge it

Enchant your tool with one of the following methods:

- Turn it clockwise (deosil) thrice over a candle flame, then waft incense over it (when used with the saltwater cleansing method this imbues the tool with the energy of all four elements)
- Thrust it toward the heavens (especially on a bright sunny day, during full moon, or during a storm; if you buried the tool in the earth beforehand, it is balanced between heaven and earth)
- Place it under the light of the full moon for one or three nights
- Breathe life into it
- Dab it with your blood, especially menstrual blood
- Leave it in the crook of a living tree or in a sacred place for a full moon cycle
- Anoint it with magickal oils or herbs
- Use another tool, a crystal, or your hands to imbue it with energy

Thank the deities, release the directions by thanking them, and open the circle.

Etiquette for Magickal Tools

- To infuse a tool with your energy, carry it near you for one moon cycle. You can put it on your headboard or under your pillow if you can't carry it with you.
- It is impolite to touch someone else's tools without their permission.
- Store your tools on a dedicated altar or wrapped in a cloth of natural material such as silk or cotton to prevent them from accumulating unwanted ambient energies.
- By tradition, tools should be buried with the Witch. (One of the stories of my tradition is that when one of the founding Witches died, the members of his coven snuck all his tools into his coffin during the viewing except his athame, which then became the coven's communal athame).

Exercise 62: Your Altar

Create a shrine embodying your beliefs in your home, utilizing whatever symbols or tools you might have. All altars are entirely personal, so feel free to be creative!

RITES

Wiccan spells and rituals are really a form of performance art. Setting, sound, color, symbols, movement, actions, tastes, smells, and feelings come together to create lovely participatory art. The more senses you bring to bear, the more effective your magick will be! A spell engages all the same elements as a ritual, but it is focused toward a more "practical" purpose.

BASIC STRUCTURE OF WICCAN RITUAL

A Wiccan ritual follows a loose pattern that leaves a fair bit of room for creativity and individual expression. Think of writing a ritual like writing a short story. There is a specific format, but a lot of different things can happen within it! I've broken it down into its component stages, and rather than giving you a specific series of actions to perform, I will list possibilities that you could combine to make a ritual of your own.

TABLE 6: Stages of Ritual

Stage	Purpose	Actions	Chants	Notes
Clearing Ritual Space	Makes a portable temple, creates a psychological liminal space between the worlds	Besom, asperge, cense, scatter herbs or salt, play a singing bowl, make a crystal grid, ring a bell, draw banishing pentagrams	"As the Besom Sweeps"; "Circle Gate"	Usually done widdershins (counterclockwise); start in north (womb of the Mother), east (new beginnings), or west (death rituals).
Casting Circle	Delineates sacred space; forms microcosm within the macrocosm	Mark the edge of the circle in some way (salt, water, incense, fire, herbs, cord, athame, joining hands)	"The Circle Is Cast"; "Circle Gate"	Usually done deosil (clockwise). Start where you started clearing. Sometimes a besom is used to make a threshold gate.

continued on the next page

continued from the previous page

Calling Quarters	Brings four elements and directions to-gether to create Axis Mundi (world navel) from which all things are possible	Invoke powers and directions using items or symbols (see appendix C); light candles; draw pentagrams (see figure 8).	"Earth My Body"; "Air Moves Us"	Usually done deosil
Invocation or Evocation	Calls the divine as you under-stand it to aid your work or be honored	Light candles; draw down the moon and/or sun; make offerings to icons.	"Silver Shining Wheel"; "Threefold God Chant"; "Goddess Chant"; "The Earth Is Our Mother"	See below
Celebra-tion or Magick	The reason you are doing the ritual	Esbats (see ap-pendix D); Sabbats (see figure 10); rites of passage; initiations; divina-tion; magick and spells.	Various, depending on purpose	
Cakes and Ale	Takes a portion of the blessing into yourself; grounding; offering energy back to the Universe	Bless (symbolic Great Rite, lay on hands, purify with salt or salt water) and consume food and drink; portion left for the deities and spirits.	"Earth My Body"; "Thanks Turns the Wheel"	Varies greatly according to tradition and perception of the gods
Thanking Divinity	Acknowledges the gods and thanks them for their help	Bow to icons; bring priestess or priest out of trance; put out candles.	"We All Come from the God-dess/Horned God"; "Hoof and Horn"; "Goddess Chant"	More details in chapter 8

Releasing Quarters	Sends your guests home, thanks them for coming and releases gathered energies	Devoke powers and directions using items or symbols (see appendix C); put out candles; kiss hand to directions; draw pentagrams (see figure 8).	"The Earth the Air the Fire the Water"	Widdershins or deosil depending on tradition
Opening Circle	Returns you to the normal world; releases the Axis Mundi	Sweep, pick up or break up whatever marked the ground; create doorway; retrace circle; rejoin and release hands.	"The Circle Is Open"; "May the Circle Be Open"	Usually widdershins

TABLE 7: Vocalizations for Ritual

Clearing Ritual Space	"With this besom I clear this space."
	"With this salt (incense, flame, water) I cleanse this space; may all negatives be walled (blown, burned, washed) away."
Casting Circle	"I cast this circle round and round; between the worlds we now are bound."
	"This is a time that is not a time, in a place that is not a place, on a day that is not a day."
	"As above, so below. As within, so without. As the Universe, so the self."
Calling Quarters	"Guardians of the Watchtower of the (Direction), Powers of (Element); I summon, stir, and call you up to witness this rite and guard this circle!"
	"By the earth that is Her body, by the air that is Her breath, by the fires of Her bright spirit, and by the waters of Her sacred womb, the circle is cast."
	"Peace to the south! Peace to the north! Peace to the east! Peace to the west! May there be peace throughout the whole world!"
Invocation or Evocation	Charge of the Goddess, Charge of the God
Celebration or Magick	Varies according to purpose
Cakes and Ale	See below

continued on the next page

continued from the previous page

Thanking Divinity	"Thank you, (name of deity) for joining me in my rite. Go if you must, stay if you will; but whether you go or stay, hail and farewell."
Releasing Quarters	"Guardians of the Watchtower of the (Direction), Powers of (Element); thank you for joining us in our rite! Return now to your earthly (airy, fiery, watery) realms harming none as you pass! Hail and farewell!"
	"Thank you (elements and powers called) for joining us in our circle. Go if you must, stay if you will, but whether you go or stay, hail and farewell."
	"By the earth that is Her body (etc.) the circle is open."
Opening Circle	"May the circle be open but unbroken. Merry meet, and merry part, and merry meet again."

Invoking or Evoking Deity

Calling upon the Divine is always a very personal matter for a Witch. We all speak to the gods in our own way. When Witches call a deity (or other spirit being) into their sacred space, this is known as evocation or summoning. We will deal with invocation (calling a spirit or deity into the body) in chapter 8.

SUMMONING

There is an art to evoking the deities. There are several books on summoning spirits out there that direct you to command and threaten the deities like common servants. That's probably fine for demons and maybe poltergeists, but it's not appropriate for any other kind of spiritual entity, especially deities, unless you are following the ancient rites of the Strega. These are gods! You show them respect.

Some deities demand more respect than others, and this should be worked into the calling you create. Zeus is pretty proud; so is Odin. They'll need a great deal of honoring. On the other hand, Zeus prefers humility, and Odin will likely want a declaration of loyalty to the Asa (the Norse gods) and an assurance that you'll be on his team at Ragnarok.

But, we have a cocreative relationship with our deities. Being friends, they should be invited, not commanded. And we might have to talk them into it. Make your ceremony beautiful, fun, and attractive to get their attention.

Like in a spell, timing could be helpful. If you're not evoking deities at Esbats or Sabbats, try looking to ancient holidays or days of the week. Both Odin and Zeus are storm gods, so a thunderstorm would be a great time to work with them! Don't evoke deities of darkness at high noon, and so forth.

Look to tradition. Use symbols. Zeus is associated with high mountains, so why not climb one to do your ceremony? Odin has two ravens that serve him: Hugin ("Thought") and Munin ("Memory"). Perhaps place a raven feather on your altar. Consider leaving culturally appropriate offerings. In Ancient Greek worship, the gods received libations of wine; in Norse worship, mead was tipped and boasts were made. In my tradition, we leave the first share of everything for the Goddess, the second for the God, the next for us, and last, a portion is left for "the children of the earth, both seen and unseen."

The evocation itself should be poetic. If you do not know how to make up such things off the top of your head, write them beforehand, or use your charges or chants. The delivery of the evocation is also important! Do not whine, grovel, or stammer over your words like you are reciting from a history textbook. Speak with authority, speak clearly with art, emotion, and poetry, speak loudly enough that everyone can hear you, and be firm but respectful. We assume our deities will come when so addressed.

When you have completed your ritual, don't forget to offer gratitude and say farewell. Don't dismiss the deities as you might the elemental powers! You are not in a position to command them. The most common devocation I know of is probably also the best for most purposes; "Go if you must, stay if you will; but whether you go or stay, hail and farewell!"

Exercise 63: Evocation

Choose a deity or deities and compose a ritual of evocation for them. You can ask for their aid in an act of magick or just honor them and make an offering.

One common method of evocation is called the Charge of the Goddess, which is the only real piece of "Wiccan liturgy" that there is. In my tradition, we have a Charge of the God as well as a Charge of the Goddess, which follow. You can find other versions online.

Charge of the Goddess

Listen to the words of the Great Mother, Who of old was called Artemis, Astarte, Isis, Dione, Melusine, Aphrodite, Brighid and by many other names:

Whenever you have need of anything, once in the month, and better it be when the moon is full, you shall assemble in some secret place and adore the spirit of Me, Who is Queen of all the Wise. There you shall assemble, you who are fain to learn all sorcery but have not yet won its deepest secrets; to thee will I teach things yet unknown.

You shall be free from slavery, and as a sign that you be free you shall be naked in your rites. Sing, feast, dance, make music and love, all in My presence; for Mine is the ecstasy of the spirit, and Mine also is joy on earth. For My law is love unto all beings. Keep pure your highest ideal; strive ever towards it; let naught stop you or turn you aside. For Mine is the secret that opens upon the door of youth, and Mine is the cup of the wine of life, that is the Cauldron of Cerridwen, that is the Holy Grail of immortality. Beyond death I give peace and freedom and reunion with those that have gone before. Nor do I demand aught of sacrifice; for behold, My love is poured out upon the earth.

Hear the words of the Star Goddess, the dusts of Whose feet are the hosts of heaven, Whose body encircles the Universe:

I Who am the beauty of the green earth, and the white moon among the stars, and the mystery of the waters, and the desire of the heart calls unto your soul; arise, and come unto Me. For I am the soul of nature Who gives life to the Universe; from Me, all things proceed, and unto Me, all things return; and before My face, beloved of gods and men, let thine innermost self be enfolded in the rapture of the infinite. Let My worship be in the heart that rejoices; for behold, all acts of love and pleasure are My rituals. Therefore, let there be beauty and strength; power and compassion; honor and humility; mirth and reverence within you.

And you who seeks to know Me, know that your seeking and yearning will fail unless you know the Mystery; if you do not find that which you seek within yourself, you will never find it without. For behold, I have been with you since the beginning, and I am that which is attained at the end of desire.[4]

---

4. The original Charge of the Goddess appears in Charles Leland's *Aradia: Gospel of the Witches*. It was later rewritten by Doreen Valiente and then adapted by Starhawk. This version contains elements from both the Valiente and Starhawk versions.

Charge of the God

Listen to the words of the Great Father, Who of old was called Osiris, Eros, Ganesh, Pan, Cernunnos, Herne, Lugh, and by many other names:

Whenever you have need of Me, whether in joy or in sorrow, you shall gather together in some wooded place and call upon Me, Who is the Father of all things. For I am eternal, and as a sign that I am ever-present, celebrate and worship She Who is My Mother, and My Lover, and all things.

For with Our Love the earth lives, and that Life nourishes you Who are our children and Ourselves.

Love all things as you love Me, for I am in all things as I am in you. For Mine is the secret that opens the gates of life, and Mine is the earth that is the body of Cernunnos, that is the eternal circle of rebirth. For I am the Hunter and the Hunted. I give the knowledge of everlasting life, and beyond death I give the promise of enlightenment. I am the fruit upon the trees and the grain at harvest; but know that without planting there can be no harvest, and without winter there can be no spring.

Hear the words of the woodland God, the thunder of Whose hooves is the heartbeat of the heavens, Whose body is the center of the Universe:

I Who am the flame in the heart of every man, and the core of every star, calls unto your soul; arise, and come unto Me; for I am the flesh of the earth and all its beings. Through Me, all things must die, and with Me all things are reborn. Let My worship be in the body that is coura-geous, for behold; all acts of willing sacrifice are My rituals. Let there be pride and humility, love and strength, hope and reverence within you.

For behold My Mystery; if ever you are in need, help will not find you unless you seek it.

Cakes and Ale

Choose food and drink that is symbolically appropriate. White wine is tradi-tionally served for Esbats, while red wine is traditionally served for Sabbats. Maybe use white crescent cakes for Esbats, apples for Mabon (harvest festival), or beer for Lammas ("loaf mass"). I've used pomegranate juice for a Persephone ritual and milk and peaches for Kwan Yin. And so on.

The most traditional blessing I know of is known as the symbolic Great Rite. The priest holds the chalice in his hands and the priestess holds the athame in hers.

She says, "As the athame is to the male,"

He responds: "So the chalice is to the female."

As she dips the athame into the chalice, they both say: "So conjoined, they bring blessedness."

This seems counterintuitive; and by all means if you'd prefer to reverse it, please do so. But there is a reason for it, which I will discuss in chapter 8.

Then they pass the food and drink around. In my tradition, we use the blessing that was coined by the Church of All Worlds: "May you never hunger, may you never thirst."

To which we reply, "Thou art God/Goddess" (whichever is appropriate).

There are many ways to do this blessing. A Dianic blessing I like is:

Bless the food and share it together.

We bless this bread. We bless this ale.

We bless the Land that nurtured it and the Sun that gave it power.

We bless all hands, seen and unseen, that have brought it to this place.

May it nurture all here, seen and unseen.

Thanking Deity

You can add a thank you and farewell to the unseen entities at your circle too, if you like. Just remember the rule: If you called them, you must send them home! Otherwise they might hang around and get under your feet, just like bad houseguests.

Releasing Quarters

There are two distinct feelings about this in Wicca, depending upon the origins of your tradition; if you are a solitary or an eclectic, you need to decide how you feel about it.

British Traditional Witches and their descendants believe that while the elementals are useful, necessary creatures, they are not human and do not understand human needs; so if you don't limit their behavior, they can get out of control and cause havoc! These traditions (like mine) mention all entities by name and send them politely and firmly home so they don't hang around and cause trouble. Traditions influenced by Feri or Dianic traditions believe that we exist in a cocreative bond with the elements, and they will never hurt us. So they invite the elements to remain if they wish. Address the elements appropriately according to your belief.

Exercise 64: Ritual Writing

Following the basic formula, write your own ritual! Create one for an Esbat; create another for a Sabbat. You can even create one entirely of chants. Use the correspondences given or research your own at the library or online. Keep in mind the power of words, and utilize all the tools you have been given: rhyme, mnemonics, symbols, colors, etc. Have fun!

SELF-EVALUATION

We have come to the end of the third chapter! Way to go for sticking with it! I'm asking a little more creativity of you than other writers, but I think that's the best way to learn. If you haven't done some of the exercises, now is the time to catch up. Everything I've asked of you is included for a reason. Let's carry on!

part two

INTERMEDIATE PRACTICES

Warning: The information in this chapter is for informational purposes. Using the substances discussed here can be extremely risky. Cannabis, most entheogens, opiates, and all hallucinogens are controlled or illegal substances in many countries. If you choose to use them, you are entirely responsible for the legal consequences. Do not drive or use heavy machinery when under the influence.

chapter four

INTOXICANTS

4) Incense, Drugs, Wine, etc., whatever is used to release the Spirit. (Note. One must be very careful about this. Incense is usually harmless, but you must be careful. If it has bad aftereffects, reduce the amount used, or the duration of the time it is inhaled. Drugs are very dangerous if taken to excess, but it must be remembered that there are drugs that are absolutely harmless, though people talk of them with bated breath, but Hemp is especially dangerous, because it unlocks the inner eye swiftly and easily, so one is tempted to use it more and more. If it is used at all, it must be with the strictest precautions, to see that the person who uses it has no control over the supply. This should be doled out by some responsible person, and the supply strictly limited.)
—Gerald Gardner, *The Gardnerian Book of Shadows*

Drunkenness is a curse and a hindrance only to slaves . . . Anyone who is doing his true Will is drunk with the delight of Life.
—Aleister Crowley

Throughout history, numerous substances have been used by mystics, shamans, and magicians to induce the magickal state of mind. Some of them cause a powerful trance state almost immediately (such as hallucinogens and opiates); some induce trance through other effects on the body (such as aphrodisiacs and alcohol); and some create emotional states that eventually, through practice and association, can aid the attainment of trance states (such as most traditional incenses and aromatherapy products). Many of the more powerful substances out there are controlled or prohibited, and for good reason. They are potent, often dangerous or toxic, and they can cause long-term damage if used improperly (or even properly!). Many of them are also addictive. Most books avoid dealing with this subject entirely. I won't.

For our purposes, "intoxicants" refers to any substance used in magick to change consciousness through external means. They fall into a few general categories:

- Aromatherapy
- Incense, sacred fires, and smudging
- Herbs
- Drugs
- Alcohol
- Hallucinogens
- Poisons and toxins (not recommended!)

In their own way, each of these types of substances expands or alters your consciousness if used cautiously and precisely for the purpose intended, and not abused.

THE ART OF SCENT

Most essential oils should be used cautiously when applied to the skin because they might actually cause chemical burns, and they should not be ingested unless you are told otherwise.

Aromatherapy is the art and science of using scent to shift consciousness and change mood. The most common substances used in aromatherapy are essential oils; concentrated, distilled, or extracted volatile oils of plants. Other substances used in aromatherapy include herbs, spices, perfumes, flowers, and incense. Many of these substances also have other consciousness-changing effects or healing properties. Some are contact stimulants, euphorics, or aphrodisiacs.

For millennia we have made use of this art in perfumery in order to increase our sexual attractiveness. Most of us now know that lavender relaxes us, and citrus scents give us energy and cheer us up. Is it any surprise, then, that to the occultist, some scents open your third eye, increase your awareness, improve your understanding, and invest you with wisdom? Accepting that, is it so difficult to imagine that some scents may also improve your wealth, increase your fertility, enhance your personal power, or psychically protect you?

Scented oils and perfumery play upon those emotional associations, and the art of aromatherapy puts those scents to work for you to alter your mood. Magickally, we can also use scent to focus our Intent. Let me give you a primer course!

Essential Oils

Essential oils are the pressed essence of plants and flowers or the extracted essence of roots, woods, and resins. When pressing, usually a very large amount of the plant is required to yield even a small amount of oil. The same holds true of extractions, in which the active substance is extracted by immersing it in oil, water or alcohol, depending on its solvency. Because such a large amount is required, and because extraction may take a very long time, essential oils are relatively expensive. Most high-end perfumes use large amounts of essential oils; this is part of what makes them so pricey. You can often make your own perfumes without the same high cost.

When purchasing essential oils, the first thing you should look for is whether or not the product describes itself on the label as a "pure essential oil" or a "fragrance oil." A fragrance oil is an artificial scent that is chemically manufactured; but in North America, a product can only be described as a "pure essential oil" if it is completely natural, aside from the agent used in extraction.

The second thing you should look for is the percentage of essential oil in the bottle. In order to make expensive oils more affordable, manufacturers will dilute the essential oil in carrier oil such as almond, grape seed, jojoba, or olive oil. Oils that you should double-check the label for include neroli, frankincense, rose, vanilla, patchouli, musk, sandalwood, elemi, and myrrh. For magickal purposes, these diluted oils are usually just as effective, but purists who are making their own perfumes, soaps, or other products may wish to spend the extra money and purchase the real thing. Often you will have to order them from the manufacturers directly. Also, double-check any commercially available essential oil blend, even ones that are homemade. Usually it is only profitable to a manufacturer of oil blends to use carrier oils as well as essential oils.

Begin by picking a plant or flower whose scent you enjoy. You can use fruit peels, flower petals, roots, leaves, or tree sap. Whatever you choose, you need enough of your chosen plant to entirely fill a glass jar that you can seal, such as a mason jar. It may help to break up the plant with a mortar and pestle if you have one, or you can muddle the plant using a round, smooth stone or the base of a wooden spoon.

Take a carrier oil, such as grapeseed, almond, or even canola oil, and pour it into the jar to fill the space between the leaves, resin, or petals. Seal the jar and put it in a cool, dark place for three to six months. Take it out at least once a week and give it a vigorous shake to disperse it. If you like, you can even open it periodically to check progress. Can you smell the plant's odor in the oil?

At the end of the three months, strain your oil through cheesecloth, or, if there are several smaller particles, through a coffee filter, and dispose of the original plant substance (usually compostable). Observe the changes in the extracted oil mixture. Has it taken on a different color? Has it absorbed the smell strongly?

If you are unsatisfied with the amount of absorbed scent, you can repeat the original process by filling the jar with more of your chosen plant, and pour your original oil over top of it, to be extracted for another three months.

This process may be repeated as often as you wish to create a stronger oil extraction. Eventually the oil will not change noticeably between extractions, and you may consider that the finished product.

This is a fantastic way to make ritual anointing oils and oil-based perfumes! Gardner used a vervain extraction in his rituals. Oil of Abramelin, a traditional magickal oil blend first popularized by Aleister Crowley, is an extraction of galangal root, cinnamon bark, and myrrh, extracted in olive oil for six months. In contact with your skin it is a euphoric that encourages divine contact and inspiration and increases magickal power. In magick it is used by applying it in small amounts to the temples or third eye.

Getting Started with Essential Oils

If you have an interest in essential oils, you may find the following list helpful. I am going to suggest a few oils to start with, the magickal correspondences they represent, and the uses they have in aromatherapy and natural first aid.

Cedar

Elements: Earth, Fire
Planets: Sun, Earth
Astrological Signs: Leo, Virgo
Chakras: Base and solar plexus
Magick: Grounding, banishing, cleansing, protection
Aromatherapy: Cleansing, protection, reducing stress
Beauty: Astringent, antiseptic
First Aid: Antiseptic, astringent; emmenagogue, expectorant, sedative, stimulates circulation. Inhale cedarwood steam to clear congestion. Add to bath to ease urinary infections and speed healing. Use as a salve to treat dermatitis, eczema, and psoriasis. Use as a tincture for insect bites.

Cinnamon

Element: Fire
Planets: Mars, Venus
Astrological Signs: Aries, Sagittarius
Chakra: Sacral
Magick: Money attraction, psychic awareness
Aromatherapy: Stimulant, concentration
Beauty: Anti-inflammatory, skin warming (Warning: Do not use in cosmetics.)
First Aid: Anti-inflammatory, arthritis and muscular pain, spasms. Put a single drop in your bath (but no more!) or add to pain salves.

Clove

Elements: Fire
Planets: Venus, Mars
Astrological Signs: Aries, Virgo
Chakras: Base and brow
Magick: Courage, protection
Aromatherapy: Sensuality
Beauty: Do *not* use in cosmetic or bath products; irritates skin.
First Aid: Anti-inflammatory. Numbs toothaches when directly applied to gums.

Cypress

Elements: Earth
Planets: Venus, Earth
Astrological Sign: Virgo
Chakras: Base and heart
Magick: Blessing, consecration, protection, healing
Aromatherapy: Grounding, grief, tension, stress, and anger
Beauty: Astringent, eases water retention, treats cellulite
First Aid: Antiseptic, astringent, deodorant, rheumatic pain, muscle spasms, cramping, bleeding, circulation problems, menopause, edema, wound healing, expectorant, skin circulation, muscle pain and cramps.

Eucalyptus

Element: Water
Planets: Moon, Neptune
Astrological Signs: Pisces, Cancer, Scorpio
Chakras: Solar and heart
Magick: Healing, purification
Aromatherapy: Dispels mental fatigue
Beauty: Astringent, antiseptic
First Aid: Antibacterial, antiviral, deodorant, expectorant, liniment—rheumatic, arthritic, and other types of pain. Flu, fever, sore throat, skin and muscle pain. Contraindicated in asthma attacks.

Ginger

Element: Fire
Planets: Mars, Aries
Astrological Signs: Leo, Sagittarius
Chakras: Solar
Magick: Sexuality, love, courage, attracting money
Aromatherapy: Memory, willpower, protection, aphrodisiac, courage
Beauty: Anti-inflammatory and skin warming. Use sparingly.
First Aid: Anti-inflammatory, flu aches. Put a few drops in your bath (but no more!).

Lavender

Element: Air
Planets: Mercury, Jupiter
Astrological Signs: Libra, Aquarius, Gemini
Chakras: Brow and crown
Magick: Health, love, peace, conscious mind
Aromatherapy: Relaxation, calm, sleep and dreaming, depression
Beauty: Topically applied; heals skin conditions, moisturizes skin, reduces wrinkles
First Aid: Apply to temples to relieve tension headaches and migraines. Apply to skin to relieve muscle tension, heal scars, or soothe aches and bruises. Safe to apply undiluted to even an infant's skin. Every basic aromatherapy kit should start with lavender.

Lemon

Element: Water
Planets: Moon, Neptune
Astrological Signs: Pisces, Cancer
Chakras: Solar and brow
Magick: Lunar energy, full moon, healing, purification, psychic awareness
Aromatherapy: Dreams, improves mood and energy, fights depression
Beauty: Do not apply topically; may cause burns and irritation! Dilute and splash on skin for astringent. Put in hair rinse for golden highlights.
First Aid: Dilute with water and place on insect bites to relieve stinging.

Lemongrass

Element: Air
Planet: Mercury
Astrological Signs: Aquarius, Gemini, Libra
Chakra: Solar
Magick: Psychic awareness, purification
Aromatherapy: Headaches, drowsiness, memory, creativity
Beauty: Skin and hair astringent
First Aid: Antiseptic, deodorant, antifungal, astringent, relieves rheumatic and other pain, nervine, indigestion, especially effective on ringworm and skin infections.

Lime

Element: Air
Planets: Venus, Uranus
Astrological Signs: Aquarius, Cancer
Chakra: Heart
Magick: Purification, protection
Aromatherapy: Refreshes, enhances energy and alertness, opens blocked
    heart chakra
Beauty: Tones and refreshes skin
First Aid: Mental alertness; restores consciousness like "smelling salts."

Orange

Element: Fire
Planet: Sun
Astrological Signs: Aries, Leo, Sagittarius
Chakras: Sacral and solar
Magick: Solar energy, Sabbats, purification
Aromatherapy: Energy, well being; enhances mood and libido
Beauty: Enhances red-gold highlights in hair
Special: As a natural cleaning product orange oil can't be beat! Will remove
    oil and strip wax from furniture.

Patchouli

Element: Earth
Planet: Saturn
Astrological Signs: Taurus, Virgo, Capricorn, Aquarius
Chakra: Base
Magick: Money, fertility, lust
Aromatherapy: Grounding, enhances libido

Peppermint

Element: Fire
Planets: Mercury, Venus
Astrological Signs: Aries, Leo, Sagittarius
Chakras: Base and brow

Magick: Purification, psychic awareness
Aromatherapy: Sleep, tension
Beauty: Astringent
First Aid: Muscle and flu aches and bruises, inflamed joints, sinuses. A couple drops (no more!) drunk in hot water eases an upset stomach.

Rose

Element: Water
Planets: Venus, Moon
Astrological Signs: Gemini, Virgo, Libra
Chakras: Base, heart, and brow
Magick: Love, psychic powers, healing, divination, protection
Aromatherapy: Aphrodisiac, relaxant
Beauty: Skin conditions, especially scars, stretch marks, and wrinkles
First Aid: Soothes insect bites. Can be applied directly to infant skin
Special: Very expensive, but some qualities just can't be beat. Try in carrier oil, second pressing, or as rose water when possible.

Rose Geranium

Element: Fire
Planet: Venus
Astrological Signs: Virgo, Libra
Chakras: Base and heart
Magick: Love, healing, fertility, protection
Aromatherapy: Aphrodisiac; stimulant
Beauty: Perfumery
First Aid: Insect repellant; skin stimulant
Special: Less expensive substitute for rose in magick, but not effective for psychic work.

Rosemary

Element: Air
Planets: Venus, Uranus
Astrological Signs: Gemini, Virgo, Libra
Chakra: Throat

Magick: Love, healing, concentration, consecration
Aromatherapy: Intellect, memory, alertness
Beauty: Astringent and disinfectant (use sparingly). Treats acne.
First Aid: Muscle aches, bruises. Natural disinfectant when applied topically
    to a wound or diffused. Insect repellent.

Spearmint

Elements: Air
Planets: Mercury
Astrological Signs: Aquarius, Gemini, Libra
Chakras: Brow
Magick: Concentration, focus
Aromatherapy: Intellect; stimulates appetite
Beauty: Astringent
First Aid: Muscle aches and bruises, inflamed joints, flu aches; clears sinuses.

Vanilla

Elements: Water
Planets: Venus
Astrological Signs: Aquarius, Gemini, Libra
Chakras: Heart
Magick: Intellect, love, lust
Aromatherapy: Intellectual stimulant, aphrodisiac, relaxant
Special: A less expensive "love" oil than rose

Exercise 66: Magickal Oil

Blend oils for use in magick by putting together a combination you find pleasing with appropriate correspondences. Use my list, the books in the bibliography, or research online! Record your recipes.

BURNT OFFERINGS

Probably the first use of sacred burning things was in prehistoric times, when humanity learned that different woods, leaves, barks, saps, and twigs released different scents when burnt in a fire, and each of these scents had an effect on our senses and emotions. Because many of the gods were seen as being in the sky, burnt offerings carried prayers to the gods, and burning the dead released their spirits to the otherworld. In magick, only items that produce scents or intoxicating fumes are relevant. The point is not only to communicate with the Divine, but to change our consciousness in a way that focuses our Intent to a specific purpose.

SMUDGING

Smudging is the use of sacred smoke to cleanse and consecrate. Modern Witches get the use of smudging from the Native Americans, and the practice has become part of many North American spiritualities. Most metaphysical stores carry smudge sticks, but you can make your own in any desert climate.

Major ingredients of smudge mixes and sticks include:

- Bay leaves: You have likely used bay leaves in cooking. Native Californians used bay leaves in their smudges to keep away colds and flus in fall, and bay laurel wreaths were given as a trophy for victories in Ancient Greece. Bay leaves have a protective solar association, symbolizing both victory and peace.
- Cedar: Cedar, an evergreen tree, has soft, rounded needles and grows in semidry climates. It has a pungent odor, similar to but warmer than that of pine. Cedar's wood is soft and reddish or golden in color, and it burns hot and quickly. It is fairly common for people to have contact allergies to cedar oil. It creates a barrier of protection wherever it is burned, and it is another wood used in consecration. Cedar was holy to Egyptians, Jews, Druids, and numerous African cultures, as well as Native Americans.
- Conifers (various)
  - Cypress: Used in similar ways to Cedar. Cypress trees grow best in flatlands, like prairies or swamp deltas. Cypress oil is used frequently in voodoo and hoodoo recipes for love and prosperity. It is a more pungent, less sweet, and more lemony scent than Cedar.
  - Fir: See Spruce.
  - Hemlock: See Spruce.

- ○ Juniper: Used in similar ways to Cedar. Junipers were holy to the Egyptians, and their berries are one of the ingredients in the sacred incense of Egyptian temples, Kyphi.
- ○ Pine—See Spruce.
- Spruce is largely used for purifying and cleansing. It is very strong, and its odor when burnt can really be overpowering. Please use it sparingly—it is likely to produce allergic reactions in sensitive people.
- Copal: Copal is a generic term for tree resin that is in a state between gel and amber form. In smudging it refers to local conifer tree resin. It is used as incense, and it creates positive energy and prosperity wherever it is burnt. It smells light, airy, and sweet.
- Fennel: Use of fennel as a smudge is fairly recent and has only occurred since the Europeans brought it over to North America and naturalized it. It is used for the same reasons it was used in European folk magick: to repel sickness and negative energies. It smells faintly like licorice and creates hard seeds that are used in cooking.
- Lavender: Lavender's light purple flowers on spiky stems are a common sight in any herb garden. They smell light, fragrant, and airy. They relax and raise the spirits in aromatherapy and increase psychic ability. The stems are used in a smudge stick, and the flowers are used in smudge mixes.
- Mint: There are many different species of mint, and most grow wild like weeds all over North and Central America. In my area, I get more spearmint than peppermint, and it can be overpowering if not used in moderation when smudging. Mint is cleansing and uplifting.
- Mugwort: Various species of mugwort are found all over the world. Since it is a consciousness-altering substance, it has been used by many cultures to heal and induce visions and dreams. Mugworts like damp climates. It has frond-like leaves and smells a little like spruce and hyssop. Some metaphysical stores will carry bundles of it for smudge, or they may carry the oil or the dried herb. If you get really lucky, you might find some in an herbal store, but you will likely have to plant and/or wildcraft it yourself.
- Mullein: It is said that mullein's special work is to heal damage caused by human interference, which is why it tends to grow wild in areas of new development. The roots and furry leaves help maintain and restore soil damaged by erosion. You may have seen spears of its fuzzy,

gray-green leaves and yellow flowers or seed clusters growing overtop most other plants in the fall. Traditionally, only a single leaf is taken from each plant for smudging and dried. Mullein is grounding, healing, and calming when used in a smudge, and it heals damage caused by relationships. Its smoke is used to treat asthma, so it may be a good alternative for those with sensitivities. I find that it smells a bit like dust or mold, and a bit like old shoes when burnt, but I don't find it totally unpleasant.

- Resin: Basically any resin, which is solidified tree sap, can be used in a smudge. This includes such exotic resins as frankincense. When used for smudging, resin symbolizes the balance of the four elements: Water is pulled from the earth and transformed into sap, trees grow from earth to sky so they are balanced between Earth and Air; and when Fire is introduced, the smoke also represents Air.

- Sage or Sagebrush: Sagebrush, and/or silver sage, grows wild. Note that this is not the culinary sage that you grow in your herb gardens. It is a tough and hardy plant that likes sandy soil and limited water. It smells a lot like culinary sage; very strong and pungent. In the Okanagan Valley where I live, it sprouts new shoots in April, blooms about August, and goes to seed by September. Some people really like to include flowers in their smudge sticks because it creates a softer, more fragrant scent; others don't like them because they crumble and leave a mess. Sage, when burnt, clears and removes negative and unwanted energy or entities from one's tools, environment, and self. It is the primary ingredient in any smudge.

- Santo Palo: This tree grows in Central and South America. Some metaphysical stores carry it because it is used in Central American shamanism. It is also used in funeral pyres. The clear, pleasantly soapy scent of the wood is effective even in small amounts, and it purifies and consecrates.

- Sweetgrass: Sweetgrass is a tall, gray-green, thin-bladed grass that grows in prairielands. It smells sweet and almost like honey, like crushed or cooked lemon. Most metaphysical stores will carry braids of sweetgrass, which adds positive energy any place it's burned. It grounds, protects, and consecrates.

- Tobacco: Many traditions make offerings to the spirits and celebrate community using tobacco. It makes connections and empowers magick. It is smoked, used in smudge, offered, and added to medicine bags.
- Arctostaphylos Uva-Ursi: Also known as kinnikinnick, Indian tobacco, or bearberry, this short-leafed green shrub is very calming and grounding. It is a key ingredient in peace pipe smoking mixtures because it facilitates peace and cooperation. It smells faintly green and earthy when burned.
- Yerba Santa: "The saint's herb" is a traditional smoking and smudging herb in the Southern U.S. It only grows in wild places, so it can be difficult to find. It is used for protection, nurturing, and connection to ancestors or ancient knowledge. Only a single leaf from each plant is used.

The Intent of a Smudge

Energetically, a smudge does three things.

First, it banishes and clears negative energy from the area or auric field. This is the basic ingredients of most smudges, and this is what the sage bundles that you buy at metaphysical stores are for. It's a little like vacuuming or cleaning the carpet. It's a good start, but if you want it to last, you need other things too.

Second, smudging replaces the negative energy with positive energy. You do this because nature abhors a vacuum. If you don't fill the auric field you have just cleansed with something else, the negative energy likes being there and it's just going to creep back in. This is a little bit like adding carpet freshener to the shampoo. It removes the old stinky smells and replaces them with fresher, more pleasant ones. This is what sweetgrass braids or lavender are for.

Third, it creates a protective barrier that prevents negative energy from creeping back in. This is like applying a stain guard to that carpet, which protects it from getting as dirty or smelly again. This barrier is helpful, but it's not permanent. You'll get better results if you use it in your smudge than if you don't, though! Cedar and juniper are often included in commercially available sage bundles, and this is why.

Exercise 67: Sacred Smoke

In this exercise you will be making your own smudge stick or mixture. You will be harvesting the ingredients from your local area. If these items do not grow in your area, skip this exercise, or purchase the relevant items from your local metaphysical and/or herbal store and make the ground mixture instead. (Tip: herbal stores are usually less expensive than metaphysical stores.)

Smudge Sticks

First, acquire sage or silver sage from the surrounding countryside. Always use a consecrated tool when harvesting plants intended for sacred purposes. The boline would be appropriate. If you do not have a boline, consecrate and bless a knife before you use it.

When harvesting sage, make sure you are mindful. Take only the fresh shoots whose absence will not harm the larger plant. Sagebrush grows in large bushes along awkward, hilly slopes, so getting the biggest and best stuff may be difficult and you may have to climb. Always ask permission of the plant before harvesting, and wait until you feel it is right before doing so.

You have about a week to work with sagebrush before it becomes too dry to easily use. Take several pieces of sage about the same size, laying some in one direction and some in the other, and tie them into thick bundles. Squish them with your hands a little, but do not make them too tight, or they will not burn effectively because they won't get enough oxygen. Do not make them too loose, either, or the bundle will just disintegrate when you burn it. Use natural twine or yarn to wrap up and tie the bundles; then trim the ends so they are flat. Set the bundles aside to dry for about ten days. Alternatively, put your bundles in a food dehydrator and they will be dried in two or three days.

If you want to include other things in your sage bundles, such as cedar, lavender, or copal, make sure that you have also harvested the twigs or stems recently, and in a similar mindful fashion to how you harvested the sage. Lavender needs to be used within a couple days of harvest, while cedar can be used up to a week later without falling apart. Pack the additional item into the center of the sage stems, surrounded and contained by the sage like a pig in a blanket. You do not need much! Tie the bundles as previously instructed and set to dry. Cedar takes longer than sage to fully dry, so leave those bundles for two weeks or so. Lavender takes less time, so your lavender and sage bundles will be ready to go when the sage bundles typically would be.

Smudging Powder

Powders can be as effective as sticks and sometimes are easier to make. Acquire the same ingredients as above, and harvest them in the same careful and sacred way. Grind up the appropriate herbs with a coffee grinder or a mortar and pestle. This is a good way to use up the crumbling snippets off smudge sticks too! Here's a sample recipe used by a local healer:

- 1 tbsp sage
- 1 tsp lavender
- 1 tsp juniper
- 1 tsp uva-ursi
- 1 tsp copal

To use the mixture, pour it into a fireproof dish and pinch the top of it into a thin line. Light the line and the rest will burn evenly from the top down.

SACRED FIRES

Many woods are thought to have sacred properties, and many cultures have made use of them, from Beltane balefires, funeral pyres, and wicker men, to sweat lodges. Whole books have been written on sacred woods and plants, but I'll include a few basic recipes here that you can modify as needed. You can also refer to Table 4: Sacred Woods. Note: I recommend Scott Cunningham's *Encyclopedia of Magical Herbs* and *The Complete Book of Incense, Oils and Brews,* as well as Ellen Evert Hopman's *A Druid's Herbal for the Sacred Earth Year* for further research.

Beltane Balefire

Balefires were used to bless and purify. A large fire was kept lit on a hilltop all of May Eve to guide in the summer sun and, in some traditions, the Seelie Ride. Cattle and women trying to conceive jumped over or between balefires to encourage fertility.

Oak, ash, and hawthorn are sacred to the Druids and the coming of summer. "By oak, ash, and thorn" is an oath you have probably heard, which swears on the most sacred of trees. In North America, true ash is in short supply, so many use rowan (also called mountain ash) or locust as a substitute.

Stack these three woods in equal parts and light them without artificial fuels. Keep the sacred fire free of contaminants for your Beltane celebration. When the rite has ended, extinguish the fire and keep some ashes from it to scatter on the site of your sacred balefire next year!

Samhain Fire

Use any five of the following woods depending on local availability:

- Apple
- Ash
- Cedar
- Eucalyptus
- Hazel
- Oak
- Rowan

In one tradition or another, all these trees were considered "trees of life," which bridge the gap between this world and the next. Most of them were also used in funeral pyres or divination. Samhain is the time when the gates between the worlds are thinnest, and so we call back our ancestors to celebrate with us, and call upon the Dark Goddess or God to help us see into the future and the past. Lay these woods in either a pentagram pattern or a great big bonfire, and keep burning all Samhain night!

Yule Log

To prepare a sacred log to burn in celebration of the Winter Solstice, which represents renewal, start with a half-log of any of the following woods:

- Apple
- Cedar
- Eucalyptus
- Oak
- Pine
- Spruce

Drill three holes in the rounded part of the wood large enough for taper candles (the standard taper candle diameter is 7/8 inch).

Insert candles:

- for the Triple Goddess—white, red, and black;
- for the Threefold God—gold or yellow (the newborn Sun King), green (god of life), and black (god of death);
- for the Holly and Oak Kings—red, white, and green.

Decorate with the natural evergreen foliage of your area in winter (which symbolizes the promise of life in death). Burn on the Winter Solstice.

There are many more sacred woods out there. If you'll remember from chapter 3, the Druids had a list of particular ones. You can find information about them in some of the books I list in the bibliography or online. Keep in mind the different meanings of woods and trees in differing cultures when creating your sacred fires.

A word of caution: Remember the Rede of the Wiccae. "Elder is the Lady's tree / Burn it not or cursed ye'll be!"

Try to take only deadfall if possible. Your impact on the land is lessened.

INCENSE

Incense is the name given to anything that can be burned to create a scent. The simplest incense is made of herbs, woods, and resins burned on charcoal. Commercially available incense also includes charcoal and saltpeter, or makko powder, to make them self-igniting. They come in cones and sticks, which you can make yourself. Sticks are much more difficult to make than cones because it is impossible to get the proper bamboo sticks, so I will provide a basic recipe for cone incense.

A *resin* is anything that was once the sap of a tree. It often comes in "tears," which are little irregularly shaped hard balls. Some examples are: frankincense, myrrh, copal, colophony (pine resin), dragon's blood, benzoin, and anything with "gum" in the name. You can get more exotic resins from different suppliers.

A *wood* was obviously part of the wood or bark portion of a tree. This should be ground into tiny pieces or a fine powder. Sometimes poorly separated resins will already have wood fragments in them (myrrh and colophony in particular). Commonly used woods include: sandalwood, cinnamon, wood aloe, storax, and cedar, though any wood or bark can be used. Sometimes, particularly tough roots, such as galangal, behave like wood when burnt and can be used in lieu of wood.

An *herb* is, essentially, anything else; usually leaves or flower petals, and occasionally roots, which have been dried and ground into powder. Commonly used herbs include: rose, lavender, rosemary, patchouli, pine, sage, vanilla, clove, lotus, and nutmeg.

A special note: Be wary of asafetida (sometimes called for in old grimoires for psychic protection), cayenne, ginger, rue, sulphur, pepper, garlic, and other peppery substances, because they burn with a strong, acrid scent that can be irritating to the nose and eyes.

Intoxicating Incense Herbs

The following is a list of herbs that, when burnt, create a specific intoxicating effect. Never use the ones that are marked as toxic without very specific guidance from someone who knows the right dosage and techniques to utilize them!

Aconite or Wolfsbane—an opiate. Used in magick for gaining visions, protection, shapeshifting, and astral travel. *Toxic!*

Cannabis—a psychoactive herb used to open the psychic senses. I don't suppose I have to remind you that it is still illegal in most of the Western world. It can be mildly addictive.

Galangal—a stimulant. Used in magick to increase personal power and for psychic protection.

Henbane—a psychoactive herb used to study past lives and banish illness and negative influences; also for shapeshifting. *Toxic!*

Mandrake—an opiate. Used for personal protection and power. Also used in love magick. *Toxic!*

Mugwort—a strong psychoactive intoxicant used to seek visions and for underworld journeys. *Toxic in large doses.*

Opium Poppy—a powerful opiate. Used in magick for astral travel and visions. Highly addictive and generally illegal. *Toxic in large doses.*

Tobacco—a strong stimulant. Used as in smudging. Extremely addictive when inhaled, even over charcoal.

Wormwood—a strong psychoactive intoxicant used to seek visions and steady nerves, and for underworld journeys. Moderately addictive. *Toxic in large doses or when built up over periods of time.*

Exercise 68: Holy Smoke

Make your own incense using a combination of resin, wood, and herbs. You can find your supplies at incense suppliers online, a metaphysical shop, a Catholic shop, or herbal stores. Choose ones whose scent you enjoy according to magickal purpose. For the best results, use the following ratio:

- 1 part resin
- 2 parts wood
- 3 parts herbs

Grind your materials together with a mortar and pestle. *Note: any mortar that has ground resins cannot be used again for food, because resins will build up in your liver over time if ingested and can be toxic. It is best to have a mortar and pestle especially dedicated to incense making.*

If making loose incense, the best mixtures still have some texture to them (ground leaf fragments, tears, wood bits, etc.). If you are making cones, make sure they are ground as finely as possible or they won't stick together well.

Cones

This recipe is adapted from Scott Cunningham's Cone Incense Base in *The Complete Book of Incense, Oils and Brews.* Begin with the following:

- Gum tragacanth, gum arabic, or, for the cheap (like me), xanthan gum

You can acquire these at incense suppliers or natural food stores.

Place a teaspoon of the gum in a glass of warm water. Mix until all particles are thoroughly blended (you may find a whisk helpful) and let it sit for a few minutes. It should turn into a paste with the consistency of phlegm. Set it aside. This will be your binding agent.

In a bowl that you intend to use for nothing else, mix the following:

- 6 parts ground charcoal (not self-igniting)
- 1 part resin
- 2 parts wood
- 3 parts herb
- A few pinches ground orris root (to fix the scent; again, available at suppliers or health food stores)

- 6 drops of essential oil from one or more of the incense components you are using
- Optional (these should be added as empowering agents and for their symbolic value):
  - A little liquid (such as wine or honey)
  - A pinch of powdered stone. (You can powder stone by filing it with a metal file or smashing it with a hammer.)

If you aren't able to find charcoal pre-ground, you'll need to grind it yourself. If you do this, do it outside and cover your mouth and nose because the black dust gets everywhere, and it is not good for you.

Mix thoroughly in the order listed.

- 10 percent of the completed incense weight in potassium nitrate

Using a small kitchen scale, weigh the entire bulk of the incense powder you have made and add one tenth of its total weight in potassium nitrate. You will probably have to acquire this from a compounding drug store. It comes in plastic bottles and it is a heart medication. But because it is also an ingredient in explosives, you may be required to sign for it. Be very careful with the measurements; too much of this and your incense will burn too quickly (or even shoot off sparks); too little and it will not burn at all. Blend thoroughly into the mixture.

When blended, use your mucilage binding agent and mix by hand into a thick putty; the less wet, the better. Shape or mold into cones and dry on a piece of wax paper for one or two weeks. Note: Xanthan gum is, in my experience, the cheapest and easiest to use, but it can get moldy if it is too wet, so be sure to set your cones in a dry room.

MAGICK AND MEDICINE OF PLANTS

Most Witches make a detailed study of the use of herbs. They can be dried; ground into powders; steeped in infusions, teas and tinctures; mashed fresh into poultices; or cooked into ointments.

You can find reams of information online and in books (see some suggestions in the bibliography) that cover common household or medicinal herbs, so I am better off leaving you a couple guidelines that will teach you the basic principles of herbal preparation, and allowing you to do your own research.

Guidelines of Herbal Medicine

- The most important thing to remember is that just because something is natural does not mean it is entirely safe! Drugs are drugs. They often have side effects, may be helpful in some situations but dangerous in others, can be hazardous when mixed, and should only be used for their intended purpose.
- When researching the medicinal (or magickal) use of herbs, always look for a heading called "contraindications," because this will tell you the side effects and when using it might be dangerous. For example, many things are potentially harmful when mixed with blood thinners or pregnancy; in those situations, I would say it's a good rule of thumb to avoid anything your doctor doesn't specifically tell you to take. Also, be very careful of any psychoactive substance if taking any medication for mental health, from the most mild sleep aid and antidepressant to the most potent antipsychotic.
- Don't go through a book and throw together a pile of leaves in a cup with the idea that if one thing is good, several are better. Not only are there potential side effects of mixing numerous herbs, but often, a simple preparation will work better.
- Don't ever take more than the recommended dose! Some herbs are good for you in the typical dose but can be poisonous in large amounts (like thyme and parsley). Don't take anything in a way that is not recommended. Rue, for example, is fine as a tea, but it can cause blisters if it comes in contact with your skin.

Herbal Intoxicants

Here is a brief list of some of the more direct consciousness-changing herbs, available at most herbal stores and some metaphysical shops, and how they're used in Witchcraft:

- Damiana—associated with love and lust; an aphrodisiac tincture or tea that stimulates the cardiovascular system and blood flow to the mucous membranes, which includes the genitals. Do not use if you have a heart condition. Sacred to Aphrodite.

- Galangal root—for magickal power and protection; makes a euphoric, stimulant oil infusion. You can get this cheap at Asian food markets if you're willing to grate it yourself.
- Mandrake root—magickal power, protection, and love magick. A powerful opiate-style sedative. It is toxic. Use it sparingly in topical ointments. Do *not* ingest!
- Mugwort—for visions and astral travel; works as a tea, oil infusion, incense, or ointment. It's a powerful sedative like an opiate, toxic in large doses. Sacred to Artemis.
- Rue—a sedative. Traditionally used in love magick. Rue can blister the skin if used topically.
- Sweet woodruff—a euphoric when added to alcohol, it is a traditional ingredient in May wine.
- Verbena—a mild nervine that does very little on its own besides increase mental alertness; acts as an enhancer when added to other psychoactive compounds.
- Wormwood—almost exactly like mugwort. Sacred to Hecate.

HARVESTING HERBS

Take care that you can correctly identify what you are harvesting, and collect from areas that are unlikely to have gathered pollutants and chemicals. Roadsides and large farms often teem with useful weeds that are full of toxins. Never use flowers from a florist if you are going to take them internally; they use preservatives that are poisonous if consumed.

Harvest respectfully, and never by taking everything you can. It's unsustainable and disrespectful to the land. Shamanic traditions will tell you that the plants' spirits might turn against you and cause allergies, poisoning, or other mischief! This is a good time to put your boline to work. Leave an offering when possible.

You already know that moon phase and sign can be significant, but so can season. Harvest buds and leaves in the spring and summer, when their juices are most potent. Harvest seeds in the summer and early fall, and flowers when they are freshly bloomed. Harvest roots in early spring and the late fall, preferably when the plants they support are denuded so that they are concentrating all their effort into those roots. Last, harvest fruit its peak ripeness; and if possible, wait until after first frost, especially for rosehips and grapes, because it brings out their vitamins and sweetness and improves their flavor.

It is thought that harvesting herbs on the Summer Solstice imbues them with the greatest magickal power; and that anything left on the field after Samhain belongs to the faeries, so it is best left alone.

Herbal Teas

Making herbal tea is the easiest thing in the world. Take 1 tsp of the dried herb and pour steaming hot water over it; the hotter the better, because more of the active volatile oils will be released. Keep it covered while serving to prevent those same oils from evaporating. No matter how many different herbs you use, the dosage is one teaspoon per cup or three tablespoons per pot.

If you don't like "floaties" in your tea, use a tea ball or basket, strain it after steeping, or get linen tea bags from the herb store. Steep five to ten minutes before straining.

Following are some magickal teas for your perusal.

Aphrodisiac Tea

To get you in the mood, use equal parts of each:

- Rosehips
- Rose petals
- Jasmine flowers
- Sweet woodruff
- Damiana

Awen Tea

For insight, clarity of thought, and creativity, use equal parts of each:

- Spearmint
- Peppermint
- Verbena

Euphoria Tea

To improve mood, steep the following along with a bag of Earl Grey tea:

- 1 part lavender
- 1 part sweet woodruff

For the best effect, sweeten the tea with a touch of honey and a little lemon juice.

Mana Tea

For an extra boost of magickal power, add the following to a spicy tea, such as chai:

- 1 part ginseng
- 1 part verbena
- 1 part galangal

Psychic Visions Tea

To open your sense, mix equal parts of the following:

- Peppermint
- Lavender
- Mugwort

Exercise 69: Potions

Make an herbal tea for a magickal purpose following the instructions above. Make use of it in ritual, and record your results.

WISDOM OF DIONYSUS

Wine, alcohol, and spirits have been around since before recorded history. It usually symbolizes the blood of the gods, up to and including its use in the Eucharist today. I imagine that its popularity in ritual is due to availability. Fermenting things is easy, and just about anything that contains natural sugars can be fermented. Wine is particularly simple. Let me give you an essential recipe!

Ingredients:

- Grapes, fresh picked and as free of pesticides as possible
- Cold distilled water

Optional:

- Sugar or honey
- Camden tablets (available at any home brewing shop)

Take a large, clean container (such as a plastic garbage can) and sterilize it with bleach and hot water. Set it in a place that won't freeze; the warmer the better, because it speeds the fermentation process. Select your grapes. Red or purple grapes make red wine, while green grapes make white. Generally, the sweeter the grape you start with, the sweeter and more alcoholically potent the wine will be! Give the grapes a quick rinse and add them to the bucket. You might feel drawn to wash off the "dust" that collects on the grapes, which will be a dull blue or green, depending on the type of grapes you have chosen, but you actually want this stuff. This is naturally produced yeast and it is what causes the grapes to start fermenting.

Squish the grapes. You have probably seen people stomping grapes in paintings. I have found that for home production, this is still the most effective method of breaking up the grapes so that mold will not gather and the juice will flavor your water. You could also put them in a food processor or invest in a wine press. You don't have to stomp hard; just use your feet to gently guide and press them.

When the grapes are pressed, pour just enough water overtop to cover them completely. Then put a towel or cheesecloth over your bucket and let them sit for one to three weeks. The longer you leave the primary mash to ferment, the stronger your wine will be, but leaving it too long may cause mold. The cloth you cover it with needs to be porous to allow fermentation, but it must also be secure so bugs can't get into it.

After the end of the primary fermentation, strain out the grapes and add the Camden tablets. Then pour the liquid into a glass carboy with an airlock or an oaken barrel, both of which are available at home brewing shops. Oak barrels add a distinctive flavor more commonly associated with red wine. If you want more alcohol, add sugar or honey at this stage. Leave your wine fermenting for three to six months in a dark, preferably warm place.

Afterward, strain one more time, add sugar or honey to taste (it will still ferment a little, but at this stage you are adjusting sweetness) and bottle! Your wine should be clear (so strain it for particulates if necessary), stable (so be sure it's finished fermenting), and free of carbon dioxide (so stir it well). Your bottles must be sterilized. Many people invest in proper sterile wine bottles, but you can also clean out old glass pop and wine bottles with bleach water and then run them through a very hot dishwasher. Don't forget to include the caps! Use a siphon hose to drain the carboy or barrel to avoid agitating the wine (which causes oxidization). Leave a full inch between the wine and the bottom of the cork or cap, which gives the wine room and prevents your bottles from popping open or exploding.

These are the very basics of wine making. Vintners have tried to perfect this art for thousands of years, so if it interests you, I encourage you to research, explore, and experiment!

Exercise 71: Libations

Here are a few sacred drink recipes for you to experiment with. Make one or all of them as you prefer!

Aphrodite's Nectar

You will need:

- Small bottle of sherry or sweet red wine
- 1 tbsp damiana

Steep the damiana in the sherry overnight and strain out. Take 1 tsp at a time as an aphrodisiac. Traditionally used in circle to consummate a handfasting by the newlywed couple.

May wine

You will need:

- 2 bottles of sweet white or blush wine
- 1 tbsp dried sweet woodruff
- Strawberries

Macerate the sweet woodruff and steep in wine for three days to one week, shaking periodically. The night before Beltane add sliced strawberries to taste. Serve as a punch for a mild euphoric.

Samhain Absinthe

You will need:

- 750 mL of vodka, brandy, or other high-test alcohol (traditionally, Ouzo or other anise-flavored drink would be appropriate)
- 1 tsp wormwood

Macerate wormwood and steep in alcohol for three days to one week. Drink at Samhain or the dark of the moon for visions, precognition, and underworld journeys.

Wassail

You will need:

- 1 jug apple cider
- 3–5 sticks cinnamon bark
- 5–10 whole nutmegs
- 1 tsp whole cloves
- 1 whole dried ginger or galangal root

Heat the apple cider in a slow cooker. Add herbs and simmer on low heat for a few hours. Drink at the Winter Solstice as a stimulant and mild euphoric.

Tinctures

Tinctures are alcoholic compounds that have absorbed the qualities of an herb that has been added to it. You make them in pretty much the same way you make an extraction; macerate the herbs, fresh or dried, and allow them to leech their qualities into the alcoholic mixture for at least a month, shaking periodically to release more herbal juices. For best results, use a high-test alcohol such as whisky, brandy, rum, or vodka—whichever you prefer. You can generally leave the herbs in the tincture without straining if desired because the alcohol preserves them. Tinctures may be used topically (such as a myrrh tincture to fight infection, which is the best such compound I know) or internally, depending on the herb. When intended as an internal medicine, take a tincture in a dose of four drops at a time under the tongue once or twice daily.

ENTHEOGENS

Anthropologists call a culture's sacred psychoactive substances *entheogens*. They include pretty much any substance with a measurable psychoactive effect that is used religiously. The word means "creating the divine within us." The root of the word, *entheos*, translates as "full of the god, inspired, possessed" and is the root also of the word "enthusiasm." Entheogens are present in nearly every culture and faith, including modern Christianity.

Throughout history, entheogens have been used to produce feelings of euphoria, changes in consciousness, and enhanced creativity. From a magickal point of view, they have been used primarily to open the third eye and be aware of alternate realities, universal oneness, the fabric of the Universe, and the impermanence of space and time. They are also used for divination, to achieve enlightenment, and to connect to the Divine, or as they say in some circles, "to see God."

We've already covered one entheogen of the ancient world—alcohol. There are many others, including:

- Kykeos—a substance imbibed to achieve enlightenment in the Eleusinian Mysteries
- Soma—an entheogenic compound mentioned in the Rig Veda that likely contained fly agaric
- Ambrosia—the drink of the gods granting immortality; in Greek literature, it may have contained henbane, and in Norse mythology was likely a drink containing wormwood
- Manna—from the Bible (which may have been psilocybin mushrooms)
- Even common household drugs like caffeine and nicotine, in the form of coffee and cocoa beans and tobacco, have been used for centuries to raise consciousness and stimulate the senses.

There is a long history of the use of entheogens among magick practitioners. Aleister Crowley advocated the use of a variety of drugs in his magickal practice, including heroin, opium, hashish, mescaline, and cocaine and wrote about his experiences—and his struggle with drug addiction—in his fictional work *Diary of a Drug Fiend*. Dion Fortune described how taking opiates for asthma caused vivid visions of the Goddess and of magickal insights for the protagonist of her novel *The Sea Priestess*, leading her to experiment with creating similar visions in a waking state.

Carlos Castaneda wrote several books about his experiences training with a Yaqui shaman. While much of his later work deals with what he calls the "shamanic reality," his thesis, *The Teachings of Don Juan: A Yaqui Way of Knowledge*, dealt extensively with the use of entheogens in Mesoamerica and his personal experiences with them. These included peyote, datura, and a smoking mixture containing psilocybin mushrooms. They were used to open the mind to the shamanic way of seeing and thinking.

Terence McKenna, philosopher and ethnobiologist, advocated the use of natural psychoactive substances in mysticism, such as ayahuasca, cannabis, psilocybin mushrooms, and the plant derivative DMT. He believed that their use taught people to reestablish a more harmonious relationship with Mother Nature. In his book *La Chorrera* he describes how he found "the Logos" through a psychedelic experiment, which he believed was a helpful voice of the Divine that is universal to all mystic experience. The use of psychoactive substances gives the mind an opportunity to make connections and insights that may not have otherwise been made, and they can also be used to heal trauma and harmful patterns absorbed by the subconscious. They can invoke amazing mystical insights and experiences.

But it is my personal feeling that entheogens, especially hallucinogens, are a shortcut. Using them is a lot like using the dark side of the Force: "quicker, easier, more seductive." You do not have to work to achieve the altered state necessary to do magickal work, and it is possible (though the training can take years) to achieve similar altered states and mystical insights without them. I advise anyone undertaking the study of magick to train their minds first before venturing into this realm. Without appropriate shamanic training, starting with intoxicants might lead to you becoming dependent upon these substances to achieve the magickal trance state. Or, you will simply not be able to achieve magickal insight through the use of these substances at all. This will impair your development as a Witch.

This by no means implies that learning to use entheogens is easy! There is a rigorous training process in any shamanic tradition which involves specific methods of harvesting or preparing plants (or both), as well as controlling your altered mind to focus on the magickal work you are trying to accomplish. Also, if you use these substances on a regular basis (such as smoking cigarettes) you may not be able to use them in magickal work without taking an enormous (and potentially dangerous) dose.

Tobacco and Caffeine

Tobacco is one of the ingredients in the sacred "peace pipe" of Native traditions. It is also smoked as cigars in voodoo ceremony (usually to honor the loa, or deities). South American shamans eat it to keep the spirits in their bodies—enough, in fact, that they literally vibrate. That same dose would likely kill a typical North American.

Caffeine is used in tea, and therefore, to obtain changes of consciousness in meditation and in tea leaf reading. It is also a significant component in chocolate (a euphoric). Its use in sex magick is ancient, and recently it has also seen use in such meditative disciplines as "chocolate yoga" (practicing aerobic hatha yoga and eating chocolate at intervals to raise consciousness).

As stimulants, tobacco and caffeine are utilized in magick for beta and, optimally, gamma consciousness. They are best combined with high levels of physical activity (such as dancing, yoga, or sex) to move them through the system and excite the synapses. They raise kundalini and improve trance channeling.

You have likely already experimented with caffeine in magick through Exercise 33: A Cup of Tea, and you might have experimented with tobacco in smudging; now let's experiment with putting our psychic powers to work!

Exercise 72: Tea Leaf Reading

Brew yourself and your subject each a cup of caffeinated loose-leaf tea in cups with saucers. Any green or black tea will do. Do not use a tea ball or strainer. Chat while the tea steeps and try to get a feel for what information your subject is looking for. Making an emotional connection is important.

When ready, have your subject drink the tea. Rather than drinking the last swallow, however, whirl it around in the cup clockwise three times; then dump the tea into the saucer. Remove the cup without tapping it or doing anything else to encourage leaves to fall out, and turn it over.

Look for patterns in the leaves. Begin by interpreting patterns that stand out on the saucer because they are of the most immediate importance. A bird might mean freedom for some, travel for others. Trust your intuition.

Next, read the cup. Again, interpret the symbols that appear in the leaves according to your intuition. Visualize the cup as a clock face, with the handle as your starting point in the six o'clock position. If the cup has no handle, use the spot where your subject's lips touched to drink. The closer to the top of the cup a symbol appears, the more immediately in the future it will occur. Refer to figure 13 for reference:

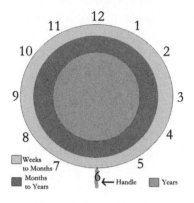

Figure 13: Tea Leaf Reading

All this is based on subjective interpretation and intuitive senses, like cloud watching. Record your reading and results in your Book of Shadows.

Cannabis

Gardner specifically mentioned hemp (cannabis) in his Book of Shadows. He said that it was "especially dangerous" because it "unlocks the inner eye swiftly and easily," tempting the Witch to abuse the substance. He recommended someone else should control the supply.

It is very effective as an antispasmodic and pain reliever, especially for nerve pain, as well as inducing theta and delta consciousness. Cannabis can be smoked (which is its most common form), ingested, burned in incense, or taken in a tincture or ointment. If you do not habitually use cannabis, a very small amount will be sufficient for psychic work and just a little more is needed for journeyworking; more will likely just knock you out. I have offered a recipe later on in the chapter that includes cannabis.

Vision Vine and Magick Mushrooms

The use of hallucinogenic plants in magick is as ancient as the sea. I will share with you what I know. Some of this is based on my own experience; some is grounded in research or the experiences of others.

The purpose of using hallucinogens for magickal intent is not to have a "good trip," but to open one's consciousness to a heightened state of awareness (4.5–6 theta Hz) in which an alternate reality is possible. The aim is to see through the cracks in beta consciousness. The Intent is not a good party. The Intent is enlightenment. This is important in learning about the shamanic plants.

A Word of Caution

While the use of such chemical hallucinogens as LSD (lysergic acid diethylamide, commonly known as acid) or XTC (MDMA or 3-4-methylenedioxymethamphetamine, also known as E, Adam, Roll, Bean, and X) will accomplish the same purpose as some of the shamanic hallucinogens I will be discussing, I urge you not to use them. LSD can actually cause enough changes in the way your brain produces dopamine that you can acquire psychotic disorders. You can also develop permanent difficulties with abstract thinking, memory, and awareness. E interferes with the way your brain produces serotonin, and can cause permanent brain damage and memory loss, permanent changes in sleeping habits, appetite, sensitivity to pain, and perception, as well as all kinds of dangerous stimulant effects you might not be prepared for.

This does not imply that natural hallucinogens are entirely safe, either! There is the potential for side effects, including heart problems and permanent changes in perception.

Much of what happens under the effects of hallucinogens depends upon one's perceptions and mood when using it. So, a positive environment is crucial! Do not experiment with these things when you are depressed, anxious, or alone. You are setting yourself up for the proverbial bad trip. Ideally, never use any of these substances without the mentorship of someone who already has. Just remember that it is exactly like Yoda said when Luke asked, "What's in the cave?" The answer is, "Only what you carry with you."

Magic Mushrooms

There are a couple different species of "magic mushrooms." The active psychotropic chemical is psilocybin. 190 different species of "magic mushroom" have been identified to modern scientists, and they grow literally all over the world. According to Terence McKenna, people started using magic mushrooms for magickal purposes as far back as 1 million years ago. They were used in shamanism and ritual by Africans, Mesoamericans, and possibly the ancient Mesopotamian cultures. Names used by the Aztecs and Mazatecs for psilocybin mushrooms included *teonanácatl,* "divine mushroom," "genius mushrooms," "divinatory mushrooms," and "wondrous mushrooms."

A wave of research in the fifties led to the establishment of Dr. Timothy Leary and Dr. Richard Alpert's Harvard Psilocybin Project in the sixties. During the time they were in operation, the project discovered evidence that hallucinogens were effective in the treatment of addictions, neuroses, post-traumatic stress disorder, and other mental illnesses, reportedly with results equivalent to years of therapy, and with a considerably higher success rate in treating alcoholism than Alcoholics Anonymous. This is a point of note for occult practitioners; the reason why this was effective was because the hallucinogens reportedly forced people to process the muck of their subconscious minds all at once, as opposed to the slow, gradual process of therapy. Expect that they will do the same to you. If you are not prepared to deal with that, do not use them.

Everyone's experience with magic mushrooms, like with most hallucinogens, is very individual, even from one trip to the next. Most visions sound comical when described, but they often have great meaning for the person experiencing them.

Castaneda describes his own experience with psilocybin. He was not terribly fond of it. He saw the walls around him dissolving, and himself dissolving into the walls. His spiritual leader, Don Juan, interpreted this as a fear of losing control. Though he was urged to experience the smoking mixture again, he never did.

My Own Experience

I have never been a drug enthusiast, but in the course of researching this book I experimented with using two kinds of hallucinogens for sacred purposes: magic mushrooms and sticky salvia. I chose these because they are relatively safe. I have not ever heard of someone overdosing from mushrooms or suffering a long-term change in perception, as long as they took the right ones and not something that looked similar. They can cause nausea, but since they are a strong euphoric this isn't as unpleasant as one might imagine. For this reason, and because it is believed to make the high better, it is generally advised to take them on an empty stomach.

The standard dose for magic mushrooms is approximately one or two grams, ingested or drunk in a tea. Half a gram was sufficient for me. Mushrooms are horribly bitter and taste roughly like moldy Aspirin, so they are often eaten with squares of chocolate or drunk with honey, both of which speed absorption of the drug and enhance the initial euphoric effect. Make sure you know and trust your source, and never just randomly eat some mushroom that you think might be the right one; a mistake can be fatal.

My experiences with magic mushrooms have been very positive, though I have only tried them three times, all with a specific shamanic purpose. The first time I was simply looking for enlightenment, and I understood with perfect clarity a personal issue that had been causing strife in my household, and thus was able to resolve it. The second time I was intending to have a sacred bonding experience with my family, and we all had amazing, insightful visions of past lives that we participated in together. The third time I was just looking for a vision, and a weak tea combined with some cannabis led to some intense dreams in which I foresaw the publication of this book and the workshops I would teach as a result of it. Less than a week later, I received an email from Weiser Books, and the result is the volume you now hold in your hands.

My experience of the initial effect is that light seems brighter as the pupils dilate, and then I begin to notice colors and details I did not notice previously as the senses are seemingly enhanced. Then come the giggles, as the euphoria takes effect, and after that are the odd sensory experiences that mushrooms are noted for: tracers, hallucinations, loss of balance because the room is spinning, and so forth. It was at the moment that the high ends, just after the peak when I started coming down, that the shamanic insights and visions began to affect me.

STICKY SALVIA

Sticky salvia, known as *salvia divinorum*, or "diviner's sage," is currently legal in Canada but illegal in the United States. You can get it at hemp shops or online, usually in standardized dosage packets. It produces potent hallucinations that only last for a few minutes at most. The most common form of use is to smoke it in a pipe, but you can also eat it or take it as a tea. It is horribly bitter.

I experimented with salvia with my husband and my initiator. We gathered in a cast circle in my front yard in the middle of summer, and my son, who had tried it previously, was our guide. We each took turns smoking it with an intention of honoring the Esbat and doing sacred work together. I initially had little effect, but on the second round, for a few minutes the whole world looked like a watercolor painting, and I marveled at the beauty of the sacred Earth.

AYAHUASCA

Ayahuasca is the drug of choice for South American shamans. Also called "vision vine" or "ghost vine," it is harvested from the jungle and cooked up in a foamy, foul-tasting tea. Regional differences between mixtures exist, because it is not just the ayahuasca vine that is included in the tea. Illness is thought to be associated with evil spirits, or magic darts sent by other shamans. Ayahuasca grants visions to show the shaman the entities or darts causing the problem. Those entities can then be fought, or the darts removed.

The use of ayahuasca is becoming more common in North America as people seek out shamans to take the ayahuasca brew and gain visions and insight. A determined person would be able to find a practitioner, but as with every other movement of this kind, there are those with next to no training in the use of the vision-vine who are promoting themselves as skilled shamans. Use caution if you intend to pursue this route.

As of this writing, I have no personal experience with ayahuasca. A modern metaphysical author who has frequently used ayahuasca is Stuart Wilde. His work has been extensively influenced by his experiences.

DATURA

To my knowledge, there has never been an overdose of ayahuasca or magic mushrooms. There have, however, been many overdoses of datura, also called Jimson weed and "devil's weed." Teenagers manage to poison themselves every year. Dosage and preparation are important, so if you really insist that you must experiment with this temperamental entheogen, find someone who has used it regularly and knows what they are doing. Do not try it on your own. Preferably, please don't try it at all. Carlos Castaneda experimented with datura in his apprenticeship with Don Juan. This was his favorite of the drugs he tried.

Peyote and Mescaline

Castaneda originally found Don Juan by seeking to study the use of peyote in Mesoamerican shamanic practices. Peyote is well documented for its psychotropic effects, largely because its use by certain Native American tribes in sacred ceremony, especially the famous Ghost Dance, is partially protected by legislation in the United States. Aleister Crowley specifically recorded using mescaline, so it has been linked to the Western occult tradition as well.

Reputedly some states permit ceremonial use of peyote by non-Natives, but since my only source for that is Wikipedia, I would advise you to double-check your local state laws before attempting to justify your use of peyote in Witchcraft to the local police! In Canada at the time of this writing, mescaline in raw form is illegal, but anyone may grow and use the peyote cactus.

I don't have any personal experiences with peyote or mescaline either, but Castaneda and Crowley have both described it extensively in their writings.

LSD and XTC

Many people seem to have had positive experiences with acid. Some have had powerful life-changing visions that have cured them of addictions or neuroses, or brought them into intense, direct contact with the Divine. There are numerous movies from the sixties that detail what being in this state of consciousness is like. But most synthesized drugs, such as LSD and XTC, and any opiate are dangerous. I chose not to experiment with them because of this.

Poisons and Toxins in Magick

Even more exotic intoxicants have been used historically by ancient Pagans and magicians, such as volcanic emissions, flowers, the poison of frogs, snakes and insects, mercury, ergot (a toxic mold that grows on grain, from which we get LSD), and other dangerous, usually poisonous substances. In her book

Poisons of the Past, Mary Kilbourne Matossian tells us that the oracle at Delphi gave prophecy after inhaling toxic volcanic fumes, and there is evidence that the Witch craze in Salem, along with many other incidences of mass hysteria in history, have been caused by ergot poisoning. Poisonous substances might really work for psychic insight and astral travel, but I cannot stress strongly enough how utterly stupid and dangerous using them actually is. Just don't.

WITCHES' FLYING OINTMENT

You have probably read somewhere by now about Witches' Flying Ointment. It is an entheogenic ointment that contained a variety of intoxicating substances, the most notable of which were belladonna and aconite. There really is a formula to mix these successfully. The key is that aconite (wolfsbane) is actually an antitoxin for belladonna, and vice versa, and if you are poisoned with one of these herbs, you will receive an extract of the other one in the hospital. But unless you know exactly what the dosage is, you are likely to poison yourself. People have had success with it,[5] but an anthropologist studying the stuff managed to poison himself in the seventies, so be cautious.

There are slightly safer versions that have the same effect. They are essentially powerful opiate-like compounds (some of which even contain opium) that produce a sleeplike stupor and the feeling of flying. My own experience with the recipes that I offer you was to induce a powerful state of intoxication for astral traveling and shapeshifting. I felt lightheaded and extremely sleepy, and otherwise the effects were very similar to the early stages of mushroom intoxication: enhanced senses, bright lights due to expanded pupils, and so forth. The key difference is in the magickal experience, where for a while I became one of my totem birds—the raven—and I flew over the women's gathering I was attending and observed the goings-on. I then slept for eight hours in the back of my car where I was encamped. I have also experimented with a mandrake ointment to aid in the Great Rite and enhance sex magick, and I have found it very effective.

Witches' Flying Ointment is a topical intoxicant. According to folklore and some modern anthropologists, Witches used to apply it by slathering it onto their besoms and then riding their brooms naked to the Sabbat, or out

---

5. Sarah Anne Lawless's post "On Flying Ointments" is exceptional if you want to know more about tolerance levels and experimenting with flying ointments: *http://sarahannelawless .com/2011/09/10/on-flying-ointments*. I know her personally and her advice is intelligent and cautious.

into the fields, where they would leap as high as possible to teach the crops how high to grow. Though this is traditional, and I understand it is necessary with the original belladonna and aconite recipe to apply it to sensitive mucous membranes (but the mouth is dangerous because ingestion is highly poisonous), I found it just as effective when applied to my temples with my fingertips.

Exercise 73: Witches' Flying Ointment

Modern Witches' Flying Ointment recipes are a little less toxic, but they aren't *nontoxic*. You'll still need to be careful with your quantities and application! Knowing how to make an ointment is a valuable skill that you can use to make all kinds of healing herbal concoctions as well. I offer two recipes; the second was more effective but took longer to make.

Hot Oil Infusion

- ¼ cup olive oil
- ¼ cup beeswax
- 1 tsp cinquefoil
- 1 tsp dittany of Crete
- 1 tsp mugwort
- 1 tsp parsley
- 1 tsp vervain
- 20 drops clove essential oil
- ½ tsp tincture of benzoin

Optional:

- 10 drops mugwort essential oil
- 1 tsp cannabis oil extraction

Melt the beeswax on your stove over low heat, preferably in a double boiler. Gently heat the olive oil in a separate pot on medium-low. When warmed, add the dried herbs to the olive oil and stir clockwise three times. Take the oil off the stove and strain through a metal sieve or coffee filter to remove herbal particulates. Discard the herbal mush. If you are using cannabis oil infusion, add it at this point. Stir in the melted beeswax three times. Add clove oil and mugwort oil if you are using it. Add the benzoin tincture to preserve your ointment, and pour the mixture into metal or ceramic containers to cool. Your oil will harden into the consistency of a solid perfume.

Cold Oil Extraction

Begin by making cold oil infusions. You will need:

- Several glass jars
- 1 tbsp blessed thistle
- 1 tbsp cinquefoil
- 1 tbsp dittany of Crete
- 1 tbsp mugwort
- 1 tbsp parsley
- 1 tbsp vervain
- Enough carrier oil to completely cover the herbs in the jars (I used a mixture of hemp, almond, and olive oils)

Optional:

- 1 tbsp cannabis "shake" (plant portion) or 1 small to medium cannabis bud

Put the dried herbs each in separate jars and make oil extractions from them. At the end of the lunar cycle, strain the oil through a coffee filter or cheesecloth to remove the herbal particulates, which can then be discarded.

Take your oils to your kitchen, and make sure you also have:

- ¼ cup olive oil
- ¼ cup beeswax
- 20 drops clove essential oil
- ½ tsp tincture of benzoin

Optional:

- 10 drops mugwort essential oil
- 1 tsp cannabis oil extraction

As above, melt the beeswax on your stove. When warmed, add 1 tsp of each of the herbal oil extractions, including the optional cannabis extraction if you have chosen to use it, and stir clockwise three times. Gently stir in the olive oil, take the pan off the stove, and add the clove oil and the mugwort oil if you are using it. Add the benzoin tincture to preserve your ointment, and pour the mixture into metal or ceramic containers to cool.

Exercise 74: Consecrating Potions

Cast a circle, call quarters, and invoke divinity according to your preference under a full moon. Take the intoxicating substance you intend to use and place it on your altar in the center of your pentacle. Point your wand at it and make a Statement of Intent. Here's an example:

> I consecrate thee, O Mushrooms, and charge thee to thy purpose; to help me gain spiritual insight, to show me doors to other worlds, and to open my mind to magickal wisdom.

Draw three Earth-invoking pentagrams over the substance with the tip of your wand.

Incant:

> By the power of three times three, as I will, so mote it be!

Conclude your ritual in the usual way. Keep your substance on your altar or stored under your pillow until your appointed time to use it. When you do use it, do so within a cast circle and in a ritual fashion for greatest effect.

SELF-EVALUATION

The substances you create are the best test of your work. Are they effective? Do you enjoy them? Then you have learned what you need to learn.

Above all, be very cautious in the use of intoxicants. Know what you are doing, and treat them with the proper respect. Blessings of Dionysus be yours!

chapter five

DANCE AND SACRED MOVEMENT

Dance, dance, wherever you may be!
I am the Lord of the Dance, said He,
I live in you, and you live in Me,
And I'll lead you all in the dance, said He!

—"Lord of the Dance," lyrics by Aidan Kelly,
C. Taliesin Edwards, and Ann Cass

The ancient practice of sacred dance predates human history in every culture and continent of the world. The earliest dances were likely acts of ritual and sympathetic magick, encouraging a good hunt or harvest by invoking the spirits of the animals and plants and honoring them. Shamans developed dances to appeal to spirits of sickness, either to encourage them to leave or to send them after their enemies. Dance is probably the most ancient form of magick that we know.

Dancing also became a social activity used to bind the tribe together, to greet other tribes, or to court potential mates. It celebrated such things as Rites of Passage, a good harvest, or the return of the sun; in short, everything we would celebrate in the modern age (like weddings, harvest festivals, and Christmas). Ancient civilizations also made dancing into a performance art intended for viewing rather than participation, which originated from large-scale religious rituals.

The modern tradition of Pagan dance draws on a variety of sources, and I've included a lot of photos and diagrams to show you some of them. These are not always the best ways to learn dancing, but I will do my best. I will also do what I can to adapt the dances I teach to all levels of physical ability whenever possible.

DANCE AND TRANCE

Dancing changes consciousness in five significant ways:

- By stimulating trance through repetitive movements or disciplines, such as spinning in place
- By creating visual stimulation for the observer through movement, body positioning, set, and costume
- Through repetitive rhythmic induction
- By raising the body's energy and endorphins, creating ecstatic trance.
- By exhausting the body of the dancer

We're going to experiment with numerous dances and other forms of sacred movement.

THE FIVE TIBETAN RITES

There is a series of five yoga moves reputedly practiced by Tibetan monks. Known as the Five Tibetans or the Five Rites, these are an excellent daily yoga practice, and they only take about ten minutes to do. Supposedly they expand lifespan but being only thirty-nine at the time of this writing, I wouldn't know. What I can tell you is that often this is the only exercise I get for days at a time and I am in very good shape. Another excellent physical practice that teaches energy work is Tai Chi.

Exercise 75: The Five Rites

For daily practice: Begin with an odd number of each of the five movements. Consider which one you have the most difficulty doing and how many repetitions of that particular movement you can handle; then limit all the exercises to the same number. Once you have begun the exercises, do not quit until you have completed them. Work up to performing twenty-one repetitions of each movement.

Counterintuitively, with these movements you inhale during the contraction and exhale during the release. You will find that there is a point at which you can no longer inhale in each contraction; that indicates that you should stop and release.

The First Rite

Figure 14: The First Rite

Begin with your arms straight out at your sides and your gaze forward. I like to turn up one palm as the dervishes do. (This is a trick I learned from my yoga teacher. She switches hand from day to day for a balance of energies, though the dervishes always use the right palm to receive the blessings and wisdom of heaven.) Fix your gaze on a distant object at eye level that is easy to see and focus on.

Spin in a clockwise direction, keeping your arms out and your gaze fixated on that same object. There is no need to spin so quickly that you fall down. Turn your head around to find the object of your focus again when you are halfway through each spin. This will help prevent dizziness.

When completed, stand in place until the dizziness has mostly passed, then move on to the next one. You will find that your tolerance will increase with time. If you need to adapt this rite, simply spin in place to the best of your ability.

Figure 15: The Second Rite—Part One

Begin by lying on your back with your arms and legs straight. Inhale and bring yourself up into a V shape sit-up:

Figure 16: The Second Rite—Part Two

When you run out of air, exhale and return to the original position.

If you need to, this exercise can be adapted initially to bend your knees and do low-impact sit-ups; or you can keep your arms at your sides to mitigate the impact slightly. If you are in a wheelchair, you can simply bend forward instead.

Figure 17: The Third Rite—Part One

Begin on your knees with your back straight, your gaze forward, and your hands just below your buttocks.

Figure 18: The Third Rite—Part Two

Inhale, lean backward, and turn your gaze to the sky while arching your back and sliding your hands down the back of your thighs. Exhale and return to the original position when you run out of air.

Some people will not be able to achieve as much of an arc in their backs. That's fine; just do your best. This is difficult to adapt to a wheelchair because most of them have high, unyielding backs. Just sit on a stool or your bed and bend backward as best you can.

The Fourth Rite

Figure 19: The Fourth Rite—Part One

Begin in a seated position with your legs and back straight, your arms at your sides, and your palms to the ground, as shown.

Figure 20: The Fourth Rite—Part Two

THE WITCH'S EIGHT PATHS OF POWER

Brace your feet and hands, and push yourself into a bridge position as you inhale. Exhale and return to the original seated position. You will likely find that your rear end slides along the ground so you may want a mat beneath you!

My husband has muscular weakness and a bad arm, and is incapable of doing this exercise. But there are ways to adapt it. One is to kneel and bend upward on your knees. Another is to brace your arms on your wheelchair handles and bend up and back (provided your chair is heavy enough not to tip). A good solid easy chair would work just as well.

The Fifth Rite

Figure 21: The Fifth Rite—Part One

Begin on your stomach. Extend your legs relatively straight behind you, and balance on the tips of your toes and the palms of your hands. Your arms should be straight, your head up and your gaze forward. In yoga this is known as the serpent asana.

Adapt this position by bracing up on your elbows instead of the palms of your hands, and your knees instead of your toes, if necessary.

Figure 22: The Fifth Rite—Part Two

Inhale and push yourself backward, keeping your legs and arms straight and aiming the top of your head so that it is between your hands and tipped toward the ground, putting your crown chakra toward the earth. Your back should be as straight as possible, and your butt should be up in the air, forming a pyramid shape. Your goal is to have your heels on the ground, but they may not necessarily be that flexible yet. This position is known as downward facing dog. This is a classic yoga position that many people find very difficult to master.

To adapt it, remain on your elbows as you push back, touching the top of your head to the ground, and if you remained on your knees, sit over your feet. When you run out of air, return to your original position.

If you are built large or you are pregnant, you can also do this exercise by leaning on a wall instead of the floor, and you can bend or straighten your elbows as you choose while tipping your crown chakra toward the wall. If you are in a wheelchair, this movement will push your chair back and forth.

I've made a video for my YouTube channel which demonstrates these exercises and suggests ways to adapt them; search "Witch's Eight Paths of Power: Five Rites."

INDIVIDUAL DANCE

If you have followed me this far and practiced the exercises as given, you have accepted by now that there is more to the world than meets the eye; that spirits exist, ideas have form and identity, and thought can change reality.

So it should come as no surprise that we can access these ideas, give them identity, channel them through us, and gain strength and wisdom from them. Conversely, by doing so we lend strength to their reality and purpose, and we honor them on a spiritual level. This can be accomplished through dance.

Exercise 76: Elemental Dance

Choose one of the cardinal elements. Perhaps challenge yourself by choosing one that you have an aversion to rather than an attractive one. Consider how that element might move and act. Choose costume or makeup that suits that element (perhaps blue silk scarves for Water, or glow stick bracelets for Fire) and a song that captures the essence of that element for you. Then consider how your element might move, and invent a freeform dance to call upon its essence and channel it! This exercise can be used for invocations as well.

TOTEMIC DANCING

Is there a creature of the natural world that you feel an affinity with? Aboriginal cultures believe that we can access aspects of our fellow creatures, and when we feel an incredibly strong affiliation to a particular creature, we call that being a totem. Chances are that there is at least one animal that already holds your fascination and admiration. Let's develop a relationship with that animal through dance.

Exercise 77: Mask Making

Make a mask that you will use to embody an animal you feel an affinity with. You can make it out of papier-mâché leather, cardboard, or you can get a paper mask from the dollar store and dress it up with feathers, fur, sequins, etc. Do your crafting within a cast circle and try to draw some of your totem within yourself so that you can express its identity well.

Exercise 78: Totemic Dance

Consider the creature you have chosen. How might it move? What does it do in a day? What might it be concerned with? Invent a dance to embody your totem, making use of your mask. Don't be afraid—no one is going to see it except you (and maybe your coven or friends). Embody your animal spirit and enjoy it!

Invent a devotional dance to match a chant you have chosen (again, YouTube is an excellent resource, and you might also search for a site called *Pagan Chant of the Month Archive*, which is maintained by Ivo "Panpipe" Dominguez Jr.). Here is an example:

- Isis—stretch your arms over your head, legs together.
- Astarte—arms overhead, legs apart.
- Diana—mime drawing and firing an arrow.
- Hecate—squat into the birthing position and hang your arms down.
- Demeter—stand up and cradle an infant in your arms.
- Kali—spiral your hand up in front of your body, representing kundalini serpent energy.
- Inanna—power stance: arms raised to your sides and legs apart.

For another example, there is a video on my YouTube channel (search "Witch's Eight Paths of Power: Sacred Dance") that demonstrates a dance I invented for the chant "Mother of Darkness."

GROUP DANCES

Dancing is one of the best ways I know to raise and direct power toward a common purpose in a group. These dances can be performed with friends or a coven and you will find them at Sabbats and Pagan festivals.

FOLK DANCING

Folk dance is hundreds of years old and varies from region to region, but there are some basic steps that seem to be universal—we'll learn some of those here. Most dances at Pagan events will fall into one of two categories. They will either be circle dances or line dances. Circle dances represent cycles: the cycle of the seasons, the cycle of the moon, or the cycle of life, death, and rebirth. Line dances represent community and continuity. By performing the actions of the dance together, you harmonize your intent.

CIRCLE DANCES

When you're doing a circle dance, direction is important. In the northern hemisphere, clockwise (deosil) is the direction of the sun and the upperworld;

counterclockwise (widdershins) is the direction of the moon and the under-world. Often, Witches in the southern hemisphere reverse this. Keep this in mind as you read about the dances given.

Exercise 80: Vine Step

The vine step gets its name from how the legs seem to move and crawl over each other. This prevents a circle dance from being a simple runaround in a circle. Even the most uncoordinated klutz can do this if he or she is sober.

Figure 23: Vine Step—Part One

Step 1: Begin with your feet slightly more than shoulder width apart, your knees loose, and your feet turned slightly outward.

Figure 24: Vine Step—Part Two

Step 2: If moving deosil, step to your left by crossing your right foot over your left. Widdershins would of course mean doing the reverse.

Figure 25: Vine Step—Part Three

Step 3: Step in the direction you are going with the foot that is now in behind. You should be back in the original position.

Figure 26: Vine Step—Part Four

Step 4: Now take the foot you originally crossed over and step in the direction you are going by crossing it in behind the other foot.

Step 5: Just like Step 3!

That's all there is to it! Repeat this until the dance is done.

THE WITCH'S EIGHT PATHS OF POWER

LINE DANCES

I am going to share with you an example of a line dance called a bridge dance. You can perform this with all kinds of modifications. For a spring celebration, you can each carry boughs of leaves or fruit blossoms, forming the bridge with them instead of your arms. For a wedding, you could do the same, or form an honor guard with drawn swords.

Exercise 81: Bridge Dance

Decide which direction you are going (east to west? north to south?). Begin by forming two lines of equal numbers facing each other. It is traditional to pair men with women in this fashion but it's not strictly necessary, depending on your group.

If you have an odd number, everyone lines up in pairs except for one person, who begins as an extra on one side. (Traditionally, the right raises power while the left banishes, so you may want to put that to work for you.) All pairs (except the first pair in the line, if you have one) join hands and raise them up, forming an archway. You can cross branches or swords if you have chosen to use them. Either your singleton, or the first pair, now dances through the archway with hands joined at about waist level (or branches or swords crossed carefully, or clasped at the wrist with the sword point or branch pointing down).

The first pair now tacks itself on the end of the line and forms a new arch. The second pair in the line is now the first pair and the cycle repeats. If you had a singleton, she now joins the line on the opposite side from the one she started on (so if she was on the right hand line, she now joins the left one). Everyone shifts up, and now there will be a new singleton at the beginning of the line the first person just joined (so in this example, the left line). You may also wish to do this if you have limited space.

People all join hands with their new partners and the new singleton dances through the archway, repeating the cycle.

DANCES OF UNIVERSAL PEACE

The Dances of Universal Peace are a recently created multitraditional spiritual practice that bring religious traditions together and honor them in sacred greeting dances. They are designed to be performed in groups, with simple movements set in time to a sung verse or chant. Their creatrix, Amara Karuna, teaches them all over the world. I will share a dance in the Pagan tradition. For more information, check out Amara's songbook and her YouTube channel.

Exercise 82: Hoof and Horn

This dance appears courtesy of Amara Karuna.

All participants join hands in a circle, and hands stay joined throughout the dance.

> Step back (outward) and bow low to each other, singing,
> Hoof
> Step inward and raise your arms above your heads, singing,
> And horn
> Repeat these steps, singing,
> Hoof and horn
> Step back (outward) and bow as low as you can, singing,
> All that dies
> Step inward and raise your arms as high as you can, singing,
> Shall be reborn
> Swing your raised arms to the right side, then the left, and repeat, singing,
> Corn and grain, corn and grain
> Swing your arms in a clockwise circle, singing,
> All that falls shall rise again.

Don't forget that your hands remained joined! Repeat until you get weary.

SABBAT DANCES

Pagans incorporate a lot of celebratory seasonal European folk dances into their practice, such as Morris Dancing and Mummers' Plays, maypole dances, and the Wheel Dance. A few of these follow.

Exercise 83: Merry Maypole

This dance is performed on Beltane (May Day, which you'll recall is a seasonal celebration of sex and fertility), or sometimes Litha (the summer solstice and celebration of the Goddess and God at the height of their life-giving powers). You will need a maypole, which is a pole with streamers or ribbons all around the top. Sometimes a ring is fastened to it (coat hangers twisted into position to form a ring and a "cap" for the pole work nicely, especially if you cut a slot in the pole's head) and sometimes the streamers are attached right to the top of the pole. You can cap it with flowers (tradition uses hawthorn or seasonal fruit blossoms). I advise you not to use crepe paper party streamers because they dissolve completely when wet and they don't have good tensile strength to begin with. The ribbons are traditionally red (for the fertile menstrual blood of the Goddess) and white (for the God's fertile seed) or multicolored.

You need to have as many streamers as there are people, and there needs to be an even number of them. I find it is better to err on the side of caution rather than have a whole bunch of unused streamers, which means not everyone might be able to participate. The maypole dance is physically demanding, so your less mobile folk may prefer to chant or drum anyway. I can tell you as a healthy asthmatic I find it challenging!

At one annual Beltane celebration I attend, the women dig the hole in the earth to hold the pole while the men chop it down and put it in. Both groups help to cap it with the ring of ribbons before it is propped up. The symbolism here should be fairly obvious!

Traditionally, everyone forms a circle, alternating men and women, though this convention will depend on your group. It is a fertility dance, so if you have a mixed gendered group, this can enhance the experience. Men and women face each other in pairs, with the women facing widdershins (direction of the moon) and men facing deosil (direction of the sun). I imagine in the southern hemisphere this would be reversed. If you aren't alternating men and women, you still need two groups going in opposite directions.

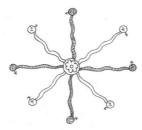

Figure 27: Maypole—Part One

Women hold the red streamers; men hold the white ones (or just pass them out in order, if your streamers are multicolored.)

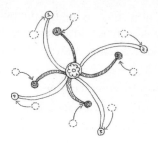

Figure 28: Maypole—Part Two

Pulling the ribbons fairly taut, the dance begins with one group moving to the outside and the other moving to the inside as they pass each other. Women, again, move widdershins and men move deosil. It is easiest to have the widdershins group start to the inside and the deosil group start to the outside.

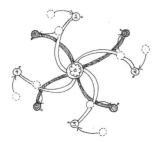

Figure 29: Maypole—Part Three

Almost right away, you will be face-to-face with a new partner. Now move past that person to the opposite side of the one you started with (so if you passed the first person to the outside, now pass to the inside).

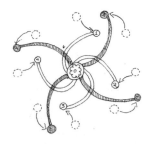

Figure 30: Maypole—Part Four

THE WITCH'S EIGHT PATHS OF POWER

When you reach the next person, pass to the other side again (so in our example, you would now be passing to the outside).

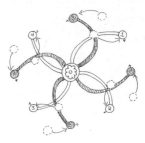

Figure 31: Maypole—Part Five

Repeat the steps of this dance, alternating inside and outside. Try to remember which way you are supposed to move next—it is easy to get mixed up! You might end up hopelessly laughing and completely lost. It's okay to replace people as they get tired if it goes on long enough, but just remember to keep alternating men and women if you started that way!

As the dance progresses, you will be weaving a pattern with the ribbons on the pole. If everyone remembers where they are, this will be quite beautiful. You will also find yourselves moving faster and faster as the ribbons shorten.

Eventually the streamers will be too short to be useful. At that point, start tying them off with other ribbons to hold them in place. People will begin to bow out of the dance as they run out of ribbon. When the last of the ribbons are tied off, the dance is done!

Exercise 84: Wheel Dance

This dance is performed on the Summer Solstice. You will need a solar cross, which is an equilateral cross with a ring around it, often mounted on a pole and decorated in seasonal greenery so it can be seen.

Figure 32: Solar Cross

Facing each other, form an inside and an outside ring by joining hands in circles around the solar cross. You don't have to have even numbers, but there should be more people in the outside ring than the inside one if there isn't. It is often more practical at Pagan gatherings to have the women on the outside, since there tends to be more of them.

Vine step together in a circle dance with the women moving in the direction of the moon and the men moving in the direction of the sun. If you aren't dividing men and women, the inside ring should move widdershins and the outside one deosil. The trick is to keep moving faster and faster; and by tradition, you kiss each other as you pass! Eventually the dance will collapse in a heap and a cheer, and you can use it to raise power for the seasonal cycles and healing of the earth, or other magick besides.

Exercise 85: Corn Dance

This dance is performed for the harvest festivals (see figure 10); Lughnasadh/Lammas (August Eve, the first harvest festival, celebrating the grain harvest), Mabon (autumn equinox, the second harvest festival, for fruits and vegetables) and sometimes Samhain (Halloween, the third harvest festival, which celebrates the blood harvest—slaughtering the animals that won't be fed over the winter—as well as ancestors and the dead, when the veil between the worlds is thinnest). You will need sheaves of corn or wheat, bundled so that they may be carried easily by the dancers. If your tradition is polarity based, you can alternate men and women if you like.

One version simply uses the corn sheaves in a bridge dance.

In the other, the dancers form a circle. Facing the direction of the sun, they take their inside arms and extend the corn sheaves toward the center, forming the spokes of a wheel. They move in a deosil circle in this fashion, at least once around the ring. It works well if you can do it to a count of eight.

At the end of the rotation, the dancers stop and alternately raise and lower the corn sheaves by reaching up and squatting down. If you have alternated men and women, first one group raises and the other lowers, then it is reversed. If you haven't, just be sure the pattern in the circle is raised, lowered, raised, and then lowered, at any given time. This represents the growing and harvesting of the corn. Repeat up and down within a count of eight.

Repeat the wheel and continue in this fashion to the end of your song or chant.

Exercise 86: Underworld Journey

This dance is performed on Samhain or the dark of the moon. Dancers form a circle and begin a solemn processional widdershins. This is a meditative process, with each footfall stepping to a steady, slow drumbeat. Be sure to return to the living world by circling deosil when the dance is done, and don't forget to ground! (It wouldn't hurt you to eat something either. It is important that you remind yourself that you are still alive.)

Exercise 87: Kings' Dance

This dance is performed on either the Summer or Winter Solstice, or sometimes Beltane.

Two men don costumes representing the Oak King (representing the waxing half of the year) and the Holly King (representing the waning half of the year.) They engage in a mock combat, using staves or swords. The Holly King is symbolically killed at the Winter Solstice, and the Oak King is symbolically slain at Beltane or the Summer Solstice.

Exercise 88: Spiral Dance

Our most important Pagan dance tradition is the spiral dance, in which the group spirals in and out around a center point, representing destruction and creation. You might see it at any Sabbat or Festival. Spiral dances can involve hundreds of people or only a few, and they are an incredibly effective way to raise a cone of power (a formation of energy, visualized as a cone, directed by a group toward a specific purpose and then released) for magick. Gardnerian tradition alternates men and women, who kiss each other as they pass.

Figure 33: Spiral Dance—Part One

Step 1: The dancers join hands, form a circle, and begin to vine step deosil in time to the music.

Figure 34: Spiral Dance—Part Two

Step 2: When the dance leader is ready, he breaks hand contact with the person on his left and begins to wind toward the center in a spiral pattern, continuing to vine step. Everyone else still holds hands. A good dance leader will keep his pace at a rate that all can follow and continue to hold and direct the building energy.

Figure 35: Spiral Dance—Part Three

Step 3: The dancers gradually wind closer to the center in a spiral pattern. When the dance leader reaches the center, he turns around and begins to spiral back out widdershins. The dancers begin to pass by each other as those on the end continue to move toward the center and those at the beginning spiral away from it.

THE WITCH'S EIGHT PATHS OF POWER

Figure 36: Spiral Dance—Part Four

Step 4: When all have returned from the winding spiral, they will find themselves vine stepping in an outward-facing circle, at which point the dance leader joins hands with the person at the end again.

Figure 37: Spiral Dance—Part Five

Step 5: The dance leader leads this around at least once, then breaks contact with the end person once more and begins to spiral in toward the center widdershins.

Figure 38: Spiral Dance—Part Six

Step 6: When the dance leader reaches center, he leads the dance back out deosil once more.

Figure 39: Spiral Dance—Part Seven

Step 7: Eventually everyone reaches the outside circle again, at which point the dance leader joins hands with the end person one more time. At the end of one revolution, if a cone of power is being raised, the dancers swing their arms up as they step into the circle, then down as they step out, and they repeat this as power is being raised and directed. When ready, the dance leader lets out a shout and the energy is directed (primarily by the dance leader) where it needs to go!

SELF-EVALUATION

The only real evaluation required is: Did you have fun? Did you learn ways to improve your magick and devotion through sacred dance? Are you practicing the Five Rites to improve your health and energy? If so, consider this chapter's work successfully completed!

part three

ADVANCED
PRACTICES

chapter six

BLOOD AND BREATH CONTROL

When the breath wanders the mind also is unsteady. But when the breath is calmed the mind too will be still, and the yogi achieves long life. Therefore, one should learn to control the breath.

—SVATMARAMA, *HATHA YOGA PRADIPIKA*

Blood and breath control are essential for effective magickal practice. Ancient Eastern mystical practice called it *Pranayama,* or "control of vital force." Disciplines which make use of the control of *prana* include yoga and Tantra. In China, vital force is known as *chi;* in Japan, it is *ki.* Martial arts teach us how to use posture and breathing to control this force. Mastery of such techniques leads to amazing mystical feats, such as levitation, controlling pain and blood flow, healing, or walking on hot coals.

Magicians and Witches have also used external methods of blood and breath control, such as binding, exercise, rhythm, and trauma, and modern Wicca combines numerous traditions, Eastern and Western, to this end.

VITAL FORCE

Svatmarama, a fifteenth- and sixteenth-century yogi, developed hatha yoga, which is the form of yoga most Westerners are familiar with today. Yoga is an ancient mystical practice and physical discipline designed to facilitate meditation and the raising of Kundalini (vital energy). *Hatha* means "sun" and "moon," and it focuses on attaining balance between opposites. The postures, called *asanas,* are designed to improve health and extend life. They have measureable biochemical and physiological effects. As any regular practitioner knows, the asanas relax the mind and emotions, and induce a trance if practiced effectively. Aleister Crowley believed that every magician should practice yoga to keep in shape and learn to direct energy effectively.

Exercise 89: Just Breathe

The breathing exercises of Pranayama focus concentration, induce meditation through rhythmic driving, and improve health. In proper yogic breathing, the practitioner exhales for one count more than she inhales. Practice this process for one to five minutes a day.

For variety, block your left nostril and inhale through your right (the *ha,* or "sun" side) then block your right nostril and exhale through your left (the *tha,* or "moon" side). Do this for one to three minutes. Then switch nostrils and repeat.

Exercise 90: Microcosmic Orbit

Some Reiki practitioners are taught to create a circuit of energy called the *Microcosmic Orbit.* You can use this process to direct energy to magick or healing. Do you remember this from Exercise 6: Visualizing Energy? Try the Microcosmic Orbit now by drawing energy up from the earth. If you need help, you can "pump" it by switching back and forth from one foot to the other. When you feel you have drawn a fair bit of energy, clench your perineum and touch your tongue to the roof of your mouth. A circuit of energy will run from your perineum up the front of your body to your head, and back down the back of your body to return to your perineum. The continual circuit will keep the "battery" of magickal energy charged, so to speak, and will amplify the existing charge. Circulate the energy up with each inhale, and down with each exhale. Use your hands or tools to direct the energy where it is needed, perhaps healing, perhaps to charge talismans; it's up to you.

WHEELS OF LIGHT

Most people have at least passing familiarity with the basic lore of Tantra. For those unaware, there are numerous points of energy in the body called *chakras,* which means "wheels" or "lotuses." There are seven major chakras. When healthy, they whirl widdershins and radiate out in both directions; or straight up or down at the crown and root. Each one of these chakra points corresponds to different organs, different emotions, and so forth, and blockages can lead to all kinds of mental, physical, and emotional problems. Learning to "clear" them is an essential part of most healing arts.

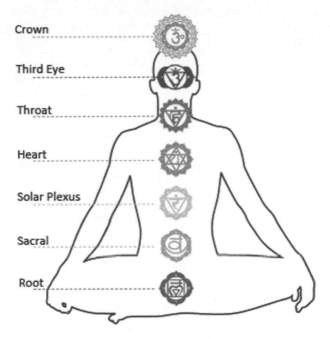

Figure 40: The Seven Chakras

TABLE 8: Chakras

Chakra:	Color:	Location:	Associations:
Muladhara (Base or Root)	Red	Base of spine between anus and genitals (perineum)	Bowels, perineum, feet and legs, adrenal glands, physical body, survival, stability, instinct, ambition, self-sufficiency
Svadhishtha-na (Sacral or Navel)	Orange	Lower belly (womb)	Urinary system, genitals, womb or testes, emotional identity, creativity, desire, pleasure, procreation, relationships, sense of humor
Manipura (Solar Plexus)	Yellow	Solar plexus	Pancreas, liver, stomach, sense of belonging, mental identity, self-esteem, personal power, stamina, will, success, ego

continued on the next page

Anahata (Heart)	Green or pink	Center of sternum (heart)	Heart, lungs, circulatory system, thymus gland, social identity, trust, emotions, forgiveness, love, wisdom, stability, patience, compassion
Vishuddha (Throat)	Blue	Throat	Throat, neck, mouth, teeth, thyroid, sinuses, communication, creativity, personal responsibility, faith, truthfulness, self-knowledge, intuition, expression
Ajna (Brow or Third Eye)	Indigo	Between the eyebrows (third eye)	Head, brain, eyes, ears, self-knowledge, wisdom, insight, intellect, clairvoyance, detachment, understanding, intuitive reasoning, visualization
Sahasrara (Crown)	Violet/ white	Top of skull	Soul, higher self, intuitive knowing, spirituality, duality, integration, awareness

Exercise 91: Chakra Breathing

Begin this exercise by sitting on the floor in the classic cross-legged or lotus positions, or sitting in a chair. You can practice Exercise 5: Tree Meditation and/or Exercise 90: Microcosmic Orbit first if you wish.

Draw red energy up from the earth's core, and as you inhale bring it into your base chakra through your perineum. Breathe out, carrying all the negative things you have stored in that chakra with it. It may appear in your visualization as a muddy brown color. Inhale bright red color back in from the earth; exhale negativity. Continue until you feel this process is complete.

When you can breathe out red energy as bright as it was when you inhaled it, exhale it, and then inhale it into your sacral chakra as pumpkin orange energy. Exhale the negativity again (a different muddy brown.) Repeat until it is clear.

Change the orange to a bright sunny yellow and inhale it into your solar plexus. Exhale the blockages and gunk, which may appear to you as a greenish-black. Clear this chakra completely too.

Transmute yellow to emerald green with pink undertones, and inhale it to your heart chakra. Exhale what needs to be cleared. Repeat as necessary.

Continue through your throat chakra (sapphire blue), brow chakra (indigo), and crown chakra (so white it is almost amethyst).

From there, see a golden glowing cosmic egg above your head. Transmute white to gold, and breathe into it. This represents union with the Cosmic Creation force, and if you have given this exercise the attention it deserves, this will produce a wonderful feeling upon contact, like an orgasm in the head. It does not need to be cleared.

When you have enjoyed this contact for as long as you think you can stand, begin to bring the energy back down the same way you brought it up; through the crown chakra as white, then the brow chakra as indigo, and so on, inhaling energy and exhaling blockages. You will likely find this easier than raising it, but there will still be things left that the cosmic energy will remove.

Exhale the last of the red energy into the earth's core, and complete the circuit. Be aware of the energetic flow going up one way and down the other in an endless loop. Enjoy this until you decide that you are ready to quit. Record your results.

KUNDALINI

Some hatha yoga exercises are designed to raise kundalini energy. Kundalini resembles a white serpent, and it dwells at the base of the spine. The goal is to unite the goddess Shakti (earth energy) with the god Shiva (sky energy) to achieve a powerful state of religious ecstasy in the body. This is known as Tantra, which you have been practicing in the previous exercise.

Tantrics use various methods including breathing, meditation, and sexual contact to wind energy up from one chakra into another. The end result resembles a double helix pattern or a caduceus. Did you notice this at the end of the exercise?

You probably also noticed that your body was generating heat. This is because your body is like a frayed wire; it is a bad conductor. When electricity (or other energy) moves through a conductor that resists it, heat is produced because some of the energy is left behind and heat is how it disperses itself. Many Reiki practitioners notice the same effect, while their client is often cool. This fades with practice as we learn how to be better conductors.

Exercise 92: Kundalini Awakening

At a festival I attended recently, a local tantrika taught us the daily afternoon meditation they used in Osho's ashram in India. For fifteen minutes, shake your body like a rattle. Everyone's shaking is different; mine looks a bit like I'm on one of those vibrating belt machines. Then, dance intuitively and freeform for fifteen minutes. Last, sit and meditate for fifteen minutes. You can play music for each of the fifteen-minute sections to facilitate the change. (At the festival, for example, the shaking music sounded like somebody shaking a cowbell, so I imagine any fast rhythmic rattling would work; the dancing music had a steady and rhythmic beat; and the meditation music was slow, relaxing, and involved a lot of repetitions of *om*.) I found this exercise very effective and have incorporated it into my regular practice. If you are looking for something more intense, give this a try!

BIOFEEDBACK

Numerous experiments with biofeedback prove that we can exercise control over many of our autonomic body functions, including breathing, heart rate, brain waves, and pain or other nerve responses. You have already experimented with this for yourself in chapter 2 in your work with brain wave entrainment. There are many other things we can do. Controlling your heart rate controls your level of calm and concentration and can also aid healing and pain resistance; controlling breathing focuses your mind. It all comes back to the breath.

Exercise 93: Heartbeat Drum

Drumming, dancing, and other methods of rhythmic induction change the movement of the blood and the breath through the body. Your heart rate tries to match any rhythm you hear, especially if it sounds like a heartbeat! Allowing your heart rate to slow resists bleeding and pain; accelerating it increases healing and physical vitality.

For this exercise, you will need a partner and a drum with a deep bass tone. One partner drums while the other does the internal work, and then you change off.

If you are doing the internal work, take your pulse. You can do this by laying your fingers lightly against the inside of your wrist or in the hollow between your windpipe and the thick muscle of your neck. If you are drumming, time one minute so that your partner can count the number of beats per minute. The first partner then gives this count to the drummer, along with the sound of the beat. The drummer then begins drumming out the beat as it was given, systolic pressure (maximum pressure, when the heart muscle contracts) in the accented beat, and diastolic (minimum pressure, when the heart muscle relaxes) in the backbeat. Change the beat when you perceive that your partner is relaxed and comfortable. Start by slowing it down gradually. For the best results, be very patient and do not rush this; the body takes time to adjust.

If you are doing the meditation, take your pulse again while your friend times one minute and see if it has changed.

Now, if you are drumming, start speeding up the rhythm, perhaps eventually drumming even faster than your partner's original pulse. If you are meditating, take your pulse again once it has been sped up.

Bring the drumbeat back down to the meditating partner's original rate so that she doesn't leave cold or anxious.

If desired, you can now switch places.

Exercise 94: Breath of Fire

The Breath of Fire is something you might have heard of. It raises kundalini. You may have heard of Tantrics inducing orgasms by simply concentrating; this is how that is accomplished.

Sit in a comfortable position with your spine straight. Touch your tongue to the roof of your mouth to prepare the Microcosmic Orbit. Make your connection with the core of the earth and draw the energy up into your base chakra. As you do, begin to breathe in short, rapid pants. Breathe properly; allow your belly to expand with each inhale and contract with your exhale. You will feel the energy building with each breath. Allow it to expand in a winding serpent pattern up from your base chakra into the sacral chakra; from the sacral to the solar; and so forth. When it reaches your crown, you can either expand it up into the cosmic egg, allow it to explode in a fountain around you, or focus it into some magickal purpose. You can use this energy to resist fire and pain, empower healing, enchant talismans, or achieve divine connection; the possibilities are endless! Make sure to direct the energy into something, however, before you allow your breathing to return to normal.

Exercise 95: Yin Yoga

Yin yoga holds single positions for extended periods; perhaps as long as ten to fifteen minutes. It is designed to stretch the body, and it can be used to direct blood flow for meditation and magick.

Choose one of these asanas each day to hold for ten to fifteen minutes:

Cobra is the part of the Fifth Rite in which you lift your upper body up on your hands while keeping your legs back, your belly to the floor, and your eyes up (see figure 21).

Sphinx is essentially the same position, only you prop yourself up on your upper arms instead (this is less intense on the lower back). This encourages sluggish kundalini to rise.

Figure 41: Sphinx Pose

Downward Facing Dog or Dolphin

Downward facing dog is the second part of the Fifth Rite (see figure 22).

A variation is dolphin, in which you form a triangle on the ground around your head with your upper arms and place your forehead on the floor. You can also do this on your knees if that is more comfortable. This is good for relaxation and meditation.

Figure 42: Dolphin Pose

Child's Pose

To get to child's pose, go from a posture such as downward facing dog and sit back on your legs so that your rear is over your feet, stretching your arms out in front of you, and putting your forehead to the ground. Most people find this very comfortable, and it is good for meditation.

Figure 43: Child's Pose

Warrior

Spread out your legs to form a V. Turn to face one side. The forward foot should be straight, and the backward one should be at an angle. Bend your knees and extend the arm that is on the same side as the forward foot straight out in front of you, while you reach behind you with the other. This should make you feel very powerful and grounded, and it is an excellent pose for anything in which strength or courage is important. Make sure to practice for the same amount of time on the other side as well.

Figure 44: Warrior Pose

Tree

You are unlikely to be able to hold this for ten minutes, but try it! Focus your gaze on something slightly distant from you and directly ahead, as you did for the First Rite. Lift one leg up and rest the foot just above or below your other leg's knee. If you want something more challenging, press the outside of your raised foot on the mid-thigh of the other leg; then point your knee downward, forming a triangle. This is good for balancing you between heaven and earth. Practice with both sides for an equal time period.

Figure 45: Tree Pose

Corpse Pose

Remember this one? I bet you haven't done it for months at this point! Well, do it again. Lie on your back with your arms at your sides and your legs straight out, feet relaxing outward. It is good for relaxation and grounding.

INVERSION

Any posture in which your head is below your heart is an inverted posture. Most people do this to gain insight by focusing blood flow to the brain instead of the body. You have already practiced this in downward facing dog. Mystics do this for hours at a time. As a child, likely so did you, by hanging upside down on trees, monkey bars, or swing sets. I am going to suggest some simpler ways to do this now that require no training. Be cautious, especially if you have any kind of disorder related to equilibrium or circulation. Though a certain level of discomfort is expected and even desired, if you find yourself in pain or your vision is blacking out, come slowly out of the posture and sit or lie down while things readjust.

Exercise 96: Inversion

Choose one of these to practice:

- Handstand or teddy bear stand—hold this position for at least one to two minutes, but no longer than five.
- Lie on your couch with your head toward the floor in such a way that you won't fall off. With practice you should be able to work your way up to staying like this for up to fifteen or twenty minutes.
- Inversion machine—if you are lucky enough to own one of these, they work very well for this with little effort or risk.
- Suspension games—those who are into kink likely have some experience with swings or suspension. There is no reason why this cannot be put to work for meditation and mystical enlightenment, especially with a little judiciously applied pleasure and pain.

HEAT AND COLD

Changes in temperature affect blood flow, breathing, and consciousness. You have already experienced this to some degree in dancing, kundalini awakening, and the Breath of Fire! Martial arts training sometimes includes sudden temperature changes, such as running in the snow and then throwing oneself onto a snow bank. Sweat lodges heat the body and reduce respiration because of the smoke and thickness of the heated air, punctuated by breaks in the outside world with much cooler temperatures.

Exercise 97: Hot Yoga

Most yoga studios have "hot yoga" classes that you can attend, but if one isn't available, try this: Turn the thermostat in your home up to tropical temperatures; about 77 degrees Fahrenheit (25 degrees Celsius). To make it more effective, set a pot boiling on the stove to increase humidity in your house. Then, do your Five Rites and compare the experience to normal conditions!

Exercise 98: Waterfall Kata

You've probably seen movies in which a martial artist in training stands under a waterfall and does his basic exercises (kata). You can do the same with Tai Chi, the Five Rites, or any other basic routine. If there's no waterfall near you, try standing in snow or cold water. The movement is important to avoid hypothermia.

Spinning, Binding, and Other Traumas
Spinning
Exercise 99: Child's Play

Do you remember being a child at the playground? Many of your favorite activities were trance-inducing, and that's why you liked them. Find a favorite and practice it with a specific magickal Intention in mind. Changing your equilibrium means changing blood flow to the brain, which can alter your consciousness.

- Merry-go-round—spinning on a merry-go-round causes dizziness; and if practiced for long enough, a trance. This is why children will ride them until they are ill. If you would feel silly on a merry-go-round, try spinning in place or riding a zipper.
- Swinging—I used to swing on the swing set for hours, and it made me feel very relaxed and at peace, even ecstatic. If you don't want to swing, try a fair ride or a Ferris wheel. If you want to combine this with fear and trauma, try a roller coaster or the Drop of Doom. Intense!

Binding

Binding is used in a First Degree initiation. Most covens teach how to do binding safely. Be careful; binding too tightly or for too long can result in nerve damage or asphyxiation.

Buckland's Complete Book of Witchcraft refers to a device called a *Witch's cradle,* reputedly used by Witches to alter consciousness through sensory deprivation, binding and suspension. It actually came from the renegade scientific work of John C. Lilly. A safer design is made of canvas or similar, lined with fur or something thick and soft, suspended from a pulley. The mystic sits in the cradle and is swung around in a circle. There is no information about how to make one in Buckland's book, so use it at your own risk.

Binding and scourging the skin cause changes in the body's surface temperature and shocks to the system, so they definitely control the blood and breath. If you'd care to take a walk on the wild side, let's do some more work together.

Exercise 100: Wisdom of Yggdrasil

For this exercise, you will need a partner whom you trust implicitly, a chair, and soft cord or rope. Please be cautious with this if you have any circulatory conditions, head injuries, equilibrium problems, claustrophobia, PTSD, or seizures.

In the Poetic Edda, the classic Norse myths, Odin hung himself from Yggdrasil for nine days to acquire the secret of the runes. In that spirit, we're going to use binding and some limited inversion to seek enlightenment.

Seat yourself on a solid chair that will not tip over if you lean forward; then do so. Grasp the front legs with your hands and press your chest against your knees, allowing your head to dangle below. Have your friend fasten your arms and legs to the chair legs firmly enough that you can't escape, but not tightly enough to cut off any circulation. Remain there, bound and with your head down, for at least five full minutes. There will be a moment when this will be extremely uncomfortable; allow it to pass. There will be another moment when you will feel very anxious and claustrophobic; allow this to pass too. When all your resistance has ceased, open your mind and allow messages to come.

If your companion is willing to dare this, switch places after you are untied and the dizziness has passed. Journal about your experience in your Book of Shadows.

Trauma

Strangulation and asphyxiation have been used for changing consciousness, and I am sure they are effective, but they are not recommended. There are simply too many opportunities for something to go horribly wrong.

Sudden frights and other shocks to the system do this as well. The Challenge at the Threshold of a Wiccan First Degree initiation is one example. A blindfolded candidate is escorted to the edge of the circle, bound and naked, and the blade of an athame is suddenly pressed to the initiate's chest, with an admonishment to not come with fear or falseness; then a promise of trust is elicited, and the candidate is permitted to enter. We'll cover some work with traumatic driving in Chapter 7.

SELF-EVALUATION

The Witch who masters control of her blood and breath masters the direction of vital energy. The only effective gauge of self-evaluation for this chapter is your results. Which methods were the most effective for you? Which were the least?

We are now venturing into some advanced Witchcraft practices. A good teacher is very strict about the exercises at the beginning but allows more flexibility as studies progress. While I certainly don't expect that you will use all of what I have offered, I hope you were at least willing to try it.

The final two chapters of this book cover concepts that are challenging even in advanced Witchcraft practice, and will teach you everything you need to know to prepare you for the Second and Third Degrees of Wiccan initiation, aside from whatever a specific tradition might require (more on this in chapter 7). Take it slowly, take your time, and don't do anything until you are ready. And congratulations! You are to be commended for persisting.

chapter seven

THE SCOURGE

Art thou willing to suffer in order to learn?
—GERALD GARDNER, *THE GARDNERIAN BOOK OF SHADOWS*

Everyone carries a shadow, and the less it is embodied in the individual's conscious life, the blacker and denser it is. At all counts, it forms an unconscious snag, thwarting our most well-meant intentions.
—DR. CARL G. JUNG

Let's talk about pain. Let's talk about fear, darkness, anger, and "things that go bump in the night." Let's talk about the suffering we'd rather not endure, the things that make us shiver to the marrow of our bones, the worst and most harrowing moments of our lives.

Let's talk about those bones, too! Every living person has a grinning skull awaiting them, because let's face it; none of us are getting out of this alive, are we? Death is the heritage that awaits all of us, no matter what we did or did not do in our lives, no matter what diets we go on or which cigarettes we smoke or don't smoke, no matter whether we are lucky or unlucky. Sometimes we anticipate it—we all know that we are destined to die of old age eventually—but often we don't. We are diagnosed with terminal ailments before our time; we get run over by a bus . . . we don't know. Sooner or later, we dance with the reaper. So we're going to practice the steps in this section. We're going to take Death by the hands, look into his empty eye sockets that see right through us despite our best efforts to hide, and I hope in the end, you will be able to do so with only the slightest thrilling chill that makes your hair stand up on the back of your neck, as opposed to gibbering in terror and panic.

Let's talk about things we keep hidden, even from ourselves. Let's talk about our dark sides; the aspects of our personalities that we don't like. Part of our growth as individuals involves confronting and accepting these unloved and unwanted parts that frighten us too.

We're going to dig all the skeletons out of our closets now. We're going to accept our dirtier, uglier aspects; and with any luck, we will be able to make them start working for us instead of against us. Maybe we'll even find that they aren't as horrible as we thought! We're going to retrieve some of the pieces of our souls that we have left behind through fear, grief, anger, disappointment, and humiliation. We are going to look right into the heart of the abyss, and we are going to accept its own pitiless gaze without fear.

We're also going to confront the forces of the primordial chaos. We're going to face the fact that there will always be some things that we simply cannot control. We're going to come to grips with the fact that sometimes you can do absolutely everything right, and it can all go horribly wrong anyway. We're going to proceed through this dark and scary territory on the premise that "what does not kill us makes us stronger."

In short, we're going to confront fear, and through our confrontation and acceptance, we are going to triumph over it. We will leap with both feet into the Dark Goddess's cauldron of transformation; and through our "boiling and cooking," we're going to die to our old lives and be reborn to a new one in which we are stronger and more complete. We're going to learn to get out of our own way, and in so doing, become better Witches, and, I hope, better, more authentic and wholehearted people. Are you ready?

THE SCOURGE AND THE KISS

The scourge is a tool used in British Traditional Witchcraft to ritually flog Witches, especially in an initiation ritual. Not all Wiccan traditions use it. It symbolizes the authority of the high priestess and the Goddess, as well as the willingness of the Witches of the coven to learn, no matter the difficulties. The scourge also represents the suffering and pain of life, while the kiss represents joy and pleasure. Their symbols are often depicted together on Wiccan ritual tools, symbolizing the balance between comedy and tragedy, life and death.

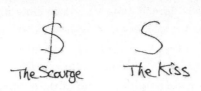

Figure 46: The Scourge and the Kiss

British Traditional Witches receive a lot of criticism for their use of the scourge, but scourging is still used in many religious traditions all over the world. The scourge used in the craft is more accurately described as a flogger or cat-o'-nine-tails. It is soft and made of cloth or leather. Its use is precisely described in Gardner's Book of Shadows ("The scourgings are 3, 7, 9 (thrice three), and 21 (thrice seven) 40 in all") and is never intended to actually cause harm. It changes consciousness through rhythmic and kinesthetic driving and by controlling blood flow. Scourging in Wiccan ritual probably descends from the mystery cults of the ancient world. In the Dionysian Mysteries, the initiate was scourged to symbolize his death and rebirth. A similar rite was used in Greece, Rome, Egypt, Assyria, and Persia, and it may have been the beginning of Christianity. Traditional Witches retell the Sumerian tale of the descent of the goddess Inanna, who went to the underworld to retrieve her dead lover, died, and was reborn, as part of our Second Degree initiation rite.

The scourge is also linked to fertility, perhaps because of its similarity to a grain flail. During the Roman festival of Lupercalia, women were whipped by the priests to make them fertile. Osiris's crook and flail are echoed in the wand and scourge, clutched by the high priestess or priest when drawing down the deities into their bodies during the circle.

The use of the scourge is a method of purification. The number of strikes are thought to have numerological and spiritual significance, and conducted in this pattern scourging is an effective method of traumatic and rhythmic driving. If you dare, let us explore it.

Exercise 101: The Scourge

For this exercise, you will need a scourge as described in the introduction. Adult stores or ritual and Witches' supply websites are the best places I know to get them. You can also make one by fastening nine knotted thick silk cords to a stick.

In circle, or with a partner, remove as much clothing as you are comfortable with. One of you kneels before the other one with back exposed but most of one's front covered to protect the genitals and face.

The other partner takes the scourge in hand. There is a trick to its use. If it is relatively solid, one swings it back and forth in a crisscross or figure eight pattern of perpetual motion. This keeps a good rhythm and level of force, and is less likely to accidentally catch something painful. If it isn't solid, take the tails in one hand and pull them slightly taut, then release when swinging the hand that is holding it to strike. Be careful to strike on a diagonal so that you are less likely to cause hurt or injury.

Strike your partner's exposed back and/or buttocks in the following pattern, with breaks in between. The symbolism behind this has been translated into more modern language from Gardner's Book of Shadows.

- 3: Three is the number of the Goddess as maiden, mother, and crone; the three stages of life, and the number of Fate.
- 7: Seven is the number of the gates of heaven and of Inanna as She descended into the underworld, the original number that represented the planets; and it is the number of the Goddess combined with the number of the earth (four elements.)
- 9: Three threes make nine, always a powerful number in Witchcraft. That's Fate intensified, and it is a prime number squared.
- 21: Three sevens make 21.

Forty is the total number of strikes given, and this is five (the number of the Fivefold Kiss, humanity, and the pentagram,) times eight (the actual number of kisses in the Fivefold Kiss, and the number of the elemental weapons), and this represents a balance of humanity: male and female, each with twenty digits.

If needed, repeat this pattern until the desired trance effect is achieved for your magickal work.

THE SHADOW SELF

The psychologist Carl Jung wrote about the "shadow self," the parts of our personalities that we keep repressed because they make us uncomfortable. Often, what we repress are things that are good for us in some situations but are regarded as socially unacceptable, like desire or anger. As a Witch, it is important—even necessary—that we learn to deal with our shadow selves. Lying to ourselves and refusing to admit to our darker sides is only destructive. It leads to hypocrisy and arrogance, and worse yet, our repressed urges sabotage our magick.

In chapter 1 emphasized the fact that we create a lot of our own reality through our perceptions. The shadow self is how our desire to effectively manifest is undone. Do you remember Exercise 9: Know Thyself? Have you been working with it regularly, or have you relaxed your discipline? It is time now to take it up again.

It is not uncommon for this sort of work to dig up sensitive, buried elements of a traumatic past. There is no shame in going to a therapist if this turns out to be the case for you; and indeed, many Witches and magicians eventually do in order to clear subconscious sludge and free their spirits. The work is worth the effort.

Fighting Fear

Fear is our greatest enemy. Most of the time when we are prevented from accomplishing something we want to do, it is fear that stops us. These exercises will aid you in facing that fear, and ultimately emerging triumphant.

The Rust and Gilded Pentacles

Do you remember Exercise 49: The Iron Pentacle, back in chapter 3? Have you been working with it? If not, you may have found one of its darker reflections: the Rust or Gilded Pentacles. They occur when fear prevents you from manifesting Iron.

The Rust Pentacle is the decayed and demeaned reflection of the Iron Pentacle. The Gilded Pentacle is the flip side of that. It is also based in fear, but aggressive fear as opposed to passive fear. It looks good, but is every bit as damaging as the Rust Pentacle. Just remember that "all that glitters is not gold."

Exercise 102: The Rust Pentacle

The Iron Pentacle rusts when our flight response is triggered. Instead of dealing with things with courage, we run away from them. We do this either because we have always been punished for manifesting iron, or because we are afraid to because we see how people who manifest iron are treated by others.

Rust is what happens when we neglect or drench the Iron Pentacle in too much Water. If we do not actively clean, polish, and use iron, it will rot.

Symptoms of rust include depression, whining, blame, excuses, anxiety, hopelessness, disempowerment, avoidance, numbing, addiction, and running away.

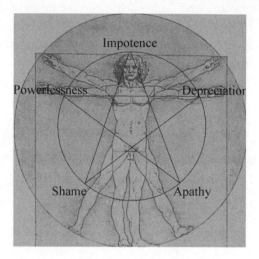

Figure 47: Rust Pentacle

Impotence

Sex exposed to rust becomes impotence. Is there something you wanted to do but felt was beyond your power? Were you in a middle management position where the boss kept undermining what limited authority you had? Did you ever have to watch as your teenager became involved in something questionable? Have you ever been stuck in a rut and it seemed like you just could not get ahead, or that the Universe was out to get you? The danger phrases indicating that you may be sliding into impotence are "There's nothing I can do," and "That won't work."

The cure for impotence is to work with the energy of sex and reclaim it; feel that life force connection. If you have been miring yourself in a depressing situation, seek out ways to alleviate that depression. Practice sacred orgasm and revel in life energy. Immerse yourself in joy! If a problem seems too overwhelming to overcome, break it down. How can you do things in pieces as opposed to all at once? Consider the possibility that something you have been struggling with may not really be your problem at all!

Shame

Pride left to rust becomes shame, which keeps us from sharing ourselves with other people and defeats connection. We numb shame with addiction, avoidance, and denial. Are you ashamed of anything? The warning phrases are "No one can know about," "I can't tell you," and "I am humiliated."

The cure is to clear your conscience and confess your vulnerabilities to others. Sounds like a paradox, doesn't it? But confession really is good for the soul, as long as it is done in a safe environment with people you trust. Find a good therapist, a good friend, or a good clergyperson to talk to, or share your secrets with others who have the same ones.

Depreciation

Rusted self is depreciation. Do you ever feel like you are invisible? That nothing you say or do matters, and that if you were to disappear no one would notice or care? Some employers excel at depreciation as a form of control. They have no praise no matter how hard you work, and if you show initiative, they will cut you down. Some teachers and parents are good at this too. And some of us are good at encouraging depreciation by dressing to blend in and trying not to be noticed. The warning phrases that indicate you are suffering from depreciation are "No one cares about me," "I'm not good enough," or "I don't deserve X."

The cure is to accept your own worthiness and find your right-sized ego. If you believe you are worthy, then others will also believe it. How do you do that in a culture or environment that fosters depreciation? Go back to the tools of the first two chapters. Use Exercise 8: Affirmations and Exercise 22: Self-Hypnosis to your greatest advantage!

Powerlessness

Power rusts into powerlessness, which is connected to impotence. We've all felt powerless at one point or another, that we had no power to change something we disagreed with, or that something was out of our control. Even if a situation is in someone else's hands, you are still not powerless. You can always choose how you will react. Most doctors will tell you that the will to live is the only real deciding factor as to whether someone will live or die. Even in a terminal situation, loved ones can strengthen will by being present and offering their love in a difficult time. The danger phrases that indicate powerlessness are "I can't," and "There's nothing I can do."

The cure is to take back your power. Practice the art of affirmation by repeating this simple and elegant phrase, "Yes, I can!" And remember Margaret Mead's wise statement: "Of course a small group of committed people can change the world. Indeed, it is the only thing that ever has."

Apathy

Rusted passions become what is perhaps the most difficult, and the most dangerous, element of the pentacle to clean: apathy. It is very difficult to spark the fires of passion once they have been extinguished. Apathy is the numbing of our emotions to avoid hurt. It manifests frequently in the "compassion fatigue" that plagues our society. The danger phrases to watch out for are "It doesn't matter anyway," "It won't do any good," "Why bother?", and "I don't care" (or its modern incarnation, "I could care less").

The cure is to actively practice compassion. Reach out to others. Feel, even if it hurts. Get involved. Listen. Offer to help. Try to see things from the perspectives of others. Care! "There but for the grace of God, go I."

Exercise 103: The Gilded Pentacle

The Gilded Pentacle is actually iron pyrite, or fool's gold. It looks prettier than the dull and gritty Iron Pentacle, but its gilt is a false coating that hides the rusted iron beneath. It appears when we engage the fight instinct in response to fear. This is what happens when you expose the iron to more Fire than is required. And we sure like to feel as though we are better than others when we are gripped by it!

Symptoms of the Gilded Pentacle include self-importance, superiority, denial, obstinacy, defensiveness, aggression, and rage.

THE WITCH'S EIGHT PATHS OF POWER

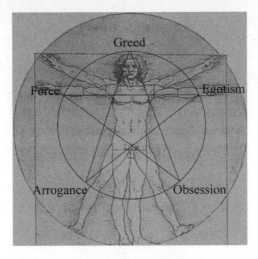

Figure 48: Gilded Pentacle

Greed

Greed sometimes looks like sex to us. Rather than connecting to life force and being enriched by it, we try to control and possess. We hoard and acquire because we hope this will protect us against lack. This urge infects our lives, our relationships, our very culture. Our desperation does not help us. He who dies with the most toys wins nothing but loneliness, and the only way to truly love something—indeed, the only way you can truly claim that you do—is if you are willing to set it free. The danger phrases to warn that we are being greedy are "I must have," or "That is/you are mine."

To fight greed, we must be willing to let go and trust. We need to tap into the energy of sex, the life force, and remind ourselves that lack is something created by inequality. We are meant to have enough, and there will always be enough if we manage it wisely, whether we are discussing food, money, or love.

Arrogance

Arrogance is gilded pride. When our parents and educators told us not to be proud, they really meant for us not to be arrogant. It is hard to draw the line sometimes. Pride is about knowing your integral worth and being comfortable with that; arrogance is being smug about it. I have a problem with arrogance because pride was something I had to fight tooth and nail for due to an excess of shame that I used to carry around with me, so now I overcompensate. The danger phrase to watch for is the word "better." If you think you can do something better than someone else, that you know better or you are better, that's arrogance. If you are the kind of person who insists on doing everything herself, you struggle with arrogance.

The cure is humility. Laugh at yourself! Allow yourself to fail. Be open to the ideas and methods of others, even if you wouldn't do it the way they would; you might learn something. Give credit where it is due. If you do not do this work, life will make sure to provide some humiliation for you, especially when you are doing the work of the scourge.

Egotism

Gilded self is egotism. Egotism and arrogance are often confused, but when you are falling into ego, it means that everything is always all about you. Right-sized egos do not overcrowd the room. If all conversations somehow become about your troubles or your successes, or you think that the world is literally out to get you, then you likely suffer from egotism. This often becomes a problem for Witches working through their Second Degree. It, again, is overcompensation for the lack of self that we had before we began this work, but it is just as dangerous. The warning phrases of egotism begin with "I" or end with "me." These indicators are not worrisome in and of themselves, but frequency of use is a bad sign.

The cure is to practice shifting your perspective. Do you really believe that the world is out to get you specifically? Do you think maybe your friends would like to talk about their problems once in a while? Please do keep in mind that a relationship involves give and take, and if it does not, then you are using someone. Try to visualize how you would feel in the same situation. Listen to yourself talk and consider your phrasing, your tone, your attitude, and your subject matter.

Force

The iron pyrite version of power is force. David R. Hawkins wrote an entire book about the topic, and Reclaiming and Dianic Wiccan traditions talk about "power within" as compared to "power over." Force manifests in many ways. Any time you are arguing, you are manifesting force instead of power, because you are no longer trying to communicate, you are just trying to browbeat the other person into giving in. Manipulation and passive aggression are other ways in which we try to force others to do what we want. Contrary to Machiavelli's beliefs, you do not have to dominate someone else. If you have "power within," others just do not affect you in that way. The danger phrase to indicate force is "You have to." Perhaps you have heard it said, and it is true, that the only things in life that we have to do are to pay taxes and die.

The cure is to learn how to be assertive instead of aggressive or passive aggressive. I'd suggest Dr. Manuel Smith's book *When I Say No, I Feel Guilty* as an excellent introduction in assertiveness; we'll be working with parts of it soon.

Obsession

Last, gilded passion manifests as obsession. This is what happens when something dominates our every thought and we just can't let it go. We fall into a trap of using our self-talk in a negative way, or we grasp something tooth and nail that we can't hold on to. This could be a lover, our youth, a job we loved, or an outfit we have been too fat to wear for ten years. The danger phrase to avoid is, "If only."

The only cure for obsession is acceptance, and that is the hardest work I know. Mourn, grieve, and release. Give yourself time to do that, but know that if you are unable to move on, you will stagnate. The only constant in life is change.

Exercise 104: True Courage

You have probably heard this saying: "Courage isn't about not being afraid. Courage is about feeling the fear, and doing it anyway."

All of us have things that we fear. Most of us give them greater concern than they deserve. So I issue you this challenge: Choose something that you have always wanted to do but up to this point have been too afraid to, and just do it. It can help to start with something smaller and work up to greater acts. For me, it was an act of courage to learn to drive, something I only did a couple years ago, after my husband's accident forced me into the situation. Whatever you choose, be patient with yourself, and above all, do not give up!

You will find that your panache grows stronger as the years go on and you will be willing to try bigger and scarier things. Confronting your fears successfully gives you strength to confront bigger issues until there is not much that frightens you any longer, and even the stuff that does seems less scary. Give it a try!

Anger Is Good

Most of us have been taught that anger is bad and wrong. But anger exists for a reason. If you are angry, a need of yours is not being met. You have a right to be angry! It's all in how you channel it.

The first thing you must do is learn to accept, rather than repress, your anger. When you repress a "negative" thought, you lock it in a little box. Then you throw it deep into the well of your subconscious, where you hope it will disappear. This will work, for a while. But eventually, the box will start to rot, and the festering poison will start to seep into the water. If you have been working with the Rust or Gilded Pentacles, you will find that your negative thoughts will start to bubble to the surface. It may feel overwhelming at first—the more you have suppressed your feelings, the worse it will be. Sometimes, you might experience outbursts of emotion that can put your relationships in a compromising position; you may feel compelled to do horrible things that you don't understand. You can't store your fear and anger in boxes. They have to be dealt with; preferably at the time, but certainly, they must be dealt with eventually.

Exercise 105: Dealing with It

When you are given something that makes you feel bad, you have three options as to how to deal with it:

- You can confront it.
- You can throw it away.
- You can store it to be dealt with later.

Notice that "bury it and forget it exists" is not an option for the human psyche. You have only these three options, and the last involves a promise to yourself; that you will bring it back to the forefront and handle it when you are ready to do so.

Sometimes the psyche enforces this choice upon us because the issue is simply too much to face at the time. This is known as acute traumatic disorder. Symptoms include severe depression, staring into space, increased startle reaction, nightmares and night terrors, panic attacks, and unprovoked or disproportionate rage or violence. We have learned to associate these symptoms with the horrors of war, but other horrible events can cause this as well; it really all depends on how difficult a situation is for you. I have seen it result from abusive relationships, car accidents, bullying at school, and even messy divorces.

If we refuse to deal with a conflict because it is simply too much, or because we do not have the opportunity given the circumstances (as often happens in war), it festers and turns into post-traumatic stress disorder, or PTSD, which I am sure you have heard about. The difference between acute traumatic disorder and PTSD is that the latter lasts for years.

If you choose to throw the conflict away, you can't hold on to pieces. You must choose to rid yourself of it completely. So ask yourself: Why am I angry? If it seems insignificant but it angers me anyway, why is that? Is it just that I am under too much stress about other things, or is there some need not being met that is represented in the issue?

If you choose to deal with it, you can't do it by half-measures. You must throw yourself into it with your whole being and complete the work, no matter how uncomfortable it might make you feel. You might be forced into confrontations you would rather avoid; there could be losses; and a grieving period may be needed.

Applying these principles, work through an issue that has been bothering you for a long time.

Exercise 106: Anger Management

When you get angry, you have two options to stop:

- You can change your thoughts.
- You can change your environment.

If changing the way you look at things doesn't work, try changing your location! Go for a walk. Go to the bathroom. Do the dishes. If you are in the middle of an argument, remove yourself from the person you are arguing with. Come back when you are ready to discuss things reasonably.

If you find that you are too attached to the emotions and energies of others (a common problem when you are a psychically sensitive person) then practice your shielding work! If you find that negative energies are clinging to you (for instance, you had a bad day at work and you came home and yelled at your husband), then practice energetic cleansing methods. Smudge, center, ground, besom, do chakra clearing—whatever works for you! It's a good idea to practice some method of psychic cleansing daily.

SAYING NO

"No" is a very liberating word that more of us should know. I recommend picking up a copy of Dr. Manuel Smith's book *When I Say No, I Feel Guilty* to teach this particular skill.

Exercise 107: Assertive Rights

Smith's book contains a code called "The Bill of Assertive Rights." All of us are entitled to these rights. Here is a ten-day itinerary to practice each of them in turn.

Day 1: Consider your own judgment. If someone tells you that you should (or should not) do, feel, or say a particular thing, ask yourself, Do I agree, or disagree? Make your own decision, no matter how much you respect his or her opinion.

Day 2: Practice not explaining yourself when you have made a decision. For the first little while, err on the side of caution and explain nothing at all.

Day 3: When someone comes to you with a problem, from your boss to your spouse to your child, ask yourself if you really feel this matter is actually your problem. If you don't, inform the other party of this loud and clear. If you do, clarify how much of the matter you are willing to accept.

Day 4: If you have a change of heart, be informative right away! Do not just avoid the situation.

Day 5: Concentrate on laughing off any mistakes you have made. If damage has been caused by this, do what you can to correct it.

Day 6: Admit when you don't know the answer to something. Don't try to find the answer immediately—at least not today.

Day 7: Focus on doing something for yourself regardless of what other people think (making sure that you harm none).

Day 8: Trust your feelings. Offer no explanation to yourself or others for doing so.

Day 9: Focus on not pretending that you understand something that confuses you. This includes directions, advice, actions, or even just a thick accent!

Day 10: Consider whether or not you care about anything you are told today. This is great practice against psychic vampires. Admit it out loud. Be as blunt or as tactful as you like.

Exercise 108: Advanced Shielding

There are many ways you can refine your basic psychic shield to fit any situation.

- Add a holy symbol (I usually use a blue pentagram) to your forehead for divine protection.
- Make the outer edge of your shield spiky, like a puffer fish. This prevents people from pushing you.
- Let the shield refract light, like cloaking devices in science fiction. This makes you invisible and people are less likely to notice you.
- Visualize the barrier around your shield like a reverse osmosis filter. An RO filter has microscopic holes in the shape of water molecules, so only water (and hydrogen and oxygen, which comprise water) can get through. Your shield can be attuned to only allow certain energies through it and keep out all others.
- Experiment with colors. Try blue for protection and boundaries, red for irritation, or pink for love. If you don't want to be affected by the color you are working with, make an outer skin around your shield.
- Make the outer skin of your shield into a mirror so it reflects back what is directed at you.
- Make your shield flexible and "bounce back" the things you don't want. You are only limited by imagination!

Exercise 109: Protecting Yourself from Psychic Vampires

A psychic vampire is someone who feeds on your energy. You likely know at least one of these people. They call you up to complain constantly about their lives on the premise that "only you can understand" or "they need you to be a friend," but when you try to rely on them in the same way, they are unavailable or they turn the topic back to themselves. Their pain and suffering is always worse than yours (if you believe them) and you always feel tired or crabby after being in their presence. When they call or come over, your heart sinks. Most of them have no respect for boundaries. They want to hug you all the time, even if that isn't appropriate, or find some other pretense of making physical contact, like offering massages. Paradoxically, they tend to thrive in metaphysical communities because we are compassionate people who want to help others, and we are more likely to hug, heal, or make other physical contact (in short, we are ideal targets).

There are techniques you can practice to protect yourself from them:

- Above all, practice boundaries. Saying no is your best defense, since psychic vampires often play upon your sense of guilt, obligation, or compassion.
- Avoid anyone who relies on you for emotional support that you cannot rely on in return, unless they are your offspring. You will be amazed at how effective this simple rule is!
- Cross your arms around your heart chakra and your legs over your genitals. These are sensitive areas that are easy to establish energetic connections to. If you don't want to give out the angry body language of crossed arms, you can lean your face on your hand and make sure to rest your elbow on a counter so that most of your arm is between the vampire and your heart chakra.
- Don't permit people to push your physical boundaries. Only hug if you wish to. You have no need to apologize.
- A psychic vampire establishes connections to you that drain your power or energy, which manifest in your aura as shadowy tendrils attached to a part of your body. When the psychic vampire has left, sever any connection tendrils by forming a karate hand and using it to slice repeatedly through your aura. It is amazing how quickly vampires, especially if they have been around you a while, will try to reestablish the connection when you do this!
- If the vampire is persistent, get rid of anything she may have given or lent to you.
- Smudge or practice some other form of energetic cleansing regularly.

EGO DEATH

As we are learning to reclaim our power, sometimes we become a little drunk with it, especially those of us who came to the craft because we felt disempowered. This is commonly called High Priestess's Disease, and it is associated with the work of the shadow, and the Second Degree in Wicca. This is the stage of development that causes most of the "Witch wars" that happen in our small communities. It is good to recognize that you are divine; but so is everyone else. It seems that humility should go without saying, but my experience in training priests and priestesses tells me that it mostly falls on deaf ears. Witches in this process are like teenagers. They must leave home while they still know everything!

Many teachers of the craft have become disillusioned when their students reach this point, but I have learned to try to take it with a grain of salt, though like a parent on the receiving end of teenage angst, I am not always successful. I have come to believe it is a necessary and important stage, just like adolescence. I went through it too. If we didn't, we would be sycophants our whole lives and never develop our own beliefs and opinions. Just like parents, teachers of Witchcraft make mistakes, or don't do things as efficiently as they otherwise could, and a new approach is often needed to improve upon the Old Way. But the Old Way is often so because it works, and when we grow out of adolescence, especially when we have children of our own, we learn that Mom and Dad had reasons for doing the things they did and some of them make great sense.

There is only one way to grow up enough to be a high priest or high priestess: you must experience the death of your ego. It is never fun or easy. Whole lives can be rearranged by this process; you might leave your marriage or relationship, move across the country, take a new job in a totally different field; but whatever you do, there will be huge change. You have already begun this process, and you cannot turn back; but be sure you do not leap through the door to the remainder of this book without being prepared for the climax of the story. Good luck! I'll see you on the other side.

Exercise 110: The Hero's Journey

Joseph Campbell is a mythologist who expanded on the work of Jung with his theory of the Hero's Journey. The Hero in any myth (Campbell called it the "Monomyth") descends into the underworld to obtain wisdom, which he then brings back into the living world. Whenever you face a crisis in your own life, you become a Hero of myth, and you give your trials meaning if you learn from this and bring that wisdom out of darkness to benefit others. Initiatory Wicca invokes these crises through initiation rituals, which confer the degrees. When you find yourself faced with a situation that, for you, represents a crisis, research Campbell's Monomyth and cast yourself in the role of the Hero. How can you transform this experience into a quest for enlightenment?

Pain As Teacher

Sometimes a traumatic or unhappy event induces the necessary ego death to confront the shadow. Witches can tell you that if you don't have one at your Second Degree, life will soon provide one! Suffering can bring enlightenment. It all seems to depend upon how we react to, and process, the experience afterward, something called "post-traumatic growth." Think of it like a bee sting or a snakebite. Venom introduced to the body forces it to heal at an incredibly rapid rate, or the organism that has been stung or bitten will die. It is excruciatingly painful. But as beekeepers can tell you, the introduction of all that rapid healing often unintentionally heals previously existing conditions in the site of wounding, such as arthritis, nerve pain, and scar tissue. A traumatic event can be like a healing bee sting to the soul. Characteristics include a changed sense of priorities, warmer and more intimate relationships, a greater sense of personal strength, and a willingness to recognize either a new path or new possibilities in one's life and spiritual development.

My own journey with post-traumatic growth took place in the wake of my husband's accident. I suddenly found that many things that once seemed to matter to me were no longer important. This included seeking approval from casual acquaintances and my community. I began to give greater priority to my family, my love, and doing things to make a difference in the world. I wanted to leave a legacy, and I gave myself to my spiritual path. I started writing again.

I began to be more honest with myself and my feelings. I stopped answering the phone if I didn't feel like it. I took more time to appreciate the beauty of life and the world all around me. I stopped worrying about making mistakes, and I became more apt to try new things.

Every trauma is an initiation, a journey into the underworld, a trip through the Monomyth. How you react is up to you. Will you find the great boon deep in the heart of the underworld to bring back to the earth? Or will you become trapped there?

RITES OF PASSAGE

Any passage into a new stage of life represents a loss and a sacrifice, as well as a new beginning. Such is the cycle of death and rebirth. In our ancient roots we made sacred ceremony to mark those transitions. I believe this is something woefully missing from our culture. The only real rites of passage that we maintain are marriage and graduation.

A rite of passage is characterized by:

1. A shift in the existing order;
2. A liminal state for the initiate, when he or she is neither one thing nor the other;
3. An ordeal, test, or task to indicate worthiness;
4. And finally, formal acceptance by the new group.

A girl having a first moon ceremony might be both welcomed by a group of women she loves and trusts, and admonished on marriage, love, sex, and so forth. A boy becoming a man was often driven from his mother's house or kidnapped by the elder men, taken into the woods to conduct a first hunt, or marked or scarred in some way, and then accepted by the adult males.

Maiden, Mother, and Crone

Women have a few natural rites of passage to mark the course of their lives. It all has to do with the blood. The onset of menstruation marks the transit from child to maiden, and the beginning of adult awareness and sexuality. Motherhood introduces a new concern with leaving a legacy, whether it is children, ideas, or causes that are birthed. Menopause marks the waning part of life, where autonomy and sharing hard-earned wisdom with future generations becomes paramount. Many Witches look to the Dark Goddesses for inspiration and celebrate their croning.

Youth, Father, and Sage

Men also have three stages of life. Wet dreams mark the transition from child to youth; fatherhood marks a shift in the male psyche from self-interest to the protection and preservation of future generations; sagehood indicates that a man is ready to impart his hard-earned wisdom to those who come after him. These transitions were also marked by sacred ceremony, but no longer, and I believe this is a significant contributor to the prevalence of the Peter Pan Syndrome which many women in relationships complain about; our boys never really grow up.

Wiccan Degrees

Throughout this book, I have referred to three degrees of initiation in Wicca. Loosely, the First Degree, traditionally taken after a year and a day of study in the craft, is both recognition that you understand the basics and a declaration that this is your chosen path. The Second Degree recognizes that you are ready to teach, and declares that you wish to understand the deeper mysteries. The Third Degree, often not taken at all, indicates that you are ready to lead a coven and teach the teachers. Each of them is a mystery: the first is about birth, the second about death, and the third about love. Initiatory traditions have rituals for these rites of passage, which also link you to a Witchcraft lineage. Each tradition will have its own requirements to be considered for these rites, some of which can be quite difficult. Many Witches never seek initiation. If you do, ask covens in your area about what sort of Witchcraft they practice and if initiation is part of it.

Exercise 111: Rite of Passage

Write a rite of passage ritual for someone you know who is about to begin a major life transition. If possible, ask if you might perform this ritual.

DON'T FEAR THE REAPER

Death, of course, is the ultimate mystery and initiation. But we won't know anything about it for certain until we get there ourselves.

Many people have come very close to dying but have returned to life. This is known as a near-death experience, or NDE. It is characterized by out-of-body experiences, followed by visions of a bright light at the end of a dark tunnel, or of what life would be like for their loved ones without them. They chose not to go to it, or were told that it was "not their time," and then they were back in their bodies. Sometimes they experienced a sense of unity with divine consciousness and all things. This is a life-changing event that results in the gaining or losing of faith, the sudden advent of psychic or mediumship abilities, and above all, an appreciation of the beauty of life.

Exercise 112: A Taste of Death

For the most part, proceed with this exercise as you did with Exercise 100: Wisdom of Yggdrasil, only this time, tie a blindfold or sleep mask around your eyes so that no light gets in, and insert earplugs to minimize sounds. The effect is sensory deprivation. Your brain treats the absence of sensory information as a trauma, which expands consciousness.

This can be very effective when combined with a symbolic death and rebirth rite! If you wish to use it in this manner, then within a cast circle, recite the tale of a deity's death and rebirth, and then initiate yourselves into that mystery. This is the essence of the Second Degree initiation rite in Wiccan tradition.

Be careful; never abandon your bound partner—not even for a moment to use the washroom—and establish a system of communicating a need for help.

LETTING GO

If you have ever experienced great loss or suffering, you have experienced grief. The Kübler-Ross model of the five stages of grief is a popular explanation of how we move through it. We all experience grief in our own way, and as difficult as it may be, we need to give each other permission to do that without judgment. Some will experience only two of these stages, and some will experience all five; some will progress rapidly, and others will become stuck.

1. Denial—we cannot cope with the enormity of the experience and so we temporarily defend ourselves by denying it or disassociating ourselves from it.
2. Anger—our next defense is to blame someone or something else for our suffering, to rail against the unfairness of it, or to resent those not experiencing the same suffering and strike out against them.
3. Bargaining—we attempt to make an arrangement, either with others or with the Universe, to delay the inevitable. This ranges from "Goddess, I'll serve You faithfully if You spare my life," to "Can't we still be friends?"

4. Depression—the reality of the situation sets in and brings sorrow and despair. This is actually a necessary part of the process, and cheering someone up is not advised! We need a chance to grieve, to weep, to feel sorry for ourselves. It's like squeezing the pus out of an infected wound.
5. Acceptance—we accept the inevitability of the situation, figure out ways to cope with it, and move on. We come to terms with the changes. We adapt and mourn.

Exercise 113: A Rite of Grief

Come up with a ritual to help you come to a place of acceptance in a great loss in your life to aid in this process. Some ideas:

- For the death of a loved one: Perform a memorial service; drum the person across to the other side to the Summerlands.
- For a messy divorce, a handparting: Tie a cord between an image of you and your lover and cut it with your boline.
- For a difficult transition: Burn an image of the old situation in a cauldron and pick up a symbol of the new situation to carry with you.
- To come to terms with a past trauma: Meditate on the experience within sacred space and stop to allow the five stages of grief to manifest in a meditation. Always do this with a loved one who can guide you, reassure you, and listen without judgment to your tale.

Exercise 114: Food of Kali

I learned this exercise from Angelique Serpent, a friend and sister priestess who teaches Tantra all over the world. The dark goddesses represent the death and transformation principle. One of the names for this principle is Kali. And Kali is hungry. She eats things and transforms them into something new.

Consider something in your life that you want to get rid of. Visualize it as clearly as you possibly can. Use all your senses. See yourself actively involved in it. And communicate to the Divine in the form of the transformation principle, whom we will call Kali, how badly you want it gone. Wish on this dark star with all your might!

Then, give all of it to her. Don't hold back. Watch her devour it completely. She will tear at the meat with her sharp teeth. She will allow her belly to swell with the size of it. And then, it is gone. There is no turning back or changing your mind. Let it go. And watch for some amazing changes in your life!

Exercise 115: Shadow Self Meditation

A recording of this meditation is available on my YouTube page: Search "Shadow Self Meditation."

At last, you have done the preparations. Descend now into the underworld and meet your shadow. If you use music, it should be ominous, even sinister, but change to a lighter tone at the end. When you are relaxed sufficiently, begin.

You are standing on the beach of a sunless sea. You can hear the waves crashing against the shore. You turn around, and you notice that you have left your body behind you on the beach. That's okay; it's safe there. You turn back and notice there is a boat at the edge of the shore. A shrouded figure holding an oar stands at the prow of the boat. As he looks at you, you can almost see shadows of horns extending from his head. When you blink they are gone. He stretches his arm out in your direction, indicating that you should join him.

You come to the edge of the boat hesitantly. He takes your hand gently and carefully guides you into the boat. You take your time getting situated, but when you are ready, he dips the oar into the water and pushes off. You can hear the sound of the oar moving as he pushes you out farther into the sunless sea.

At first you were frightened; but now the air is exhilarating. You feel the salt spray in your face. You smell the ocean. You know that you are embarking on a great adventure to a far shore.

Before too long you can see a misty island in the distance. The rocks look a little perilous, but your guide moves the boat safely through the shoals. Before long, the boat is washing up onto shore.

You step off the boat and onto the beach, guided by the hand of the man with the oar. You let go of his hand, and as you turn around to thank him, you find that he is gone; and so is the boat, as if they'd never been.

You look about you, peering through the mist. The aura is . . . a little spooky, and the island seems deserted. You can't see very far, but rocky cliffs tower above you.

The mist clears, and a passageway opens up that runs through the mountains. Seeing nowhere else to go, you head through the pass.

The cliffsides block out much of the light, but you make your way through the misty mountains. After a time, the pass begins to descend.

As the mist clears you find yourself standing in a valley. All of a sudden, you smell the scent of cooking food, and you see an old woman, shrouded in black, making a meal in a cauldron. What do you think as you look at her? Is she compassionate? Frightening? Encouraging? Imposing? She has many faces, and she will appear to you in the guise that you need her to be in at this time. She meets your eyes with her piercing gaze, and she beckons for you.

After a moment you come toward her, and then you sit by the fire. "Welcome to the underworld, child," she says. "Why are you here?"

Now take a moment, and tell her in your own words what it is that you wish to accomplish. (Allow some time for this.)

She says, "Behind me, there is a cave; but the passage down is long and winding. Still, there is nothing in there but that which you take with you. That which you seek is at the end of the passage. Go down now, if you dare."

You divest yourself of everything you will not need. This may include concerns for the world you left behind; clothing, trappings of your vanity; the symbols of your ego. Whatever you choose to cast aside the old woman takes solemnly, and without comment. Then, gathering your courage, you walk into the passageway.

It is not quite dark. There are shadows cast by the light of torches. You descend into the rock. What do you see? (Allow some time for visualization.)

At last you reach the end of the passage. A distant light is getting closer with every step.

You enter into a chamber that is lit with a phosphorescent glow. The light plays tricks; it is difficult to make things out clearly. Shadows are long and looming.

You think you see movement in the shadows that isn't quite right. You can feel the heat of the earth's core. You're close to it now; you're very deep. You can smell the scent of the smoke and molten metal of the earth.

There it is again: a movement out of the corner of your eye. What was that?

You turn and see a silhouette, a shadow; but it looks strangely familiar. And then you realize you are looking through a dark mirror. You see your shadow self. Everything you have kept hidden, everything you have denied, all your secret thoughts and fears are in this being.

And now, with that realization, you confront this shadowy figure. You challenge its existence! Perhaps you rail against it; perhaps you call out challenges; perhaps the confrontation is physical. But with every denial, the shadow meets your challenge! It has defenses against your challenges. It has arguments against your arguments. It has justifications. It is your physical match. (Allow some time for the fight!)

You stop. You realize that this confrontation is pointless. You are equals, and neither one of you will win. The shadow seems to realize this too, and it looks at you to see what you will do.

You extend your palm to your shadow, and your shadow puts its palm on yours. You see the reflection. This is your mirror; this is you. Your hand shines faintly light, its hand, faintly dark; and you realize you are two halves of a whole.

Would it be so bad to realize that you aren't perfect? Why are you afraid? After all, the dark exists for a reason. Anger is for your protection; fear also. Would it not be better if the left hand knew what the right hand was doing? Would it not be better if you worked together?

With that thought, can you find it within yourself to love every part of you, even your darkness? Can you not love yourself for who you are? Can you not forgive yourself for your shortcomings? Can you not agree to work with that dark side of yourself, accepting what is and working to improve what will be?

And with that, you reach out your arms, and your shadow does too, and you hold each other in a loving embrace. Allow yourself to feel those emotions. Release your hate and fear. Scream; weep; laugh! (Give a few moments for reactions and releases.)

But now the time has come to return. Will you leave your shadow behind you, respecting that this is your shadow's realm? Or will you take your shadow's hand, and take them with you into the light? The choice is yours. (Allow a moment to decide.)

Your decision made, you head back up the passage, which is no longer sinister; winding up, back the way you came. (Allow some time to visualize the return.)

You emerge into the light, and the mist, where the old woman awaits you. Somehow the surroundings seem brighter. You notice green that you didn't notice before. The air smells fresh and clean. You, or you and your shadow together, sit at the feet of the old woman. You speak with her as you will, perhaps telling her about your journey and what you've learned. (Allow a minute or two for this.)

She speaks to you as well. She has a message that is only for you, so listen. (Allow time to hear the message.)

She gives you some food to take with you so that you may bless the ritual feast with its energy. And then you make your way back through the mountain pass, through the mist, and back to the seashore. (Take some time for this.)

You see the boat and its shrouded pilot awaiting you. Once again, he helps you into the craft. Without speaking a word, he pushes off the shore onto the sunless sea.

You make the journey in silence, and you think of what you have learned. Or perhaps you and your shadow, made one, share information, joy, and tears.

You are triumphant in your return. You have dared to face your darker side. You know that you are stronger than you were. You bring the wisdom of the underworld back to the world of light, to benefit yourself, and to share your wisdom with others in your own way.

And now in the distance, you see the sunlit shore that you left. It gets nearer. You see your body resting in peaceful slumber on the beach. You wash up on the surf, and the boat comes safely to shore.

This time, remembering what transpired, you thank your guide before you, or you and your shadow disembark. And you sink safely into your body, and become aware of its function and being.

Take a deep breath. Welcome back!

Self-Evaluation

If you have given this chapter its proper attention, you have found it challenging, exhausting, and exhilarating all at once. If you feel as though a crushing burden has been lifted from your shoulders, then you have passed the test of the scourge. Congratulations!

Any time we confront the dark, and the fact that we are mortal, we are reminded to appreciate life even with all its thorns. Don't let those thorns stop you from grasping the rose! Jump with both feet into the Goddess' cauldron of transformation! Don't be afraid.

chapter eight

THE GREAT RITE

Assist me to erect the Ancient Altar, at which in days past all worshipped, the Great Altar of all things. For in the old times a woman was the Altar.

—GERALD GARDNER, *THE GARDNERIAN BOOK OF SHADOWS*

The Great Rite is, in my opinion, the greatest of the mysteries of Witchcraft. In the Great Rite, we transform ourselves. I don't know how effective I can be at teaching you how to access this mystery through a book. I will do my best, but you need to understand that simply reading this part will not impart the true wonder. You must practice it yourself in order to truly experience and understand it.

There are two elements to the Great Rite. The first is the act of theurgy that summons the Goddess and God to our bodies. The second is the ritual act that joins the two together; in other words, sex magick. We will examine both.

To Witches, the Divine is immanent; that is to say, divinity exists right here on earth, not somewhere else. It follows, then, that we are also at least partially divine. Our image of the Divine is female and male, and They created the Universe just as we create life in this world. So the act of making love is a holy act. In the Charge of the Goddess, our Lady says, "All acts of love and pleasure are My rituals."

The Great Rite is a ritual act of sexual intercourse, generally performed by the high priestess and high priest of a coven, who represent the Goddess and the God. It is a *hieros gamos,* a "holy marriage" of the Divine; a harmonious union of opposites.

The hieros gamos is likely not a new idea. We believe it was enacted in Sumeria with the marriage of Inanna and Tamuzi, in Greece with various gods and goddesses including Zeus and Hera, and in Tibet and India with the Tantric union of Shiva and Shakti.

Traditional Witches enact the Great Rite "in actual," especially as part of our Third Degree initiation rite. Most Witches only enact it "in token" as part of the blessing of the cakes and ale, dipping athame into chalice, or lance into cauldron. Another example of this is the maypole of Beltane. The symbolism is fairly obvious.

In the Great Rite the priest and priestess call the deities into each other, but this can also be done individually. Most traditions believe that only women can aspect the Goddess and only men can aspect the God. Some traditions believe it important that their priests and priestesses be able to aspect both.

Drawing the God into one's body is known as *drawing down the sun.* And drawing the Goddess into one's body is called *drawing down the moon,* which is done far more frequently. Both are a form of trance channeling. Effects may vary, from feeling the deity's presence to having the deity telling the priest or priestess what to say, to allowing the deity to take over and speak through the priest or priestess's body, who remembers nothing of what transpired. However, it is understood that these divine aspects come from within the priest or priestess, and not from somewhere else.

Drawing down is both a form of willing possession trance and channeling. Practitioners of various spiritualities will try to tell you these practices are different, and theirs is superior, but I would not agree. *Possession* is the name often given by outsiders to the practice of calling forth *loa,* or ancestor spirits. *Channeling* is the name given to calling forth what are believed to be enlightened spirit teachers, guides, angels, and ETs. You may also hear it called *aspecting,* which is drawing down, but with the specific understanding that the deity is an archetypical aspect of oneself. All these are forms of invocation.

I think this is such a beautiful concept! Our gods and goddesses not only aid us in our personal lives, They come to hang out with us and experience the world directly through our eyes, or offer their wisdom directly through the mouths of us, their vessels.

In my personal experience, priestesses are quite capable of drawing down the sun, and priests are equally capable of drawing down the moon, though this is a controversial subject in the craft. Once, I was honored to confer a Third Degree by drawing down the sun and engaging in the Great Rite with a priestess who was a dear friend of mine. You can even draw down the sun or moon and through masturbation engage in the Great Rite with the Goddess or God who is entirely present in the astral!

Ideally, a priestess or priest of Wicca, recognizing that each of us is divine, should be able to join with any other priest or priestess in the Great Rite. Of course, in reality there are many people we would not be comfortable being that intimate with. Sadly, there are also priestesses and priests of the craft who do not understand the depths of the mystery and corrupt it by turning it into an act of mere lust. Though lust is a good thing when properly channeled, that is not the goal of the Great Rite. Sex is the medium through which the Great Rite takes place.

Since the Great Rite is the union of spiritual opposites, the joining of yin and yang, or uniting with our anima and animus, it has been explored in many different ways: heterosexual, homosexual, masturbatory, even transgendered or cross-gendered.

ORIGINS

The Great Rite may have come from Aleister Crowley's Gnostic Mass ritual, in which the Star Goddess Nuit strokes the priest's lance to invoke the God, then later, naked, she is adored by the priest, and she kisses his lance to bestow her blessing.

Crowley is credited with the renaissance of the "left-hand path" of Tantra, which likely influenced Gerald Gardner's ideas. In this somewhat heretical discipline, initiates raise kundalini through sexual contact. The ultimate goal is to transcend the ego by achieving *samadhi,* a unity of cosmic consciousness, which transmutes a physical orgasm into a spiritual one. The magnetic polarity of male and female creates the channel of mutually exchanged and raised energy, uniting Shiva and Shakti literally as well as spiritually. Transcending the ego to achieve unity with cosmic consciousness through the sexual raising of kundalini is also the goal of the Great Rite.

In Tantra, it is the feminine polarity that is believed to be the spiritually "inseminating" force. Perhaps this is why the priestess usually holds the athame in the symbolic Great Rite. Many Pagan women find this exaltation of the sexual feminine principle liberating. There are even modern "sacred prostitutes," who teach that sex is a path to enlightenment and Divine Communion. Sacred prostitution may have been part of several ancient cultures.

The Western perception of Tantra led to the development of Western sex magick, in which sexual energy is used for magickal purposes, such as focusing on an idea or symbol at the moment of orgasm to make it manifest.

Body As Temple

If the Divine is in all things, it is in our natural bodies as well. This inspired the traditional Wiccan custom of practicing "skyclad," which, if you'll recall from chapter 3, means "ritual nakedness."

If you have not yet experienced practicing skyclad, I would advise you to experiment with it. I won't include it specifically as an exercise, but I will invite you to incorporate it into other exercises. If you are truly approaching from a place of "perfect love and perfect trust," this should always be a safe environment. There are many ways in which practicing skyclad benefits a Witch. I believe this practice is falling into disuse in the craft because most of us are solitaries and have not had the benefit of entering into a coven of initiates who always practice in the buff, so it sounds strange and unnecessary to us at first. My initial experiences with Wicca were as a solitary so I was no exception, but I am now a strong advocate for it after my experiences in a coven setting. Since it violates a social taboo, it changes our mindset immediately to be more open to magick and ritual, and it is very good for the self-esteem to realize that most of us are "imperfect" when we are naked. It also helps to facilitate the flow of magickal energy.

Exercise 116: Fivefold Kiss

Witches adore the body's temple with our ritual of the Fivefold Kiss. This practice is part of the First (and often Second) Degree initiation rite, and it is an effective tool to prepare the Witch being kissed to draw down the sun or moon. For this exercise, you will need a partner.

Traditionally skyclad, one partner kneels before the other and recites the following, kissing the appropriate body parts in turn.

Blessed be thy feet (kiss left foot, then right foot), which have brought you in these ways.

Blessed be thy knees (left and right), which kneel at the sacred altar.

Blessed be thy womb (sex), without which we would not be.

Blessed be thy breast(s), formed in beauty and in strength.

Blessed be thy lips, which speak the sacred names.

Blessed be you, (craft name), priest/priestess and Witch, son of the God/daughter of the Goddess.

You may then switch if you wish.

DIVINE FORCES

What, exactly, are gods anyway?

Pagans are undecided on this point. We believe that any or all of the following options could be true:

- They could be individual, conscious spirit beings beyond our true comprehension.
- They could be personified universal forces.
- They could be ascended beings that were once human (or other spirits)
- They could be archetypes.
- They could be our own higher self, aspects of a greater spiritual entity (or entities).

As you can see, our thealogy has some wiggle room. But whether you believe the gods are without or within, they can be many things at once, all possibilities can be true, and all individual paradigms are equally valid.

Our relationship with our deities, on the other hand, is unique. We do not believe that we must come groveling before them in the dirt. We do deeply honor, respect, and worship our deities, but it's more like a respectful friendship in which our deities are tougher, wiser mentors. Like any friendship, there is give and take.

We do not believe that the Divine is omniscient, omnipotent, and omnibenevolent. We believe that the deities see more than we do, especially in regard to their area of influence and concern—largely because they are not bound to physical reality, and therefore time and space are not limitations to them. We believe that the gods can do things that we cannot, but that we can also do things that they cannot because we are physical beings. And we believe that dark and light must exist in balance; that the gods can be cruel as well as kind; and that each will act according to their own interests, just as we do, and those interests may or may not be selfish ones.

Pagan deities have personalities, and those personalities affect how they interact with us. So, please consider when you call upon a specific deity! Do not ask Aphrodite to bless a marriage unless the intended partners do not wish to have a monogamous relationship, because Aphrodite was legendary for her infidelity. If you call upon Lilith as a symbol of feminine empowerment, because she would not submit to Adam, remember that Lilith was also regarded as a succubus who ate babies! (On the other hand, maybe you want and need to embrace that destructive potential to do your shadow work.)

We believe that the Divine exists within, and that we can access that creative power ourselves. That's what we call "magick." The gods either help us with this, or they teach us how to do it through that personal divine connection we call our superconscious or higher self. This is why magick cannot exist without some understanding of spirituality; even if that spirituality is "every man and every woman is a star" (Aleister Crowley), or, as Victor Anderson, founder of the Feri tradition said, "God is self, and self is God, and God is a person like myself."

Exercise 117: Personal Deity

Most Witches have one or two primary deities who stand for things we would like to emulate. Our relationship is a cocreative one. They work with us because we are inclined to work for purposes they identify with; we work with them because they aid us in our daily lives in return for our service.

In this exercise you will reach out to a deity of your own gender. If you are twin-souled, transgendered, or any sort of queer soul, this may not be as obvious as the body of your birth, but there are even deities who are hermaphroditic, gender neutral, gay, or have cross-gendered elements. Some examples that come immediately to mind are Hermaphrodite (child of Hermes and Aphrodite); Thor (famous for cross-dressing to recover his hammer Mjolnir); Loki (who gave birth to Sleipnir while disguised as a mare); Artemis (thought to be either a virgin or a lesbian until she met Attis); Pan (who lusts after both men and women equally); and the Buddha (once reincarnated as Kwan Yin). This is perfectly fine!

Sometimes we are chosen by deities. If that is the case for you, research to identify the god or goddess that has chosen you and try to determine why. Consider what you like about him or her, and what you do not. Are the qualities you dislike actually challenges that would enhance your personal development?

THE WITCH'S EIGHT PATHS OF POWER

Make a list of what you consider to be positive and negative attributes. Don't be afraid of offending; a realistic picture of our deities is important in working with them. You do not want to ask the gods to help you with things that don't concern them; you will waste your energy, and they will be annoyed.

Work on developing a personal relationship with your deity. Some suggestions:

- Leave appropriate offerings
- Study your god or goddess' culture and relationships
- Consider similar deities from other pantheons and speculate on how your deity would relate
- Buy or create a statue or other icon
- Work at projects in your deity's honor

Note that you may have to adapt some cultural traditions. Wicca is called the Old Religion, but it is called that because it draws inspiration from ancient ways, not because it precisely preserves the Ancient Ways.

Exercise 118: Pearl Pentacle

The Pearl Pentacle takes the hard-earned self-empowerment of the Iron Pentacle, manifests our higher self, and pours the beauty of those energies out into the world to aid others. This is the end result of the Hero's Journey.

Love

Draw sparkling white cosmic energy from the center of the Universe into your crown chakra. Let it coalesce there. Let us consider the spiritual manifestation of the life energy of sex. We call it *love*, which is what happens when we come together in spirit, concerned with the well-being of someone other than ourselves. It is the feeling we get when our heart is so full it could explode. Breathing consciously, being in that place of the awareness of physical life force connection comes from sex; love is the sense of wonderment that teaches us to breathe consciously. Be in that place of love for a moment. Be aware of our universal connection to the Divine, to the world, and to each other.

Law

When you are ready, draw that white-purple energy down to your right foot, where iron's pride becomes *law*. Perhaps a better word might be "harmony."

This is literally the way the Universe works, from the laws of physics to the law of gravity to the law of attraction. This is how the Rede is manifested: "An it harm none, do what thou wilt." We learn to follow our own internal ethical compass, not imposed by others, but guided by our own True Will. As Aleister Crowley said in *The Book of the Law,* "Do what thou wilt shall be the whole of the Law. Love is the Law; Love under Will." See how love and law are connected, and how there can be no true harmonious law without love.

Knowledge

From an awareness of law, the energy of the cosmos brings us up to our left hand, the place of *knowledge.* Iron's self is about being aware of who one is and isn't. Only when we have found our authentic place in the Universe can we truly claim knowledge. This is "to know" from the Witch's pyramid; not book learning, but a sense of realization. Through a sense of self, we become mirrors for those around us to learn about themselves too. We become open to experience and awareness; we trust in the cosmos to communicate its nature to us, and we act in accordance to this. There is no knowledge without an awareness of the universal harmony of law; indeed, the current that supports true knowledge flows directly from it.

Liberty

From knowledge, spirit energy crosses our bodies to the right hand, and we gain *liberty,* the Universal manifestation of power. This is power shared with others. In other words, if all are empowered, all are liberated. We exercise discernment but not judgment, and we give others permission to be exactly who they are around us too, whether we agree or not, whether we approve or not. But do keep in mind, there can be no true liberty that does not ultimately come from love, law, and then knowledge; so discernment, and saying no, is required when freedom violates these points of the pentacle.

Wisdom

Last, from liberty comes *wisdom,* which we will visualize pooling in our left foot. The passion of iron, which is all about opening completely to life's experience, leads to the cumulative integration of these experiences in a way that makes them practical and useful. When you can take the benefit of your experiences and be an example or a teacher to others, then you are wise. It is said that a misspent youth is what leads to a wise and productive old age. And only when you can allow others to be themselves—only when you act from liberty—can you truly claim that you are wise as well.

Wisdom, of course, leads us back to love; because when you have tasted fully of life's experiences, how can you help but love? Life, the world, and all beings are by their very nature beautiful, and you innately recognize your connection to them.

Again, the locations of the points of the pentacle are no accident. Law and wisdom are foundational aspects of our higher self; liberty and knowledge are active qualities that require that we do things; love is how our higher self interacts with the world through our senses.

As you did before with iron, connect the points of the Pearl Pentacle now with a protective circle of light; from love to knowledge to wisdom to law to liberty and back to love. Thus, we manifest the powers of the Divine within ourselves, and become that which we truly are.

To step it up a notch: Do the Iron Pentacle and Pearl Pentacle meditations together!

ANIMA AND ANIMUS

Remember Isaac Bonewits's Law of Polarity and our discussion of the Anima (the female aspect at the heart of every male) and Animus (the male aspect at the heart of every female)? We require this balance for a healthy psyche. More importantly, an imbalance of these two energies makes magick difficult, if not impossible. Many cultures regarded the "twin-souled" as being magickally gifted or required their shamans to develop the other side of their nature and gain a more holistic insight. So shall you. Let's begin.

Exercise 119: The God or Goddess Within

Reach out now to a deity of your opposite gender that appeals to you. You might have been chosen by this deity too. You may be strongly drawn in a way that feels like sexual attraction. He or she may have a darkly compelling quality that repels even as it attracts. Those of you who have done your shadow work will recognize this as part of your shadow. All of the activities that were suggested to acquaint you with your same-sex deity are equally valid for your opposite-sex one. Enjoy the relationship! It may last a lifetime!

Shakti is the Tantric goddess of the earth, and of kundalini. This is why one of the most ancient symbols for the goddess is the serpent. Tantrics conceive of her as dwelling coiled at the base of the spine, in the root chakra. It is her greatest desire to be joined with Shiva, god of the heavens. Just as in the physical realm, where the male inseminates the female body with the "white serpent" of his seed, in the spiritual realm the female "inseminates" the male with the "white serpent" of kundalini. Instead of going down, it goes up; along the path of the spine, winding up the chakras in a helix, or a "cone of power," to ultimately join with Shiva at the center of the cosmos.

The sensation, known as samadhi, or *satori,* union with the cosmic consciousness, is like having an orgasm in the crown chakra. It is bliss unlike any other, and this is ultimately what the poets and mystics write about. I can tell you from personal experience that there is nothing else like it. It is why I do what I do; so that others may experience this too. You may already have done so in the course of this book by doing the exercises, especially with other activities that raise kundalini or pursue gamma consciousness. If you haven't, doing this exercise might be another way to achieve it.

Sit close to one another. In left-hand path Tantra, an opposite-gendered couple typically sits naked and connected at the genitals. You don't have to go that far; you don't even have to be naked, but it sure can make for a powerful experience! Simply gaze into each other's eyes without speaking for several minutes to open the channels between you.

Start the same grounding and drawing up earth energy exercise as you practiced in Exercise 91: Chakra Breathing. Only this time, breathe the red energy of the base chakra into the orange energy of your partner's sacral chakra instead! This process is most effective if you do not once look away from each other's eyes except to blink.

Cycle the energies between each other for a while. During this time, your breathing will synchronize so that one of you inhales to draw it in as the other exhales to expel it. When you feel that you are ready, transmute the energy to yellow and breathe it back into the solar plexus of your partner!

This process continues back and forth through the chakras until you both have bright and clear crown chakras filled with crackling power. At this point, you should be in telepathic harmony; you will likely be hot, sweating, and maybe even panting; a sense of exhilaration and divine connection should be filling your body and spirit.

Together as one, you both visualize the golden egg chakra as hovering between you and over both of your heads, and consciously mingle your energies there together as they join with the cosmic consciousness of Shiva.

If you have done this correctly, this will be an explosive, incandescent experience, like an "orgasm in your head. Just as in any kundalini awakening, there may be all kinds of physical and emotional symptoms, such as odd pains, crying, electrical sensations in strange places, sweating, effervescent laughter, and so forth. If this doesn't happen, it just means that you may need some practice!

When you have enjoyed the bliss of divine unity to your content, then bring the energy back down. Pass it back and forth in a winding pattern, creating the double helix of the caduceus and our DNA.

When the energy has reached your root chakras, ground by pouring energy back into the earth's core, and feel the circuit run in both directions between you for a time. Then let all excess energies drain through both currents, and center.

When you feel that all is as it was, without speaking lay your hands upon each other's heart chakras. Then, without breaking eye contact, clasp your hands in front of your heart and bow to your partner. This is the Namaste position, which means "The Divine in me recognizes the Divine in you."

Opening to Channel

Many people are afraid of drawing down because they don't want to give up control. I assure you there is nothing to be afraid of. The only way to reach your deity is through the part of yourself that is divine. So there is nothing in there that is not of yourself, anyway. The other thing to remember is that *you are in charge!* This is your body, and just like working with any spirit, you establish your boundaries and enforce them.

My friend whom I initiated to Third Degree is an Aphrodite priestess, and her god is Ares. Ares has a bit of a bad rep. He's thought of as being violent, aggressive, controlling, and potentially abusive. I must say that he found being in a female body to be a unique experience initially! But he adapted quickly, and I didn't find that he was much like his reputation describes him at all. He's strong-willed, but only violent in the manner of a family guardian, not a bloodthirsty murderer. When it was time to devoke, he did not want the physical sharing with his beloved Aphrodite to end. I was apologetic, but firm; and good-naturedly, when he could see that I was adamant, he bade us farewell and left me to my own body. *You are entirely in control.* You must therefore take responsibility for anything that happens as you draw down as well.

The Four Levels of Invocation

- Level 1: Primary Pilot (mid to low alpha)—Picture your body as an airplane with two sets of controls; the pilot's and the copilot's. You are the pilot, and the being you are invoking is sitting next to you in the copilot seat, giving instructions. You will hear a voice telling you explicitly what to say, or you will simply get a sense that you should say or do something. This is a state of listening and following guidance most commonly used for psychic insights and spiritual advice. You will remember clearly everything that transpires in this state and experience it like a daydream.

- Level 2: Copilots (low alpha to high theta)—At this stage, you and the copilot both have the ability to operate the controls of the plane. You will each have primary control over different parts and work together for mutual benefit. But, since there must be a primary pilot in case of emergencies, you maintain primary control of the craft. You and your copilot will take turns thinking and speaking, and you will both be aware of each other's words and actions; you might even have internal arguments! You will often find, when you are speaking as the copilot, that you know things you otherwise couldn't possibly know and use words and a way of speaking that are not your own. You will remember everything in this state, but some of it will be a little vague, like being immersed in a really good book.

- Level 3: Copilot Takes Primary Control (theta/shamanic consciousness)—This is the state where drawing down and trance channeling typically take place. The copilot has primary control of the body and will speak through your mouth (though often in a very different voice), look through your eyes, and if you are experienced, occasionally act with your body. You are in the background observing the proceedings, ready to seize control of the plane again at any time. This is used for great acts of magick and substantiation of faith. You will remember only some of this experience, and it will be fuzzy and insubstantial, like a dream. You will also experience an amazing sense of peace, calm, and bliss.

- Level 4: Copilot Flies the Plane (deep theta to delta)—This is very deep trance channeling. At this point, you are taking a nap and the copilot is flying. This is usually only possible with entities you have worked with frequently and trust deeply, although some people have had unsettling experiences in which someone has swept in and taken over! However, no matter how scary this might sound, you still have the pilot's seat and will be able to take over again in the case of any emergencies! At this point, the copilot acts with your body as if it were his own. Superhuman feats are possible, and you will likely remember nothing or only bits and pieces of the experience. This can be scary, but most of the time this will be experienced as an endless moment of exquisite ecstasy and divine unity.

Preparation

This is where all that trancework you did in chapter 2 is going to pay off.

First, define your limits. Choose an entity to work with and how much access you'll grant that entity. If you have any fear of the process, approach this as you would potentially cold swimming water; dip your toe in slowly, or dive right in if that is easier for you!

Define your motivation. Why are you asking the gods to act or speak through you? Are you intending worship, insight, or magick?

Cleanse and purify yourself, especially if it is the first time. For my first invocation of Hecate, I took a ritual bath and made offering at a crossroads. For my first Great Rite, I painted a henna tattoo of a crescent moon on my forehead. For a kingmaking ceremony, I refrained from red meat or coffee for three days (a difficult sacrifice for me!). For my Second Degree initiation, I was scourged.

Remove distractions. Seclude yourself if necessary. Meditate and relax. Clear away tension and emotional garbage.

Choose a method of trance induction. Begin with something that works very well for you. Traditional methods have included: guided meditations; spoken invocations repeated rhythmically with positioning or touch; formal ritual; invocations and scourging; incense, drugs, alcohol, or other intoxicants; drumming and chanting; dancing to exhaustion; fasting; sensory deprivation; and sex.

The Control

One more very important element in invocation of any sort, especially deep possession trances, is the control or guide. One mystic is the channel; and there is at least one helper or aid who assists the channel in going in, and coming out, of trance. In a Wiccan coven, more often than not the high priestess is the channel, and the high priest is the control. In a women's coven it may be the high priestess and her maiden. In New Age circles, often the channel is aided by a partner. Even in a Great Rite, in which both partners draw down, you will usually find that one partner goes much deeper than the other so that somebody maintains connection to the physical realm. To allow both the high priestess and priest to engage fully in the divine trance, the coven must be the control.

If you don't have a control, you need to establish some limits. The first is to always do an invocation in sacred space. Second, establish a time limit and a trigger. You can do this yourself by recording a guided meditation or giving a friend a meditation to read. You can also do it by establishing what sort of stimuli you will use to snap yourself out of it (for example, an alarm, a change in the light, or needing to pee), or only going down to the first couple levels. Also, set physical boundaries that you will not leave during this time (like a single room, or a chair or bed). Experienced channels will work out relationships with specific entities and might not hold firmly to these rules, but they are good to establish when you are starting.

A good control is almost more important than a good channel. It will be your responsibility to help your channel achieve the necessary level of trance, to care for him or her while in the trance, and to bring your channel back out when done. It takes practice and skill. Be as helpful as you can, and work at skills like chanting, speaking hypnotically, drumming, or establishing a ritual method of coming in and out.

Afterward

Trancing takes a lot of energy. Do not overstimulate yourself right away; keep the lights low and the music quiet, and don't immediately surround yourself with a lot of people. Rest, and above all, replenish your energy by eating and drinking! This is one of the major reasons for cakes and ale. It also helps you reestablish contact with the physical world. Definitely don't drive right away. Only when you feel mostly like yourself again should you dare to step back into the business of regular life.

Control: Turn down the lights and the music. Wash sweat from the channel with a damp cloth. Urge the entity to leave gently but firmly if he or she is reluctant to let go. Speak continually and softly about inconsequential mundane things to bring the channel's attention back to the mundane realm. Run interference with other people, especially when they are new to witnessing an invocation; they might get right in the channel's face right afterward to ask more questions or become fawning acolytes, neither of which is useful. Bring your channel food and drink so he or she doesn't have to try to get it in a physically weakened condition. Offer TLC.

Exercise 121: Drawing Down the Moon and Sun

Before you do step one, you must decide what you believe when it comes to deities and the Divine. Remember that your perceptions and beliefs shape your reality!

There are two ways to draw down the moon and sun. The first is to call a deity whom you prefer to work with. The second is to work with a partner, usually of the opposite gender, to use polarity as a magnet to attract a deity to you. Most people find it easiest to work with deities of their own gender, so if you've never done this before, start there.

Cast circle and call quarters. Always work in a sacred space. This protects you from potentially hostile or mischievous entities and restricts the environment. Remember, you are altering your consciousness dramatically, and the most common form of harm to people in altered states is misadventure.

Use your favorite method to induce trance. Music can be an excellent source of auditory driving, especially if it is rhythmic, arrhythmic without lyrics, or if the lyrics are repetitive (like in a chant).

Prepare an invocation, perhaps to be read by your control, perhaps even repeated over and over until it blends into the rhythm of a mantra. The charges work very well for this. There are also poetic verses from antiquity that are perfect for Greek deities. Google "Ovid" or "Sappho" to start with, or even "invocations" with the name of the deity afterward. Aleister Crowley wrote a powerful poem invoking Pan; you can always compose your own. You can also use chants, drumming, and dancing. Do keep in mind that this only works when it is repeated to the point that it becomes nonsensical.

As the channel, your job is to open yourself up to the presence of the deity and allow him or her to come through you. Sink as deeply as you can toward theta shamanic consciousness. Shut out all distractions. If it helps (and it usually does), close your eyes. Allow the driving force of the trance induction to do its work. Trust yourself, your gods, and your control.

Some people have a really powerful connection right away, but for most it takes some practice. Trust in your instincts and speak the words of the god or goddess as they are given to you, without internal censorship. Or, allow the deity who comes to your call to use your mouth to speak! This is what you have come for; to hear the divine wisdom. Let it happen. Drawing down—indeed, any kind of invocation—is more a process of *allowing* than doing.

Control: minimize the distractions for your channel and prevent him or her from staying too long in an uncomfortable position; the gods may not notice, but parts of the body can ache or go to sleep. If your channel moves, move with him or her; be supportive (emotionally and physically). Deities are not used to being physical, and the changes in energy can have dramatic effects. Once I drew down Hecate in a Samhain circle to give prophecy, secluded up on a stage area behind a curtain for privacy. But this was just after my husband's accident; he couldn't climb the steps to the stage and she had a message for him. So she marched my butt down the stairs, out into the circle to take his hands and give him the message. Then she promptly left! There was probably a split second where neither her essence nor my spirit was fully occupying my body, and I fell down! I was completely unhurt—one of the magickal effects of channeling the Divine Energy—but it illustrates my point.

If you are working in a priestess and priest partnership, you are reaching out to the Divine Couple, and using the polarity created by your male and female bodies to draw in the female and male presences. Going robed or skyclad alerts your mind that things are in the liminal stage, and being skyclad displays the physical polarity clearly. Scourging purifies your body and spirit and induces a kinesthetically and possibly trauma-driven trance. The charge, again, is a great tool. In a partnership the priest begins and the priestess recites the verses that speak from the Lady's perspective. I have, over the years, developed a personal trigger so that as soon as I begin reciting, "I, who am the beauty of the green earth, and the white moon among the stars . . ." I am transported immediately to the beginning of the trance state and open to receive the Lady however she chooses to speak, act, or appear. I have also used repeated recitation and practice of the Fivefold Kiss.

When the gods arrive, listen keenly to their messages and make them welcome. Treat the vessel as if he or she were a living embodiment of the Divine. The nature of the deity you have called will dictate the proceedings and the vessel's actions. Hecate is known for her direct crone wisdom, and she will pull no punches if you ask her what to expect in the coming year and the news isn't good. Isis, on the other hand, is patient and compassionate. Drawing her down will aid your magick, and she is likely to take her vessel around the circle to touch hands and offer loving motherly embraces. The priest or priestess may speak in a different voice and move him- or herself in a very different way than usual. Economy of movement is normal because the deities are usually careful not to injure their vessels, and hands and feet can be awkward if you're not used to them! This may change as the deity becomes more comfortable with the particular vessel he or she occupies.

You can have some very interesting experiences that confirm the Divine Presence! The first time I called Isis, the cat at the covenstead, who hated everybody, plunked herself firmly in Isis's lap for attention. Immediately upon Isis's departure, though I had not moved from the chair, she hopped disdainfully off of me. I was not the one she had come to see!

When finished, always offer your gratitude! Use the lingering divine essence to bless the cakes and ale, and eat to ground yourself. Take some time to readjust your consciousness, especially if you went deep.

Sometimes, the deity will be reluctant to depart though there is no more time. The control then urges the deity gently to "return to us your vessel, that we may call you again." It generally doesn't take much. Just give the deity and the channel time to make the transition. The deeper the channel went, the more time this will take.

Release the circle in the normal fashion and allow the channel time to come back fully to beta consciousness before going about your business.

One more gentle word of caution: Always thank and release the deity you have called, even if you think he or she hasn't come. The first time I drew down, it didn't seem that anything had happened. We broke up without releasing the circle properly. (Other Witches will shake their heads at me, but in my defense, I was a sixteen-year-old solitary who had recruited some friends to try this.) I went for a walk with two friends who were more open than others to this drawing down idea, and that's when Hecate chose to show up to speak! Again, no harm done in this case; she left when her message was given and my friends had thanked her. I was lucky.

SACRED SEX

In Wicca, our goddess charges us to "sing, feast, dance, make music and love, all in (Her) presence," and she tells us that "all acts of love and pleasure are (Her) rituals." This was a very important point of faith for me. Sex is nothing short of a holy rite in which I celebrate the Divine in myself and in my partner(s). And because I am a Witch, and I believe in the Rede, I believe that anything that is experienced by consenting adults is holy as well. For that reason, I choose to offer many different options in this section of the book.

Being a holy rite, however, one must approach sex magick with due respect. Our sexual ethic requires that we never bring harm to anyone through our actions. This means that if we are polyamorous, we must be sure that both our partner(s) and the partners of our partners are aware of what is going on. If we are into kink, we must practice the use of safe words and set ground rules. It's all about respect.

That respect includes allowing people to have different beliefs and practices than your own. Chastity and promiscuity are equally legitimate ways to observe a sacred respect of sex. Nor should we hold one standard for one group and a different one for another. I encourage you to experiment with anything that appeals to you, ignore what does not, and do not censor yourself due to fear of what others might think.

Blood Sugar Sex Magick

I will be touching only briefly on the basic principles of Western sex magick in this book, but if you have an interest, I would encourage you to explore further. One of the best books on the subject is Donald Michael Kraig's *Modern Sex Magick: Secrets of Erotic Spirituality*. Unlike many older works, it is detailed, straightforward, and inclusive, and the author tries to consider things from both male and female perspectives, as well as from a bisexual or gay perspective.

Basic Principles of Sex Magick

As most healthy adults know, sex moves an amazing amount of energy through the body. Sex is an incredible vehicle for the movement of kundalini, and therefore, the generation of magickal energy. It is also a way to connect people so they are magickally and energetically in sync with one another. Sex is also an effective method for changing consciousness and inducing the alpha, gamma, or even delta states where magick takes place. Depending on the techniques used, sex magick can involve visual, olfactory, auditory, kinesthetic, or possibly even gustatory, traumatic, or discipline-driven trancework.

Focused Sexual Rites

The primary way sex magick is used in the Western tradition is as a catalyst for raising a cone of power toward a specific purpose. This could be either to empower a spell or to achieve enlightenment through the use of sexual energy. Generally, the body is stimulated to orgasm, and the energy is directed toward the purpose like the releasing of a cone of power in circle.

Gender-Specific Sexual Responses

Ladies, we have an easier time of sex magick than men. This is because we do not have a limit on the number of orgasms we can have, and we have a longer and more gradual sexual response time. We generally have the stamina to last through whatever might be required, we take longer to achieve our initial orgasm point, and if we do orgasm before we are ready to direct it toward the purpose, we can just do it again.

Gentlemen, there are things you can do to prepare for sex magick. You can increase your stamina before achieving orgasm, you can learn how to orgasm without ejaculation, and you can learn to orgasm multiple times. The following two exercises show you how.

Exercise 122: The Razor's Edge (Men Only)

Here's an exercise that encourages you to masturbate frequently! Only when you do, practice stimulating yourself to almost the point of orgasm, then stop before you reach that point. When you become familiar with that feeling, start practicing a mental withdrawal from the experience instead of a physical one. When you can disengage your mind without disengaging your hand to resist immediate orgasm, you are ready to practice sex magick.

Exercise 123: Closing the Pipe (Men Only)

Masturbate until you have neared the point of orgasm. When you feel it coming, press firmly on your perineum with your first two fingers until the sensation passes. This will enable you to have multiple orgasms. This isn't necessary for sex magick, but it is good for Tantra and it sure can be fun!

If sex magick is something you want to experiment with, you need to be sexually healthy. You should masturbate or have sex several times a week, preferably at least once a day. It keeps your body in shape enough to handle the process, you become used to moving this kind of energy around, and it reduces stress and heals the body.

METHODS OF SEXUAL FOCUS

There are three major methods of focusing sexual energy in a rite, depending on how many people are involved and what their purpose is.

Solo Focus

In this model, there is one primary Witch who directs the magickal energy, just like in a spiral dance. However many Witches are involved in the rite, the focus is on the primary Witch and the responsibility for directing the energy is his or hers. This can be a masturbatory rite, one partner stimulating the other, a group of people working together to stimulate the primary Witch, or a group of people taking turns. I have even used this method to work multiple spells at once, directing each orgasm to a different purpose!

If you are using sex magick to seek visions or divine connection, you can make use of inversion techniques. Remember your head has to be lower than your heart. You can dangle off the edge of the bed or prop your body up on pillows.

Binary Focus

This model works more or less like the solo focus model, except that the Witches who are directing the energy are a couple working as a team. The partners stimulate each other, or they are stimulated by a group who either take turns or work simultaneously.

Binary Sexual Positions and Magick

Woman Superior is useful when the energy created will be primarily directed to the female partner's benefit; Missionary when it is to the man's.

Spooning is good for sending energy to friends of the couple.

Lying face-to-face is good for magick benefitting both partners.

Oral sex is a solo focus magickal model; except in the case of mutual oral sex, commonly called 69, which is good for healing work.

Inversions are used for the same reasons as they would be in solo focus work. The easiest method is as above; dangle one partner's head off the edge of the mattress while the other one is on top. Another position is known as the Crow, where a very strong male holds their female partner upside down.

Group Focus

In this model, a group of people simultaneously directs the energy created by the rite as they stimulate one another. A guide usually directs the process like a cheerleader or a foreman. The possibilities created by this are virtually endless. Rather than give specific rites, I will offer examples of different ways in which these varying models could be focused toward a given magickal purpose.

Exercise 124: Sex and Symbol

Create a symbol to represent your magickal goal. Make an image of it and put it on all four walls and the ceiling, if possible, so you can see it from all angles, no matter what you are doing.

Cast circle and begin your ritual.

Solo focus: stimulate yourself to orgasm. You can even use fantasies that have nothing to do with your magickal goal! Upon the point of orgasm, focus entirely on the magickal symbol. Allow it to fill your mind completely! Orgasm is not a good time for creative visualization, so allow the symbol to represent your desires entirely. When finished, end your rite in the usual way and trust the Universe to do its job. Remove the symbols.

Binary focus: as above, only both partners stimulate each other to orgasm and focus on the symbols at that moment. If you can manage a simultaneous orgasm it can add more power to your magick, but it is not strictly necessary.

Group focus: create a temple space filled with symbols. The guide will direct you to occasionally focus on the symbols as you engage in your sexual enjoyment. After a while, orgasms will begin to occur. Eventually the guide will sense that the energy is at its peak and direct everyone to focus toward one final orgasm and conscious direction of energy. Complete your rite in the usual way.

A variation of this rite involves no symbols, but a focused word. This is much easier in a solo focus model and nearly impossible in a group without significant practice.

This ritual utilizes the elemental pentacle as a tool of focus and enlightenment. If you are male, this exercise requires practice with multiple orgasms.

Make a pentagram and put it on the wall in all directions. Each point should be marked with an appropriate color, and preferably symbols or drawings of that element.

Solo focus: as you near orgasm, visualize yourself coming up to a doorway with green light behind it. When orgasm is achieved, transport yourself through the barrier on that wave of orgasm through into an earthy green forest. Feel the sensation of that element overwhelm you. As you near the next orgasm, approach a blue doorway, and use that orgasm to transport yourself into blue water. The next one takes you through a yellow doorway into yellow clouds; the one following that into red flames, and the last into a purple and white nebula, a sparkling white galaxy, or a glowing golden egg.

Binary focus: as above, only you try for simultaneous orgasm.

Group focus: this is sometimes called the Philosopher's Ring, and it is known commonly as a "daisy chain." A ring of participants engages in oral sex, connected by mouths and genitals. A guide will take you through the process of visualizing the elemental energies by reading the energy of the gathering and timing description appropriately. Not everyone's orgasm will be in perfect unison, but the unified focus will work together.

Elixirs and Magickal Children

Sexual fluids have magickal properties. They create "magickal children" (seed thought-forms) or consecrate talismans. Mixed together, they form elixirs, which can charge spells, consecrate tools, or be consumed. This may have been the original meaning of the Eucharist; consuming divine energy through the secretions of the body during sex magick or the Great Rite.

Exercise 126: Charging a Talisman

Sex magick can be used to charge a talisman.

- *Solo focus:* Use the energy of the orgasm to influence the talisman by placing it between your legs and symbolize giving birth to it; or alternatively, "impregnate" it with your sexual fluids. You can also use the energy of multiple orgasms kind of like labor pains.

- *Binary focus:* Place the talisman between your bodies to charge it with your energy during sex; or "impregnate" it with your fluids mingled together.
- *Group focus:* Place the talisman on an altar in the center of activity and focus on it while directing the sexual energy of the group.

THE GREAT RITE

The Great Rite celebrates the power of Creation. It recognizes two important elements. The first is that it requires more than one of us to create anything. Some traditions would focus on the masculine–feminine polarity. Certainly there is no creation of life in the physical realm without this biological polarity. But for the creation of ideas given form, we can develop that polarity within ourselves by balancing the *internal* masculine–feminine. And that balance extends to all things! There cannot be creation without destruction; there cannot be life without death; there cannot be light without dark. An idea needs a catalyst. Therein lies the great paradox: We cannot create anything of lasting value without the assistance of others; but we must exist independently of the good opinion of others before we can accomplish anything of significance.

And this is why it is important to recognize the second element of the Great Rite. We are divine; we carry aspects of the Divine within ourselves; and that divinity is here, now, with us—not somewhere else. When you draw down a goddess or a god, he or she comes from within you. That is why you cannot be hurt unless you wish it, and why even though it is not you, exactly, who acts when the gods do, you are still responsible for their actions.

For the realization of the Great Rite, we must simultaneously manifest these two great truths. We must aspect the Divine in ourselves, and connect to the Divine in someone else. "Thou art Goddess; thou art God."

GREAT RITE IN TOKEN

The Great Rite is most commonly practiced in token (that's symbolically, not literally). A symbolic phallus (wand, staff, stang, sword, athame, lance, maypole, mystic) is joined, head or point first, with a symbolic vulva or womb (cup, chalice, cauldron, hole in the earth, cave).

We summon the very forces of Creation to come together to make our magick. Because the biological polarity of male and female is already present, it is traditional for the high priestess of the coven to be the spiritually "inseminating" force that grasps the blade, and the high priest becomes the spiritually "receptive" force that grasps the chalice. The element of the one exists within the other in an eternal loop. If you have drawn down the moon and sun, you may be called to do the rite the other way around or without regard to gender.

Exercise 127: The Chalice and the Blade

Take a moment to aspect the deities within yourselves. If you have done an evocation rather than an invocation, attune with the appropriate deity whom you have called instead. If you did not call a counterpart of the other gender, consider how that deity may relate to a counterpart and call forth your anima or animus, whichever is appropriate. Dip your phallus symbol into your womb symbol, with the conscious awareness of what it symbolizes and the magick of these two creative forces coming together.

If you are using this for the cakes and ale, speak the appropriate blessing (you'll find a couple in chapter 3), and drip three drops of the "ale" onto the "cakes" to transfer the blessing to them. The polarity is present here as well. Just like in the Eucharist, the cakes represent the broken body of the God, given in sacrifice in the corn and the grain and the beasts of the field and the hunt, so that we may survive the winter. The ale in the chalice represents the blood that comes from the Goddess's womb to nurture us and give us life. Eat in recognition of the transubstantiation of Divine Blessing.

GREAT RITE IN ACTUAL

In the Great Rite in actual, we use our bodies as the phallus and the womb. One partner aspects the Goddess and the other aspects the God. This is often one of the most feared rituals in Witchcraft, and for good reason; it is probably the most powerful and most intimate experience you will ever have. This rite is the reason traditional covens insist that the high priest trains the females and the high priestess trains the males, since this is the rite that confers the Third Degree. I personally believe that if someone is entirely gay, s/he should be trained, or at least initiated, by a priest or priestess who is willing to aspect the other deity and be involved in a same-sex pairing. This is a controversial view in the craft; but I have spoken of my own experience with this before, and I believe it to have been powerful and successful in conferring the mystery.

There are some ethical issues associated with the Great Rite, and they bear discussion. What happens when one member of a monogamous couple is ready for the Great Rite but the other is not a Wiccan? What if the other half of the couple is a Wiccan but the priest or priestess to confer the rite is someone else? What if someone is simply not comfortable with the sexual contact? What if the priest or priestess performing the rite is legally recognized by the state and the initiate is his or her student?

Some Witches are firmly of the opinion that if you cannot get over your personal issues around this, you are not ready for the experience. Others have come up with alternatives, like performing the Great Rite in token, or drawing down the appropriate deity into their initiate, then sending her or him home to the spouse. There are issues around both of these solutions, and you will have to make up your mind for yourself.

Be cautious if a Witch insists that he or she is the only one who can confer the rite! Someone who does believe in the inviolate mystery will recognize that the Divine exists in all of us, and if you don't feel comfortable coupling with someone in particular, the high priest or priestess should find you someone you do feel comfortable with. Most Third Degree initiates know a handful of others, and you'll have some options. If you don't, that's a warning sign.

I have run into all these things in my life as a Witch and have navigated my own answers, as have the other Witches I have practiced with. No solution is perfect, and all of this requires frank discussion, but I believe many of the ethical issues stem from a cultural misperception about the nature of the rite.

What you are doing in the Great Rite is creating a *hieros gamos,* or "holy marriage," between the two aspects of divinity. You are aspecting the Divine within yourself, and that divinity is coupling with the Divine within your partner. In other words, though it is partially you, it also isn't. Many committed, monogamous Wiccans make an exception for the Great Rite, because how can you begrudge your mate a chance to couple with the gods? If you approach it from this perspective, it is truly a transcendent experience.

Unless you are in a strictly monogamous relationship and you are pairing with your husband or wife, *always practice safe sex!* Bless your condom like any other ritual tool. You owe that to your partner(s).

For this ritual you will need a partner. One of you will aspect the Goddess and one will aspect the God. If you are of the same gender, you should take this into consideration in planning (ritual strap-ons, anyone?).

Cast circle and call quarters in your usual way. Choose paired aspects of Goddess and God to work with (examples: Star Goddess and Horned God, Mother Earth and Father Sky, Isis and Osiris, Diana and Pan, Freya and Odin, and so forth). Speak or chant the invocations. The charges and appropriate chants work nicely. It is usual for the priest to call the Goddess into the priestess first, and then the Goddess calls to her mate; unless a Third Degree is being conferred by a priest to a priestess, at which point he calls the God into himself first, and then calls to the Goddess to enter the priestess. Use your favorite method(s) of trance induction and allow the Divine to enter and come through you. You can use the Fivefold Kiss to aspect them both in each other, or make a Statement of Intent or a traditional invocation.

When they arrive, you will know immediately, and at this point I have no real instruction for you except to allow and enjoy! The gods know of this ancient rite and they will do what comes naturally. Sometimes they will simply touch and kiss each other; sometimes they will couple; sometimes there will be orgasms and sometimes there won't. Just don't forget to insist on the condom; otherwise, hang on and enjoy the ride! (In the ancient days a child born from such a union was considered to have been conceived by the gods, which explains many myths of divine conceptions.)

When they are finished, thank the gods, bless and enjoy the cakes and ale, and close the rite as usual.

What does the rest of the coven do during this time? Some leave the room so the priestess and priest can have privacy. Some turn their backs or wear veils until things are completed. Some witness. And some engage in their own private sexual experiences with their partners in the coven in the same sacred space. It's really all about personal comfort level. In my tradition, a Third Degree, which is conferred by a Great Rite, is not valid unless it is witnessed by an initiated high priestess; which means that when a priest initiates a priestess (as in my case), a high priestess sits in the circle as well. In my case, my initiator's wife was the high priestess; both are good friends of mine. She drew a veil over her head while the rite was occurring to give me some privacy. It was not necessary; I was aspecting the Goddess and was not in the least uncomfortable.

Solitary Great Rite

Why not couple with your gods in the spirit realm? Essentially, this is masturbation with your deity as your fantasy lover! Think of it like calling a divine *incubus* or *succubus*. But remember to do it in sacred space; otherwise you might end up with a *real* incubus or succubus, and they are malignant spirits who will drain your life energy.

Exercise 129: Sex and the Single Deity

Cast circle and call quarters in a private space, such as your bedroom. Draw down the moon or sun as is appropriate. Then use that polarity to call to your opposite, or to a divine lover of your choosing. As a variation, do not draw down at all, but simply call to a divine lover (I have had some marvelous experiences with Herne and Diana in this way!). Masturbate, but visualize the deity you have called coupling with you instead. When you are finished, close the ritual as usual.

Alternative Great Rites

Don't let your imagination be limited! Gay couples can draw down such pairs as Pan and Dionysus or Gwydion and Gilfaethwy; lesbian couples could draw down Aphrodite, matron of lesbians according to Sappho, and Artemis, thought to be a lesbian because she was untouched by men but "preferred the company of women." This celebrates divine love rather than the raw power of physical Creation, but "all acts of love and pleasure are her rituals," so what's wrong with that? You could also approach it from the perspective of the life and death polarity instead of male and female. Holly King and Oak King, or perhaps the Kore and Persephone might work well.

A trio could invoke that divine trinity of maiden, mother, and crone or youth, father, and sage. And groups could aspect the four elements (with the optional addition of Spirit for a fifth participant), and engage in a group Great Rite; a variation on the group focus version of Exercise 125: Rite of the Pentacle. Each Witch could represent a different element (masks designed for this might make it a very powerful experience).

Self-Evaluation

There is no test here but your own heart. Do you feel you have unlocked one of the mysteries of the Universe, and touched for yourself the very forces of Creation? That, and nothing less, is the goal.

While sexual energy is certainly a significant part of the Great Rite, and I hope I have encouraged you to celebrate this also, the most important aspect is the mystical transcendence of the ego. When we realize and accept that we are divinity incarnate, there are no limits to our potential. And that is the ultimate secret to the successful practice of magick.

CONCLUSION

Congratulations! This quest, if you have worked through all the exercises and practices, has taken you months or years, and you are to be commended for your diligence and your courage. Most who step upon this path never come to this point. Was it worth the effort?

If you want to continue to explore the concepts in this book, here are some suggestions:

- Practice working with group Intent in a coven setting.
- Study shamanism and astral travel, do pathworking or psychic work to explore the limits and effects of Trance.
- Write rituals and music and study ancient symbolism to practice the craft (I recommend a detailed study of the Tarot and the Kabbalah).
- Take a course on herbalism or aromatherapy, or make use of entheogens in conjunction with other practices, to explore Intoxicants.
- Study mudras, yoga, or sacred Dance.
- Practice binding, suspension, biofeedback, firewalking, or yoga to explore Blood and Breath Control.
- Life will give you many opportunities to practice the emotional work of the Scourge, but if you want to embrace it, seek initiation, honor rites of passage, and practice the physical techniques suggested. The kink community has many ideas and resources for this.
- Draw down and work with the deities, study Tantra, and experiment with the limits of sex magick, to explore the Great Rite. There is a vast tradition of Kabbalistic sex magick to draw upon also.

These are the Witch's Eight Paths of Power. Thank you for taking this magickal journey with me. I hope you have found it enlightening. Blessed be.

ACKNOWLEDGMENTS

My instructors have been many and varied, and I cannot hope to remember them all, but some stick out in my mind: Lady Alexandra, Lady Dolphanie, Lord Grunnar, Lord Maphis, Nedra, Lord Redleaf, Lady Rowean, Satayama, Lady Vichary, Candice Balan, Mike Dion, Lois Gueret, Karen Fentiman, Lady Angelique Serpent, Kate Slater, and Victoria Willard. Thank you very much for your contributions to my body of knowledge.

Thank you also to the "PagTen" email list on Yahoo Groups for helping to define the four levels of invocation clearly, and to my students at the 2012 Wise Woman Festival for helping me find the airplane pilot metaphor.

PERMISSIONS

Chapter 1

"Exercise 5: Tree Meditation" is adapted from Starhawk's "Tree Meditation" in *The Spiral Dance*.

Chapter 3

Charge of the God © 2011 by Mistress Willow Xylona (Shanna Tulak). Used by permission.

Dianic blessing from a ritual performed by the Congregationalist Wiccan Association of BC © Mabon 2005 by Sam Wagar. Used by permission.

Chapter 5

Photos of the Five Rites © Rowean McRoy 2012. All rights reserved. Used by permission.

Photos of the vine dance step © Rowean McRoy 2012. All rights reserved. Used by permission.

Photos of the asanas © Jamie Field 2014. All rights reserved. Used by permission.

Hoof and Horn Dance of Universal Peace © Amara Karuna. Used by permission.

Goddess Dance © Myranda O'Byrne. Used by permission.

All other tables and illustrations by © Diane Morrison (Lady Sable Aradia) 2011. All rights reserved.

appendixes

CORRESPONDENCE
TABLES

Symbol	Sign	Note	Type	Element	Magick
♈	Aries	C	Cardinal	Fire	Beginnings, personality, self, authority, rebirth, leadership, rescue, courage, love, friendship, conflict, starting new things; brain, head, face; harvest root & fruit, cultivate, weed, destroy pests; good to start things but no staying power
♉	Taurus	C#	Fixed	Earth	Personal finances, vehicles, benefits, possessions, supernatural forces, love, money, real estate, pregnancy, children, art; neck, throat, ears; second best for transplanting, good for root crops and leafy vegetables; spells started now last longest & hard to alter
♊	Gemini	D	Mutable	Air	Relatives, communication, studies, writing, wit, moving, public relations, moving, travel; shoulders, arms, hands, lungs; cultivate, harvest, destroy pests & weeds; spells easily influenced by outside
♋	Cancer	D#	Cardinal	Water	Home, environment, mothers, family, emotions, end of life, nurture, hexing/binding, protection, integrity; chest, stomach; best for transplanting, grafting, irrigation
♌	Leo	E	Fixed	Fire	Love affairs, pleasure, hobbies, entertainment, sports, pets, love & friendship, power over others, childbirth; upper back, spine, heart; cultivates, harvest root & fruit, 4th quarter destroy weeds & pests
♍	Virgo	F	Mutable	Earth	Work, environment, health, service, clothing, employment, diet, details, schedules; supernatural forces, intellectual matters; intestines, nervous system; flowers & vines, destroy weeds
♎	Libra	F#	Cardinal	Air	Marriage, partnerships, legal matters, small animals, self-awareness, cooperation, compromise, socializing, balance, beauty, justice, artistic work; lower back & kidneys; balancing soil

♏	Scorpio	G	Fixed	Water	Death, taxes, inheritances, transformation, awareness, psychic power, ending connections, hexing/binding, sex, secrets, occult, insurance, soul mates, rituals, integrity, power; reproductive organs; sturdy plants & vines, transplanting, prune for better fruit
♐	Sagittarius	G#	Mutable	Fire	Religion, metaphysics, long-distance travel, in-laws, athletics, higher learning, expansion & growth, lights of imagination & confidence, adventure, philosophy, love & friendship, publishing, sports, travel, legal matters, truth; liver, thighs, hips; harvest root crops, plant fruit trees & onions, cultivate soil
♑	Capricorn	A	Cardinal	Earth	Business, career, reputation, fathers, honors, structures, discipline, order, organization, tradition, responsibility, setting boundaries & rules, recognition, ambition, supernatural forces, politics, wisdom; knees, bones, teeth, skin; plant root crops, grafting, healing, fertilizing
♒	Aquarius	A#	Fixed	Air	Friendship, hopes & dreams, groups, individualism, rebellion, break bad habits, freedom, positive transformation, science, creativity, problem solving, ESP; calves, ankles, blood; harvest, cultivate & weed
♓	Pisces	B	Mutable	Water	Inner development, revealing secrets, karma, dreaming, nostalgia, spirituality & mysticism, intuition, psychic powers, philanthropy, hexing/binding, withdrawing into self, music, gardening, creativity; feet & lymph glands, 2nd best for transplanting, root growth, irrigation

Appendix B
Color and Chakra Correspondences

Chakra	Number	Color	Location	Element	Sound	Mantra	Music	Sense	Aura	Health	Magick
(Ground)	0	Black, gray	(Feet)	Void	Silence	Silence	Silence	Nothing	Low Energy, Neurons, PTSD, Abuse, Psychosis	Damage, Cancer, Disease	banishing, binding, infertility, chaos, clearing, nothing, grounding, polarity (Black), neutralizing (Grey)
(Earth)	10	Brown	(Feet, knees)	-	-	-	-	-	Generous, Patient, Selfish	Needs Healing	Grounding, generosity, patience
Muladhara (Base/root)	1	Red	Perineum	Earth	UH	UH	C	Smell	Vitality, Sex, Anger	Bones, Genitals, Intestines, Blood, Kidneys	Passion, fire, courage, lust, life, war, anter, love, strength, attraction
Swadisthana (Sacral/ Navel)	3	Orange	Mouth/ Womb	Water	OOO	VAM	D	Taste	Extrovert, Active, Busy, Vitality	Bones, Gertains, intestines, Blood, Kidneys	Passion, fire, courage, lust, libe, war, anter, love, strength, attraction
Manipura (Solar Plexus	3	Yellow	Solar (Plexus)	Fire	OH	RAM	E	Sight	Creativity, intellect, self-esteem	Stomach, Gall Bladder, Spleen, Pancreas	Sun, healing, friendship, prosperity, productivity, feat, self-esteem, ego, inventiveness, light joy

Anahata (Heart)	4, 5	Green, Pink	Heart	Air	AH	YAM	F	Touch	Harmony, Healer, Artist (Green), Love, Compassion (Pink)	Heart, Lungs, Thymus Gland, Breast, Upper Back, Ribs, Arms, Hands	Money, Nature, faeries (Green); Harmony, love, peace, compassion, kindness, gentleness, children, healing grief (Pink)
Visuddha (throat)	5	Blue	Throat	Sound/ Ether	AY	HAM	G	Hearing	Logical, Honest, intelligent, Thoughtful	Throat, Thyroid, Larynx, Tonsils, Neck, Shoulders, Teeth, Tongue	Wisdom, patience, peace, truth, sadness, depression, protection, insight, fidelity, loyalty
Ajna (Brow, 3rd Eye)	6	Indigo	Third Eye	Light	EYE	AUM	A	Psychic	Intuitive, Wise, magical	Eyes, Ears, Nose, Pituitary	Protection, intuition, spirituality, healing broken bones & pride
Sahasrara (Crown)	7,10	Purple/ White	Crown	Thought	EEE	AH	B	Empathy	Spiritual, Pure, Innocent, Humility	Brain, Nervous System, Pineal Gland, Head	Spirit, protection, purification, consecration, blessing, clearing intuition, polarity
(Goddess)	9, 13	Silver	Anima	Femi-nine	-	-	-	-	Idealistic, Wise, Adaptable	Women, change	Goddess, moon, woman, cycles, transformation, intuition, emotion
(God)	9, 12	Gold	Animus	Mascu-line	-	-	-	-	Talented, Spiri-tual, Clever	Men, Stability	God, sun, moon, stability, healing, balance, harmony, reason, intellect

Appendix C
Elemental Correspondence Chart

Element	Direction	Color	Qualities	Guardian	Entities	Season	Time of Day	Age	Gender	Symbol
Air	East	Yellow (Purple)	Warm, moist / Movement, Intellect, Bureaucracies, Thought, Mind, Logic, Travel	Raphael	Sylphs	Spring	Morning	Child	Male	
Fire	South	Red (Green)	Warm, dry / Passion, Will, Creativity, Inspiration, Destruction, Action, Fertilization	Michael	Salamanders	Summer	Afternoon	Youth	Male	
Water	West	Blue (Orange)	Cool, moist / Creativity, Compassion, Nurturing, Love, Change, Intuition	Gabriel	Undines	Autumn	Evening	Adult	Female	
Earth	North	Green, Black	Cool, dry / Fertility, Healing, Growth, Stability, Protection	Uriel	Gnomes	Winter	Night	Elder	Female	

Moon Phase	Age in Days	Rises/Sets	Goddess Aspect	Color	Life Stage	Gardening	Magick
 New	0 to 3.5	Sunrise/Mid-After-noon	Crone to Maiden	Silver	Birth	Planting leafy & above ground annual plants	Beginnings, growth, re-newal, beauty, love, jobs, networking, and creativity
 Waxing Crescent "Diana's Bow"	3.5 to 7	Mid-morn-ing/After Sunset	Maiden, Warrior	White	Child-hood	As New Moon	Animals, business, change, choice, freedom, initiations, indi-vidualization, new ideas, challenge to status quo, rebellions, Warrior aspect
 First Quarter	7 to 10	Noon/Mid-night	Maiden	White, Black/White	Adoles-cence/Menstru-ation	Leaf growth, planting crops with seeds inside fruit above ground (beans, apples, etc.)	Balance, beginnings, health, healing, courage, ele-mental magick, friends, love, luck, wealth, fertility, psychic powers
 Waxing Gibbous	10 to 12	Mid-after-noon/About 3 a.m.	Maid-en to Mother	White, Red	Young Adult-hood	As first Quarter	Increase, analysis, evalu-ation, courage, patience, peace, har-mony, fruition, completion, finish magick 3 days before Full Moon if started as New

continued on the next page

continued from the previous page

Moon Phase	Age in Days	Rises/Sets	Goddess Aspect	Color	Life Stage	Gardening	Magick
Full Moon	12 to 15	Sunset/ Dawn	Mother	Red	Parent-hood	Plant root crops	Fruition, protection, divination, love, children, deci-sions, dreams, legal matters, ovulation, fertilization, pregnancy, lust, life
Waning Gibbous	15 to 20	Mid-eve-ning/ Mid-morn-ing	Mother, Queen	Red to Black	Mature	Transplant-ing	Remove bad habits or addictions, divorce, protec-tion, banishing knowledge, teaching
Last Quarter	22 to 25	Midnight/ Noon	Queen, Crone	Black	Meno-pause/ Midlife	Harvesting, pruning, weeding, cutting to limit growth	Banishing, re-moving illness, destruction, releasing wisdom, Underworld
Waning Crescent	22 to 25	Darkest hour/ Mid-after-noon	Crones	Black	Crone/ Sage-hood	As Third Quarter	Releasing addictions & obsessions, change, justice, hexing, quar-rels, death, reincarnation, destiny
Days of the Moon	25 to 28	First light	Crone	Black	Death/ Rebirth	Resting, weeding	Rest, medita-tion, dreams, sleep, visions

Appendix E
Numerical and Color Symbolism

Number	Meaning
0: Zero	*(Black)* Completeness, void, non-being, limitless light, Divine Essence
1: One	*(Red)* Beginnings, divine unity, wholeness, self, loneliness, erect phallus
2: Two	*(Orange)* Balances of polarities, partnerships, marriage, discord, Holly King/Oak King
3: Three	*(Yellow)* Past, present & future; the Fates, magick, Triple Goddess, trinity, the moon; life, death & rebirth; mind, body & soul; man, woman & child
4: Four	*(Green)* Elements, points of the compass, the seasons, death
5: Five	*(Blue)* The senses, balance of first even & odd numbers, humanity, transformation, pentagram/pentacle, Goddess in Venus aspect
6: Six	*(Indigo)* Balance of heaven & earth, male & female, balance, love, health, luck
7: Seven	*(Violet)* Unity of divinity & earth, days of the week, the planets, the chakras, magick, gates between the worlds
8: Eight	*(Rose)* Perfection, states of life, eternity, balance, fate, good luck, wheel of the year, eightfold path of enlightenment
9: Nine	*(Gold)* Celestial power, magick, completeness, nine-foot circle
10: Ten	*(White)* Return to unity, tree of life, balance of the Universe
11: Eleven	Master number; balance of polarities
12: Twelve	Universal fulfillment, time-space continuum, completion of the year, end of a cycle
13: Thirteen	*(Silver)* Number of member in a coven, total lunar months in a year, considered unlucky by many but lucky for witches

APPENDIX F
PLANETARY, COLOR, AND MUSIC CORRESPONDENCES

Planet	Day	Color	Number	Metal	Angel	Astrology	Powers	Music	Symbol
Sun	Sunday	Gold, Yellow	1, 6	Gold	Michael	Leo	Power, riches, glory, success, honor, faith	D	☉
Moon	Monday	Silver	3, 9	Silver	Gabriel	Cancer	Maternal love, nurturing, female mysteries, travel, psychic powers & intuition, change	G#	☽
Mercury	Wednesday	Orange	2, 6	Mercury	Raphael	Gemini, Virgo	Healing, intelligence, divination, business, bureaucracy, study, communication	E	☿
Venus	Friday	Pink, Green	5	Copper	Hagiel, Anael	Taurus, Libra	Love, romance, sex, friendship, beauty, money, art, women	F#	♀
Earth	-	Green, Black, Brown	4	-	Uriel	-	Grounding, money, fertility, growing things, motherhood, nurturing	G	⊕
Mars	Tuesday	Red	3	Iron	Kamael, Samael	Aries, (Scorpio)	Courage, war, fighting, power, defeating enemies, men's mysteries, men	C	♂

	Day	Color	Number	Metal	Angel	Zodiac	Properties	Note	Symbol
Jupiter	Thursday	Purple	7	Tin	Tzadkiel	Sagittarius (Pisces)	Money, prosperity, honors, success, grandeur, good fortune, spirituality	A#	♃
Saturn	Saturday	Gray, Black	10	Lead	Kassiel	Capricorn, (Aquarius)	Binding, hexes, psychic defense, karma, spiritualism, aiding, death, endings	A	♄
Uranus	-	Indigo	11	Uranium	Uriel	Acuarius	Transformations, free thought, magick, psychic powers, revolution	D	⛢
Neptune	-	Aqua	12	Neptunium	Asariel	Pisces	Enlightenment, visionaries, mysticism, freedom from oppression	F	♆
Pluto	-	Black	13	Plutonium	Azrael	Scorpio	Generations, karma, mysteries, sex, death	B	♇

BIBLIOGRAPHY

Andrews, Ted. *Sacred Sounds: Magic and Healing through Music & Word*. St. Paul, MN: Llewellyn Publications, 1992.

Bonewits, Isaac. *NeoPagan Rites: A Guide to Creating Public Rituals That Work*. St. Paul, MN: Llewellyn Publications, 2007.

———. *Real Magic*. York Beach, ME: Weiser Books, 1989.

Buckland, Raymond. *Buckland's Complete Book of Witchcraft*. St. Paul, MN: Llewellyn Publications, 1986.

———. *Practical Color Magick*. St. Paul, MN: Llewellyn Publications, 1983.

Campbell, Joseph. *The Hero with a Thousand Faces*. New York: New World, Library, 2008.

Castaneda, Carlos. *The Teachings of Don Juan: A Yaqui Way of Knowledge*. Berkeley, CA: University of California Press, 1969.

Conway, D. J. *By Oak, Ash, & Thorn: Modern Celtic Shamanism*. St. Paul, MN: Llewellyn Publications, 1995.

———. *Flying Without a Broom: Astral Projection and the Astral World*. St. Paul, MN: Llewellyn Publications, 2002.

Coyle, T. Thorn. *Evolutionary Witchcraft*. New York: Jeremy P. Tarcher/Penguin, 2004.

Crowley, Aleister. *The Book of the Law: Liber Al Vel Legis*. York Beach, ME: Red Wheel/Weiser, 2004.

———. "Magick in Theory and Practice." *Magick: Book Four*. York Beach, ME: Weiser Books, 1994.

Cunningham, Scott. *Cunningham's Encyclopedia of Magical Herbs.* St. Paul, MN: Llewellyn Publications, 2003.

———. *The Complete Book of Incense, Oils and Brews.* St. Paul, MN: Llewellyn Publications, 1993.

Dobelis, Inge N., ed. *Magic and Medicine of Plants.* Pleasantville, NY: Reader's Digest, 1986.

Dossey, Larry, MD. *Healing Words: The Power of Prayer and the Practice of Medicine.* New York: HarperCollins, 1995.

Fairywolf, Storm. "Queer Sex Magick." *http://faerywolf.com/queer-sex-magick.* Accessed Jan 26, 2011.

Farrar, Janet and Stewart. *A Witches' Bible: The Complete Witches' Handbook.* Custer, WA: Phoenix Publishing, 1987.

———. *The Witches' God.* Blaine, WA: Phoenix Publishing, 1989.

———. *The Witches' Goddess.* Cruser, WA: Phoenix Publishing, 1987.

Fortune, Dion. *Applied Magic.* London: Aquarian Press, 1962.

Free, Esra, HPS. *Wicca 404: Advanced Goddess Thealogy.* New Paradigm Press, 2007.

Gardner, Gerald. (1953). Gardner's Book of Shadows. Compiled by Aiden A. Kelly, Approximate date of compilation: early 1990s. From *www.sacred-texts.com* March 18, 2010.

Gawain, Shakti. *Creative Visualization.* Novato, CA: New World Library, 1978.

Gladwell, Malcolm. *Blink: The Power of Thinking Without Thinking.* New York: Little, Brown and Company, 2005.

Greenwood, Susan. *Magic, Witchcraft and the Otherworld: An Anthropology.* Oxford, UK: Berg Publishers, 2000.

Harner, Michael J., ed. "The Sound of Rushing Water." *Hallucinogens and Shamanism.* Oxford University Press, 1973, p. 25.

Harrow, Judy. *Devoted to You: Honoring Deity in Wiccan Practice.* New York: Citadel Press, 2003.

———. *Wicca Covens.* New York: Citadel Press, 1999.

Hawkins, David R. *Power vs. Force: The Hidden Determinants of Human Behavior.* Carlsbad, CA: Hay House, 2002.

Hutton, Ronald. *The Triumph of the Moon: A History of Modern Pagan Witchcraft.* New York: Oxford University Press, 1999.

Hopman, Ellen Evert. *A Druid's Herbal for the Sacred Earth Year.* Rochester, VT: Destiny Books, 1995.

Jones, Evan John, and Chas S. Clifton. *Sacred Mask Sacred Dance.* St. Paul, MN: Llewellyn Publications, 1997.

K, Amber. *Coven Craft: Witchcraft for Three or More.* St. Paul, MN: Llewellyn Publications, 2003.

Karuna, Amara Wahaba. *Inside My Heart.* Karuna Arts, 2008. CD.

———. *Inside My Heart Dance Manual: Dances of Universal Peace.* Pahoa, HI: Karuna Publishing, 2011.

Kraig, Donald Michael. *Modern Magick: Eleven Lessons in the High Magickal Arts.* St. Paul, MN: Llewellyn Publications, 1988.

———. *Modern Sex Magick: Secrets of Erotic Spirituality.* St. Paul, MN: Llewellyn Publications, 2009.

Lamond, Frederic. *Fifty Years of Wicca.* Somerset, England: Green Magic Publications, 2004.

Leek, Sybil. *Diary of a Witch.* New York: Signet Books, 1968.

LeShan, Lawrence. *The Medium, the Mystic, and the Physicist: Toward a General Theory of the Paranormal.* New York: Viking Press, 1974.

Luhrmann, T. M. *Persuasions of the Witch's Craft: Ritual Magic in Contemporary England.* New York: Basil Blackwell, 1989.

Matossian, Mary Kilbourne. *Poisons of the Past: Molds, Epidemics, and History.* New Haven, CT: Yale University Press, 1989.

McCampbell, Harvest. *Sacred Smoke: The Ancient Art of Smudging for Modern Times.* Summertown, TN: Native Voices, 2002.

Nelson, Felicitas H. *Talismans & Amulets.* New York: Sterling, 2008.

O'Byrne, Myranda. "Chant Mistress." *Book of Chants: Women's Full and New Moon Circles.* Kelowna, BC, Canada: 2010.

Penczak, Christopher. *The Inner Temple of Witchcraft.* St. Paul, MN: Llewellyn Publications, 2002.

———. *The Outer Temple of Witchcraft.* St. Paul, MN: Llewellyn Publications, 2004.

Poncé, Charles. *The Game of Wizards: Psyche, Science, and Symbol in the Occult*. New York: Penguin Books, 1975.

Rhea, Lady Maeve. *Summoning Forth Wiccan Gods and Goddesses: The Magick of Invocation and Evocation*. New York: Citadel Press, 1999.

Roman, Sanaya, and Duane Packer. *Opening to Channel: How to Connect with Your Guide*. Tiburon, CA: H J Kramer Inc, 1987.

Smith, Manuel J. *When I Say No, I Feel Guilty*. New York: Bantam Books, 1985.

Starhawk, M. Macha Nightmare, and the Reclaiming Community. *The Pagan Book of Living and Dying*. New York: HarperCollins, 1997.

Whitcomb, Bill. *The Magician's Companion: A Practical and Encyclopedic Guide to Magickal and Religious Symbolism*. St. Paul, MN: Llewellyn Publications, 2004.

FURTHER RESOURCES

My Yoga Online
www.myyogaonline.com/about-yoga/chakras/
A great resource for information on yoga and the chakras.

Sable Aradia's Magickal Music
sablearadia.bandcamp.com
You can find my two CDs, *Elemental (with Binaural Beats)* and *Elemental (with Isochronic Tones)* at this site.

Pagan Chants of the Month
www.seeliecourt.net/panpipe/oldchan.html
Pagan Chants of the Month archive, maintained by Ivo "Panpipe" Dominguez Jr.

Sable Aradia's YouTube Channel
www.youtube.com/user/SableAradia
For supplemental videos to help your practice:

- "Witch's Eight Paths of Power: Basic Chants"
- "Witch's Eight Paths of Power: Five Rites"
- "Witch's Eight Paths of Power: Sacred Dance"
- "Shadow Self Meditation playlist,"
- "Sit for a Spell Episode 7: Scrying and Divination"
- "Sit for a Spell Episode 9: Tea Leaf Reading"
- "Videos for the *Elemental* albums are also available

Amara Karuna's YouTube Channel
www.youtube.com/user/amarakaruna
Search for these dance videos:

- "Full Moonlight Dance of Universal Peace"
- "Give Thanks to Mother Gaia Dance of Universal Peace"
- "Hoof and Horn Dance of Universal Peace"
- "Mother of All Things Dance of Universal Peace"
- "Oh Earth Beautiful Dance of Universal Peace"
- "Triple Moon Dance of Universal Peace"

ABOUT THE AUTHOR

Lady Sable Aradia (Diane Morrison) has been a practicing Witch for about 25 years and is a Third Degree initiate in the Star Sapphire and Pagans for Peace traditions. She also writes music and speculative fiction. She lives in Vernon, BC, Canada, with her husband and her partner in a cabin on the edge of the woods. *www.sablearadia.com*

TO OUR READERS

To Our Readers

Weiser Books, an imprint of Red Wheel/Weiser, publishes books across the entire spectrum of occult, esoteric, speculative, and New Age subjects. Our mission is to publish quality books that will make a difference in people's lives without advocating any one particular path or field of study. We value the integrity, originality, and depth of knowledge of our authors.

Our readers are our most important resource, and we appreciate your input, suggestions, and ideas about what you would like to see published.

Visit our website at *www.redwheelweiser.com* to learn about our upcoming books and free downloads, and be sure to go to *www.redwheelweiser.com/ newsletter* to sign up for newsletters and exclusive offers.

You can also contact us at *info@rwwbooks.com* or at

Red Wheel/Weiser, LLC
665 Third Street, Suite 400
San Francisco, CA 94107